NOT WANTED ON VOYAGE

By Peter Langton

PREFACE

The history of Passenger shipping is a long and varied one. These days passenger ships are better known for their holiday or vacation cruises as a form of relaxation, or ferries to convey people and vehicles relatively short distances from one shore to another.

However, but a few years ago and up to the age of the jet aircraft which has made modern long distance travel between continents and countries so commonplace, people used ships to make these journeys whether to New York, Bombay or Sydney.

Sometimes, people travelled for migration to seek a new life on the other side of the world, some travelled on business or some purely for pleasure, but for whatever reason, they were on a mission to reach somewhere else and not just going round in circles to while away a couple of weeks of their lives each year as happens today.

Due to the passage of time there are now fewer people who remember what these ships were like and the characters who worked on them and I have been urged by many of my seagoing friends to write an account of those earlier days which are so far removed from the modern day cruise ships. I have used real first names but in the main I have omitted to use any last names.

I have recounted many a yarn which I hope

you will find both informative and amusing. There was no such thing as a 'gap year' at that time; you went straight to work from school, but a spell in the Merchant Navy was the alternative then. Something you did for a while until you decided what you wanted to do when you grew up. However, some 42+ years later, either I had still not grown up or was still undecided as to what I wanted to do in life... and now it was time to retire.

I hope you will enjoy these experiences of my own and others as we relive a forgotten past on the bosom of the ocean wave.

PROLOGUE

We stood out on the open deck under the hot Australian sun. The ship was moored at 13 Pyrmont in Sydney harbour and had been for the past 24 hours. The passengers had all disembarked the day before and now the Sydney Longshoremen were discharging the cargo from the six holds.

We, in the Purser's Bureau were taking a break, and had taken our coffee out on the open deck on this hot November morning . We watched the activity in the world's most beautiful natural harbour for 20 minutes, before going back to the dim but air conditioned confines of the Bureau to wrap up the documentation from the outward bound voyage; change the ship's currency from Sterling to Australian dollars and prepare for our series of 14 day cruises out of Sydney. These cruises would continue until the English winter was over and spring settled in, beckoning us back to the UK.

As we watched the cable from the crane jib rise slowly, out from the top of the hatch emerged a beautiful ,silver Phantom Rolls Royce, the rope netting around the wooden boards of the sling creaking as it rose higher. Having gained sufficient height to clear the ship's masts, the jib swung back towards the wharf. About half way across the water, there was an exceptionally loud creaking and snapping and we watched in awe as the rotten rope strands parted and as if in a slow motion movie, the car plunged out of its sling and into the harbour with a thud as it hit the water.

We gazed, mesmerised, as for a short while it bobbed and then sank below the surface to the bottom of the harbour leaving only a few air bubbles and surface disturbance to mark the incident.

Next came the tricky part ...The Purser reluctantly made his way to the gangway to explain to the impatient owner of the Rolls what had just gone down...literally... what had just gone down!

CHAPTER 1

In 1967 the summer school holidays promised to be different to those of previous years. The reason for that was they were not holidays, as it meant making a decision as to what to do as a career. I was 18 years old and awaiting my A Level results. University was not really an option. In the sixties you only went to university if you had pretty good grades and a fairly clear view of what career you had in mind. I didn't have either of these. Universities were still the red brick ones then and therefore limited in number. Otherwise there were Technical Colleges which had little appeal.

Well, I couldn't sit around doing nothing so I got a job on a building site which at least gave me enough money for petrol, clothes and entertainment for a couple of months but wasn't going to satisfy my quest for a career...nor that of my father. "What was I going to do?" I was constantly being asked. One day whilst the rain was pouring down and we were sheltering in a half- built house, an elderly labourer (who incidentally was younger than I am now) suddenly launched into me with such robustness, I nearly dropped my cup of tea.

"Why don't you do something with your life?" Fred demanded.   "Is this how you repay your father for giving you a good education? If you don't do something soon, you will end up like me, never having done anything and now nearing retirement". I stared at him. "But I don't have any idea of what I want to do" I said "Then go round the world ", said Fred. "Get some life experience and by the time you come back you may have an idea". I dismissed this with a short laugh. "Go round the world", I said. "How can I? I haven't got any money".

"Work your way round", Fred said. "Get a job on a ship, and let the ship take you round the world and earn money while you do it. "

I was stunned. What a great idea! I had never been outside Europe though I had been to the USSR a couple of years previously with a school trip, and I had accompanied my father to Germany when I was 12 for a wine tasting trip but as nobody had mentioned the correct way to taste wine and spit it out, there were disastrous results and further invitations were not forthcoming. Otherwise France for a limited time on a course at the University de Poitiers, winter sports holidays in Austria and a family holiday in Scandinavia were my limit. The more I thought about this the more it appealed.

"What job could I do on board?" I asked Fred. "They must have Deck Hands to tie the thing up in port, and also Stewards to serve meals and drinks. "No", said Fred, "You want to be a Purser.
"   I
had never heard of the term. "What's that?" I asked.   Fred
didn't elaborate. He merely said, "He's the guy who makes all the money".   No need for further questions at that point. That seemed sufficient information for the present. When I got home that evening I asked my father if he had ever heard of a 'Purser'. He replied that it was like a Hotel Manager come Paymaster on passenger ships and asked if I was interested. I said that I thought I might be. I went to the local library in Camberley, near where I lived and looked up all the contact details of the British passenger shipping companies. I wrote a letter of application to all of them. There was Cunard, P & O, Shaw Savill, Royal Mail, British India, Union Castle, Blue Star Line and several more.

I waited for a couple of weeks for the replies bearing job offers to drop through the letter box. One by one they arrived with the standard reply that they had no vacancies at that time and that they only wanted people with experience. I was completely despondent. They had all replied except one, when I asked my father how on earth you were supposed to get experience when nobody would give you a job? I was still feeling depressed when the final reply arrived from P & O Steam Navigation Company. They operated a Purser Cadet scheme internally within the company and did not want people with previous experience. But they wanted you at the age of 18, required 6 x O Levels and 2 x A Levels to be granted an interview, and then it was a process of selection. I had a foot in the door! Or did I? I had got the 6 x O Levels OK but was still waiting for my A Level results to arrive and wasn't expecting anything of great note. A week later they arrived. I had the required two. I filled in the application and waited.

Several days later the reply arrived and I was granted a preliminary interview in Beaufort House, Aldgate, London. I shaved off my straggly beard, had my hair cut and my suit dry-cleaned. The interview only lasted about 10 minutes and I was taken aback by how many of us there were. I later learned that they took on Purser Cadets twice a year in March and September. There were normally about 250 applicants each time, about 150 being declined by letter for one reason or another. The remaining 100 were granted the 10 minute preliminary interview, and from these, 30 were then chosen to go before the Selection Board.

The next week, I received a letter informing me I was to appear at the Selection Board later that month. I attended this which consisted of a panel of three executives and lasted about half an hour. I always remember one of the questions. They asked me why I wanted to be a Purser Cadet. I answered that I didn't really; I wanted to be a Purser! A week later the letter arrived and I had been accepted as one of just six out of the original 250 applicants. I would have to spend a year in the Head Offices in London as a probationary Cadet. Following satisfactory reports including three days of internal company exams at the end would go to sea still as a probationary Cadet for a further period of six months.

I handed in my notice to the building contractor and said a fond farewell to Fred, promising to send him postcards from exotic places when I eventually reached them. I found somewhere to live, a bedsit in St George's Drive, Victoria, a step away from the BOAC air terminal and Victoria railway station. It had a gas fire with a single gas ring for heating a pan and one electric light. There was no running water unless it rained! I had a tin jug of cold water, a plastic bowl to wash in and a plastic bucket to pour the grey water in to. There were gas and electric meters which took one shilling (5p) coins and the bedsit rental cost me three pounds five shillings a week (£3.25p). It was 13 stops on the tube from Victoria to Aldgate and a weekly ticket cost me 15 shillings (75p). I was to be paid a basic five pounds a week with a further three pounds a week (London Living Allowance), so after rent and travel, I was left with about three pounds a week for food, entertainment and general living. It was bloody miserable!

CHAPTER 2

The six of us were split into three pairs and were assigned to various departments within the Head Office for training which included Crew Pay, Victualing, Furnishings, Insurance, and many smaller ones in Aldgate. There were also the Passenger Booking and Baggage Departments in Cockspur Street in the West End where prospective passengers came to these plush offices to arrange passage.

At this stage, I must explain that British shipping lines in the sixties were part of Trade Conferences and could not compete against each other, only against foreign lines. For instance, Cunard had the East Coast of North America trade, P & O had the Far East and Australia/NZ, Union Castle had South Africa, and Royal Mail, South America. When the Suez Canal was closed at various times and P & O had to go round the Cape, they could not drop off passengers in Cape Town or Durban as this would have encroached on Union Castle's trade. However, P & O could pick up passengers in South Africa and take them to Australia. The competition would only come from foreign lines, usually the French, Dutch or Italians. Business was very gentlemanly and respectful in those days.

The company had eleven passenger ships in 1967, as well as an enormous fleet of cargo ships. The passenger ships consisted of two small ones (Cathay and Chitral) which were first class only. They were cargo/passenger and were used on the run to Hong Kong and back. These were small enough to sail up the Thames to King George V dock. Then there were seven mid-sized ships which sailed in and out of Tilbury. These were Arcadia and Iberia which were sisters, Himalaya, Chusan, Orcades, Orsova and Oronsay. Then there were two larger ones which came in to Southampton, the pride of the fleet, Canberra and Oriana. The four ships starting with the letter 'O' had joined the Fleet when the Orient Line merged with P & O to become P & O Orient lines. Later on the 'Orient' would be dropped to become P & O Lines. What was confusing was that P & O stood for Peninsular and Orient line and not Pacific and Orient as many thought. The Peninsular referred to, was the Iberian Peninsular as the company had been started in 1837 by Sir William Anderson who owned a sailing ship named the William Fawcett and secured the mail run to the Middle East. Prior to the Suez Canal being built, ships terminated at Port Said, passengers travelled overland by camel caravan to Aden where another P & O ship picked them up and continued to the Far East and Australia.

All ships started and finished their voyages in the UK and the same crew stayed with the ship from start to finish which would be anything from three to eight months. When a ship completed a voyage, the crew would be paid off and the ship would remain in port for about 12 days, sometimes in dry dock, to be maintained, renovated, stored and re-crewed before setting off again.   The one thing which was a bonus for us was when we were sent down to a ship by the department to which we were attached for experience and to assist with various tasks. If we were attached to the Booking Department we would go down to Southampton or Tilbury to assist with the passenger disembarkation and embarkation. There were boat trains of course and it was our job to ensure that baggage for the boat train did not get left behind (which of course it often did).

If we were attached to the Victualing Department or Crew Pay Department we would travel daily to Tilbury to assist with crew pay off or signing on new crew, help with checking on stores, logging minor repairs for Carpenters, Plumbers, etc, and a host of general tasks which nobody else wanted to do. This was fine for us in many ways. For a start we got travel expenses and it did not take long to work out how to get from Fenchurch Street to Tilbury Riverside using a combination of British Rail and London

Transport to save about 80% of the fare. Also we had lunch on board, working our way through the limited menu and making a 'takeaway' for the evening. If we were sent to Southampton, we stayed on board and although we did not make money on expenses we at least got to go through the menu for three meals a day. I often think this 'expense' training would have qualified me to become a Member of Parliament!

The Head Office in Aldgate had a social club for the staff and as probationary Sea Cadets we were given honorary membership. Brian, another Cadet told me one Monday that in the evening there was to be the annual meeting followed by a wine and cheese party. We decided to attend, not so much for the meeting to discuss the annual accounts but the wine and cheese party would take care of dinner. As soon as the meeting was over, we tucked in to both though the cheeses were soon gone and by 9.00pm we had both had far too much wine. We were helped out by some of the staff and taken to the Bell, a pub just across the road. Brian drew attention to us by throwing up in the saloon bar after the third pint and we were taken to Aldgate East tube, Brian being placed on an eastbound to Mile End and I, on a westbound to Victoria. Unfortunately I dropped asleep, missed Victoria and woke up in a siding in Richmond. I was the only one left on the train and went back to sleep until early morning when the train was back in use again and this time I stayed on going all the way back to Aldgate East arriving for work on time, albeit a bit dishevelled and feeling like death. Brian and I were in front of the Training Manager that morning for a reprimand but we were not alone. Another Cadet, Tony had been to a fancy dress party the night before and had come straight to work from the party. Fortunately he was wearing a suit but dressed as a gangster (Machine Gun Kelly, I believe) in a double-breasted wide striped suit complete with fedora and plastic machine gun.

After my first couple of weeks, I visited home for the weekend to see my parents. I told my father that I had to go and visit the bank in order to open an account so that my meagre salary could be paid in. Until that time, all my previous jobs had been paid in cash in a pay packet and weekly. This way I had to wait till the end of the month before being paid. Fortunately I still had a few quid left from my days on the building site to see me through the first month but such was my naivety. I also told him that I had been made to join the Pension Scheme. I was dumbfounded! I was 18 years old and earning eight pounds a week for goodness sake. I can still remember my father's words. He said to me, "Son, that's the best thing you could have done". Years later I recall his words and realise how right he was.

CHAPTER 3

One of the first ships we were sent to work on in port was the Oriana in Southampton. She was berthed next to the Queen Mary who was making preparations for sailing out to Long Beach in California where she would be permanently moored as a hotel. There was tight security during her final days in the UK but we did manage to get passes to look her over. I was agog at the size of her and it was a tearful sight a few days later to stand on the deck of the Oriana and watch her slip her moorings at her home port. She would have to sail around Cape Horn as she was too big for the Panama Canal. The docks were lined with well-wishers, the Band of the Royal Marines played her out and the RAF did a fly past as she sailed out of Southampton for the last time. I felt that I was witnessing such a piece of history, not just to think of all the passengers she had carried to and from New York and the crew who had worked on her during her lifetime but the tens of thousands of troops she had carried to safety as she outran Adolf's U-boats.

Generally, when we worked on the ships during our training, the Pursers' staff was quite amenable. After all, they had been through all this themselves at some stage and took great delight in seeing others suffer who were following in their footsteps. In February 1968 Brian, David, Clive and I were working by the old Arcadia in Tilbury for a couple of weeks. The Assistant Purser in charge of crew wages called Richard was delightful but the Senior Assistant Purser, Barry was something else. He was 6 ft 7" tall and used every inch of his height to intimidate you. He would shout 'Cadet' at the top of his voice every time he needed a task performed and we took it in turns to oblige. One morning he dispatched me to the Laundry at the aft end to find his clean uniform. I eventually found the Chief Laundryman halfway down a can of Allsopps lager and who insisted I join him. On my way back, the Chief Steward collared me for a sub-errand and by the time I returned to the Purser's Bureau, I had been away about half an hour. Barry was apoplectic! His face was red as he screamed at me demanding to know where I had been, pointing to the stripes on his shoulder and screaming something at me about insubordination.

I was no newcomer to this sort of treatment as at school, it had been compulsory to join the CCF (Combined Cadet Force). I recall one time when our Army squad was being trained for what was known as the Cert 'A' exam, we were being trained on how to drill a squad and each of us in turn had to come out in front and perform this task, having the squad do various parade and rifle drills. The Sergeant in charge was a tall lad and we used to refer to him as Granny due to his round spectacles. Eventually it was my turn to drill the squad and I asked him if there was anything specific he wanted me to have them do. He barked at me that I knew all the orders and it was completely up to me. "Right", I said and yelled at the top of my voice, "SQUAD!...DISSSS-MISSS ."

They all turned to the right and hared off down the road back to the barracks, leaving me to face the Sergeant. The veins in his red neck throbbed as he screamed at me "You bloody little snerd" and several other terms of endearment which I won't repeat here. For that minor breach I was given the job of sweeping the parade square with a toothbrush by torchlight one Saturday night. I had already completed a couple of tasks for other army disciplinary misdemeanours, namely cutting the grass on the cricket pitch using a pair of nail scissors and on another occasion after a shower of rain, emptying all the puddles of dirty water in the gravel road leading to the parade ground and refilling them with clean water. I believe this Sergeant went on to Sandhurst and finished up as a Major General before he retired. I often wonder if he remembers me with the same degree of affection.

There was a dock strike in November of 1967 and the Cathay was due in to King George V to go into dry dock. It was decided to take her over to Rotterdam dry dock, and Clive and I were to go with her. We sailed on the overnight trip to Rotterdam and experienced our first time in dry dock. Although we had a comfortable cabin each, being in dry dock in those days meant there was no water, so showers and toilets ashore had to be used. There was also no steam so most of the meals had to be cooked on Calor gas stoves for the crew. The crew on the Cathay and Chitral were mainly Chinese from Hong Kong in all three departments, Deck, Engine and Pursers but with British Officers and Petty Officers. We were under the jurisdiction of the Senior Assistant Purser called Jeremy, one of life's gentlemen and raconteur extraordinaire. One Sunday morning at 9.00am we awaited our instructions for the day and he asked what we would like to do? Would we like the day off? As we nodded, wondering what the catch was, he just said he would see us at 9.00am the next morning. Clive and I decided to go into Rotterdam which meant catching a small boat with an outboard which acted as a ferry and could take three passengers. We caught this across the river but approaching the other side there was nowhere to land as the quay was lined with empty barges all riding high in the water. 'Jump', yelled the boatman in Dutch. We jumped. The Chinese waiter and I managed to catch the side of a barge and haul ourselves up. Clive was a bit heavier and when the ferry went, he was left hanging on to the side of the barge with his legs in the water. I was laughing so much I couldn't help at first but seeing the little Chinaman struggling to haul Clive's bulk up the side, I gave a hand. Clive was heavy but we eventually hauled him over the side of the barge and he slid through some loose oil on deck. He was wearing his suit. Poor old Clive! We had to return to the Cathay so he could get changed and take his suit to Rotterdam to be dry-cleaned.

For four weeks during our training we attended the London School of Nautical Cookery in the basement of the Red Ensign Club in the East End. Every day we were given a three course menu to cook in addition to making bread and rolls. I was always being yelled at because my bread would never rise. Presumably I didn't knead it enough or leave it long enough to prove before putting it in the oven. Fed up with being bollocked daily, I shoved an extra portion of yeast in one day. When I pulled out the loaf it had risen beautifully. It was about 18" high with two barred oven shelves buried in it. It also tasted like marmite. We were always finished by after lunch and the residents of Dock Street were usually treated to six cooks playing rugby with loaves of bread on their way home as that was all they were good for. At the end of the course we all qualified for a Second Cook and Bakers Certificate.

During the year we also had to attend colloquial German classes twice a week with a lovely, elderly German lady. She did well to put up with the six of us but she persevered and we did all qualify for the Institute of Linguist's basic conversation test at the end of the year. We also had to attend night school in King's Cross two evenings a week to learn book-keeping. Then there was a 12 hour course at Sight and Sound in Oxford Circus where we had to learn to touch type to reach a basic 25 words a minute. The only trouble with this was there was an extremely attractive Australian girl running the course who would wear the shortest of miniskirts and each time she leaned over to correct someone next to you...typing was the last thing on your mind. Concentration was a problem.

The time spent in the office could be a bit boring, necessary but boring, depending to which department you were attached. The Victualling Department was one of these as their answer to training you was to sit you down with two large volumes of Policies and Procedures which you were supposed to wade through and emerge totally knowledgeable the other end. Most of this was learning how to calculate the food and drink requirements for a given number of crew and passengers to reach a certain stage of the voyage, bearing in mind price, quality and availability abroad as well as the limitations of storage space. Fairly important I suppose if you didn't want to run out of things half way across the ocean. I had to sit opposite the Superintendent Chef, a man who had spent most of his working life at sea, eventually becoming a Head Chef and in the twilight of his career accepting a position in the head office whereby he was in charge of the menus on board the ships. I used to watch him 'work' whilst studying my tomes and wishing I had his job rather than mine. His desk and the floor surrounding, was covered with piles of menus, of which all ships had to send a copy at the end of each voyage. These piles of menus I assume, were to make him look busy, although I never saw him actually look at any. His morning would start with coffee, followed by an in depth study of 'Stamp Weekly'. As the time approached Noon, 'The Sporting Life' was produced and the afternoon's hopeful winners selected. At lunchtime he would depart for whichever pub where he took his midday fare, presumably stopping off at the Turf Accountant on the way. He would return from an obviously sumptuous lunch, sometimes a little overwrought. In fact on occasions, as overwrought as a parrot, and he would doze in his chair until around 3.30pm when he would make a discreet exit to catch his train home, stopping at the Turf Accountant on his way to the station to pick up his winnings.

The Crew Pay Department was more interesting however as we had to learn how to work out crew wages on enormous sheets called a Portage Bill. One Assistant Purser had the responsibility of calculating wages, advancing wages and calculating the end of voyage payoff without allowing anyone to go into debt. This was a very responsible job and could make or break spirit amongst the crew, creating a reputation for a 'happy' or an 'unhappy' ship. We also had to learn all about the disciplinary procedures of fines and forfeitures, entries in the Official Log Book and numerous other official returns for Income Tax, National Insurance and in those days we also had Graduated Contributions (yet another form of government taxation at the time). We would also visit a ship on the day it arrived from overseas to help the Pay Department from the head office conduct the crew payoff. This was always a good day out as the crew would be champing at the bit to receive their balance of wages and get off home. After the passenger disembarkation, the entire main deck would be laid out with trestle tables and the entire crew from Captain downwards would have to travel from one table to another for the sign off process, receiving the balance of their wages, apart from the officers who were paid directly into their banks. Several of the crew would be drunk and wanting to fight the world. One of the Pay Department officials had the same surname as myself and was a real character. His name was Jimmy and was well known throughout both the passenger and cargo fleets especially with Captains and Chief Stewards. He took a shine to me and used to tell everyone I was his nephew. This was sometimes quite embarrassing when one of them would ask after my 'aunt' and my 'female cousins'. One day Jimmy took me with him to assist with the crew pay off on one of the cargo ships, the ss Balranald. I couldn't help thinking that with just the two of us this was going to be quite a work up. As it was, on cargo ships nearly all the crew was paid directly into their banks and the only person paid on board via the Portage Bill was an Assistant Storekeeper. Jimmy checked the calculations, paid the man off and we were done by 9.30am. The rest of the day was spent in the Chief Steward's cabin being taught the art of pouring the perfect gin and tonic.

Around five months of our training were spent in the Cockspur Street office at the bottom of the Haymarket. This meant a less expensive tube fare but trying to have lunch on a three shilling luncheon voucher was nigh impossible...even then. We would sit with one of the experienced Booking Clerks at first and prospective passengers would be interviewed as to where and when they wished to travel, what sort of accommodation,etc and be given an 'offer' which would remain open for 10 days. Linked to this was the Baggage Department where passengers could make arrangements for hold baggage or unaccompanied baggage. Normally manned by two persons, it was down to one on my first morning due to Hector being on holiday. Geoff, the remaining one was my designated instructor, but had flu and had to go home at 10.00am leaving me in charge of the Baggage Department. I had two desks to attend and three phones which rang permanently. I had not a clue what I was doing as I apologised to those waiting while I answered the phones and tried desperately to get information on how to have a packing case picked up in Coventry, taken to the docks in London and loaded on to a series of cargo ships via various ports in the world to eventually reach Rangoon…and then arrange haulage from Rangoon docks to somewhere in the Burmese interior. At least being dumped in the deep end, I learned quickly and by the time Geoff had returned from his bout of flu a week later, he couldn't believe how competent and knowledgeable I had become, worrying in case I might be offered the job on a permanent basis. He need not worry, I assured him.

During the summer cruising season from Southampton to the Mediterranean and the Baltic, there were always boat trains between Southampton Harbour and Waterloo. Although the old railway terminus in Southampton had been turned into offices including studios for

Southern TV, there was still Southampton Central which was now the only station and a distance from both the old and the new docks. However trains could still be diverted from Southampton Central to a line which ran to the docks and could stop at any of the berths right alongside the embarkation/disembarkation shed. For a brief period in June there was a rail strike which meant that on the Sunday when the Chusan was due to turn round, a convoy of buses and baggage vans had to be organized in lieu. Brian came to me excitedly and said they were asking for volunteers to shift baggage at Waterloo at Noon on Sunday and would pay 10 pounds. This was more than a week's wage. We put our names down.

We had to meet under the big clock at Waterloo at Noon and instead of shifting baggage the two of us were dispatched to the Area Manager's office below the concourse to answer the telephones and deal with the many queries from friends and relatives that were expected. We armed ourselves with a Sunday newspaper to share and a couple of pints of beer from the Long Bar on the station and settled down to start answering the three phones. At 1.40pm we were told it was all over and could go home which was a lot sooner than expected. Especially as the phone had not rung once!

Finding ourselves at a loose end we took my Ford Thames van, a three speed vehicle which did not have seat belts but had two free-wheeling arm chairs instead of car seats, probably completely illegal to be on the road at the time. We drove down to Sevenoaks to see Clive, my Cadet pairing. His Dad ran a garage and they lived right beside it. They were fully aware of the conditions we lived under even though Clive lived at home and commuted. His Dad took us out to the pub for a couple of pints and when we got back to the garage his Mum had made a terrific afternoon tea and we were encouraged to demolish what we could. We did. When it was time to leave his Mum had made us up a doggy bag each which would keep us going for most of the next week. I was low on fuel and asked his Dad if I could buy a couple of gallons to get us back to London before the garage closed. During tea, Clive's Dad had filled up my fuel tank and wouldn't let me pay a thing. What an absolutely lovely and thoughtful couple they were and I have never forgotten their kindness and generosity.

Towards the end of our year, we had to attend the Shipping Federation for three days in Prescott Street. The Shipping Federations were like job centres for Registered British Seafarers. Major ports all had them and the jobs available would be marked up on a blackboard. If say, a job as a Deck Hand or a Waiter advertised as being available on the Chusan, appealed, you could apply at the desk and be given a joining order for Tilbury on a certain date. Often the seafarer would have no money and would have to be given a note to be supplied with uniform at Miller Rayner's Uniform Supply and also a warrant for a rail ticket, the cost of both these being collected from the seafarer's wages by the Crew Purser during the voyage.

Another three days would have to be spent at the Board of Trade Mercantile Marine Office in Dock Street. Every British seafarer had to register here to be issued with a Discharge Book which was both proof of registration but also a record of employment. The book would be kept by the Crew Purser when a seafarer signed on the Ship's Articles and returned when he signed off. The ship's registry stamp would be there together with dates of the voyage and a report on Conduct and Ability, together with the Master's signature. A British seafarer also had to obtain a red Seaman's Book from this office which was a seaman's passport covering his travels all over the world whilst signed on a vessel. Everyone had to have these documents regardless of rank. You had to have your photograph taken holding up a number, much the same as when you are put in prison. Not an unusual experience for many. A one day firefighting course was also held at East Ham Fire Station. A fire at sea can be terrifying as there is nowhere to escape. Although we would never be qualified firemen after one day, it opened our eyes as to the dangers and we did learn which extinguisher to use on which fires. On another occasion we were sent down to assist on the Iberia when she came in to Tilbury. Unfortunately one of the fuel tanks had leaked into the First Class baggage room during the voyage and many of the passengers' suitcases were floating around in a couple of feet of fuel oil. We had to don overalls and boots and try and salvage whatever we could. Thankfully we were too junior at that stage to deal with the passengers ourselves and this was left to the more senior Purser's Officers. Not an enviable job.

Exam time approached. There were three days of them and results were promptly produced. I came second out of the six of us and as we would go in pairs to a ship, it meant that John and I would be first away. Uniform had to be purchased to our own cost and this usually came to around three hundred pounds, a fairly tall order for someone living in London on eight pounds a week. The blue uniform was the blue serge reefer suit but you had to have blue mess kit for the evenings (a uniform no longer required these days unfortunately), and due to the time the ship's laundry took to return clean clothes, it meant at least six sets of tropical uniform and four sets of white mess kit. Air conditioning was only partial on some ships which meant loads of shirts, socks and underclothes. Fortunately the uniform suppliers had an arrangement with the company so that for a twenty pound deposit, you could buy your uniform and sign a ten pound monthly standing order for the next 34 months. There was only one problem. We were to lose our 'London living allowance' and our pay would revert to 27 pounds per month less of course the 10 pounds to pay off the uniform purchase. Still, there was no rent or food to pay so we had to be better off.

John and I were appointed to the Orcades in Tilbury, a 28,000 ton ship which carried 1,200 passengers and 600 crew. She was built in 1948 as the previous Orcades had been sunk off the Cape of Good Hope during the war. We were to join by 8.00pm on the Wednesday a couple of days before sailing for Sydney. I had already given notice to my landlady and fetched my old school trunk from home in which to pack this mountain of uniform. I emptied my bank account except for one penny to keep it open so that my monthly 'salary' could be paid in as normal. I dragged my baggage on to the tube to Fenchurch Street and down to Tilbury Riverside. I had to take a taxi then as it was too far to the berth to carry a trunk. After paying the taxi, I mounted the gangway with three shillings and sixpence to my name. The ship was like a ghost ship, a power cut, cold and dark. I found the two berth cabin I was to share where John had already arrived. He was sitting in the dark, feeling and looking pretty miserable. The cabin was inside with no porthole on C Deck, only slightly larger than the two bunks it housed. There were two wardrobes about 12" in width, completely inadequate, two drawers under the bottom bunk and a washbasin. Showers and toilets were communal and down the alleyway. It did not take long before I was feeling pretty miserable too. John had already reserved the lower bunk and so I had the top one. This seemed quite acceptable at the time, though the disadvantages of a top bunk became more apparent once we started inviting girls back to the cabin for a 'night cap'.

CHAPTER 4

The concept of cruising as we know it today had not really arrived; certainly not as far as the Americans were concerned although it had been fashionable with the British and Australians for some years. The principal business was transportation, the carriage of people and their chattels from one country to another. P & O was very much in the business of what was known as the 'Ten Pound Poms". Australia was in need of Immigrants and offered a scheme whereby certain nationalities including British, if acceptable to Australia House would be eligible for the ten pound Immigrant scheme. Families looking for a completely new life the other side of the world would pay ten pounds per head for the passage, the balance of the fare being paid for by the Australian Government. Accommodation on board would be either in the tourist end of a two-class ship or on one of the two ships which had been converted to tourist Class only. Cabins were either four or six berth and down on the bottom decks. Males were berthed in cabins on one side and females on the other. This meant that mothers and daughters would share a six berth cabin with other mothers and daughters whom they had probably never met and the same for the fathers and sons on the other side. Showers and toilets were communal and down the alley-way apiece.

Baggage was in three categories. There was HOLD baggage which the passenger never saw during the voyage...but did so hopefully at the other end. This would be delivered to the dock some days before sailing and loaded by crane down into one of the ship's holds at whatever level dictated by the port of discharge. Then there was CABIN baggage which was kept in the cabin for immediate requirements. This had to be limited of course as baggage belonging to the persons on both top and lower bunks had to be stowed beneath the lower bunk. Finally there was BAGGAGE ROOM baggage. Whether travelling from England to Australia or vice versa there was inevitably a climate change about half way across and so the clothes not required for the first half were put in the Baggage Room and could be accessed for a couple of hours any day at sea.

During the English summer months from June to September, those ships not required on main line voyaging were used for Mediterranean cruising, most of the passengers being British. There were usually three months of fortnightly cruises out of Southampton before reverting to main line voyaging out to Australia again. During the UK winter months, which of course was summer in Australia, a series of two week cruises was undertaken out of Sydney to the South Pacific Islands. These were mainly for Australian and New Zealand passengers and the season would last until around March when we would set off back to the UK again. As mentioned earlier, the same crew would be on board from the UK back to the UK and this meant being away for sometimes six to eight months at a time. On arrival back in the UK you would normally get 10 days leave before returning for the next six month voyage.

The passengers embarked during the afternoon and evening of our third day on board and John and I were put on the Enquiry Counter. It was manic! Nobody liked their cabin, everybody wanted to change, nobody wanted to share, all demanding that they be moved immediately as they insisted they had paid for sole occupancy. Of course, none of them had, it was just a try-on, which we learned was standard procedure on sailing day. Many used to come to the counter before actually going to the cabin. Of course we were pretty ignorant of all this and not confident of getting into slanging matches with the paying public. Apart from not being sure of our facts, it was obvious we were young, junior and inexperienced, something of which people always take advantage. In the beginning, just about every query we took, had to be referred to the Senior Assistant Purser, Mike who was in charge of the accommodation. He was inundated and doing his best to deal with one problem at a time while the rest of us bayed for his attention to our own query. One thing I did enjoy was having a passage ticket thrust in my face and being asked how many decks they would have to go up to locate their cabin. I would take great delight in telling them they would have to go four decks down, and NOT UP.

I hated it. We sailed at 10.00pm and the desk finally closed at 11.00pm. We looked forward to a night's rest. Not to be. The number of passengers would not tally and that meant checking tickets against physical bodies to ascertain where the discrepancy was and reach the correct number. The two of us were constantly being sent to specific cabins to ascertain the names of those present and bearing in mind most people had gone to bed by midnight our cabin visits were met with hostility and rudeness. Once the numbers were correct the passenger list had to be typed before arriving in Le Havre the next morning. There were no computers in those days, not even electric typewriters, just the old manual type. Information had to be read out to the Assistant Purser typing in order to make it faster but we finally finished everything for our arrival in Le Havre at 7.00 am the next morning and then we had a full day of work ahead of us.

There was a mini embarkation in Le Havre, mainly French, German, Dutch or a few British who were unable to board in England for tax reasons. Then we had to deal with the second attempters who wanted to change cabin. Having been firmly told that they had only paid for a cabin share and not sole occupancy, they would have another try using the excuse of incompatibility with the other occupants. Often both parties would be present having come to a previous arrangement between themselves to make a joint protest and try to bully the Purser's staff into splitting them up and giving them a cabin each. Usually however, the experienced Senior Assistant Purser would fight them off with the fact that there were no other cabins which was usually true. Occasionally there might be a spare cabin as far as another port but then it was scheduled to be occupied so was technically not available. Sometimes, however, when a passenger was totally impossible, claiming he could not go back to that cabin to share with this other occupant, the SAP would relent and stick him in another cabin with a spare bunk so that he was still sharing and usually in a much noisier cabin. By the end of the second day, we were on our knees, having had no sleep and wishing we had never joined. We were only 48 hours into a six month voyage. Surely it had to get better. But we just had to stick it out, there was no choice.

Things did get better of course. As we gradually gained knowledge and got to know the ropes, life did not seem so bad. The other Assistant Pursers were good to us, having been through it all themselves and were only too aware of the little money we were paid. Once the voyage got under way, the novelty of cocktail parties, mixing with passengers, eating fine food for free, and chatting up the female passengers made the initial onslaught fade. Our Cadet training then resumed. One of us would work in the different departments on the ship and the other would assist on the Reception Desk. Half way through the voyage we would swap. I was to be on the Desk which I disliked intensely. Even once I had learned the ropes, I found many of the passengers very demanding of the impossible and quite rude when they did not get their own way. Still, it was all experience.

There were of course, as always life's lighter moments. Jeff, one of the Assistant Pursers was a born comedian and practical joker. He was the senior of the two cashiers and sometimes just prior to opening his cashier's window at 8.15am, he would take off his shoes and socks and put them just outside his safe. He would then climb inside and have me lock him in. At 8.20am when he should have been open and an impressive queue had formed, I would have to raise his shutters on the expectant public and apologise for his tardiness, explaining that he had overslept. I would then fumble around for his safe keys in my pocket and unlock the safe. The passengers would then see me disappear inside and hear me shaking him awake and urging him to get cracking as he had a queue at his window. Jeff would then stumble out of the safe, hair tousled and start to put on his socks and shoes. He would mumble an apology to the horrified passengers at the head of the line. Many a time I would hear a disbelieving passenger ask him if he actually slept in the safe and he would explain that it was part of the company's security requirements for insurance purposes as well as the fact that it saved them the expense of having to give him a cabin. Goodness knows how many actually believed him but he was very convincing and I am sure many did.

On another occasion, he would put a black glove on his left hand and keep it below the counter out of sight. When cashing a traveller's cheque, he would just count the money laboriously with his right hand and inevitably some 'helpful' passenger would suggest it might be quicker and more accurate if he used two hands. Without a word, he would produce this black gloved hand and lay it on the money to anchor the notes and proceed to count them with his right. The 'helpful' passenger would be completely overcome with embarrassment and be apologising profusely while Jeff continued to count. The trouble was he had to then wear this glove most of the time or be rumbled.

The Cashiers' windows were wide and long and when there was nobody waiting, Jeff would take a cloth and shine imaginary glass between himself and the passengers. A passenger would arrive at the window and ask if he could cash a cheque. Jeff would mouth a silent yes, and then lean round the edge of the imaginary glass and ask in a normal voice what denominations he would like. The passenger would move to the side to speak to him and the two of them would be talking around the edge of a piece of a glass screen which wasn't there.

At last, after three months, it was time for John and I to swap and he reluctantly took my place on the Desk. To start with I had to spend two weeks as a Cabin Steward. One of the experienced Cabin Stewards, 'Flossie' as he was known had the responsibility of teaching me. Having been at boarding school for 11 years, I at least knew how to make beds, though making top bunks is quite an art and pretty physical. I was taught the correct way to do things of course and not the 'cowboy' way as these chaps were no fools; they were not going to show us their tricks of the trade.

I spent time in each department of the 'Hotel' although it was not referred to as 'Hotel' in those days. That would come later when cruising with Americans took off. Most passengers did not understand the word 'Purser' and used to say 'Pursuer'. Goodness knows what they thought we did. I spent two weeks each as a Table Waiter in the classier Dining Room, as a Bar Steward in one of the Public Rooms, as an Assistant Barman, sometimes behind the Bar and sometimes in the Cellars. It was not unusual for the seasoned Stewards to play practical jokes on us greenhorns. One lunchtime, whilst working in the Dining Room, I had my table fully laid for six, with a crisp, clean white tablecloth, full silver cutlery laid out with roll bowl, water jug, glasses, butter, cruet, napkins, etc, and was waiting for the gong to go and the doors to open. Twelve Noon, the gong went and the passengers charged in like the start of the Great North Run. The poor half-starved things hadn't eaten since breakfast about three hours previously. My six passengers arrived and I pulled out the chair for one of the ladies to sit. What I had not realised until that point was that the neighbouring Stewards had discreetly tied the end of the tablecloth around the arm of a chair. With a flourishing sweep as I pulled out the chair, the entire cloth pulled everything on to the floor. The passengers stared in surprise. I stared in horror! However, to give them their due, my fellow Waiters who had arranged this trick were well organised and within 30 seconds, a new tablecloth, cutlery, crockery, glass, butter, rolls and water jug were all in place as if nothing had happened. However, it did unnerve me and I was always wondering with each meal served what would be in store for me next.

On another occasion out in the Galley, one Waiter bet another that he couldn't walk round the entire Dining Room with his penis hanging out. He collected a plate of mixed salad and took out his penis, burying it in the salad. He then held the plate directly in front of him and walked right the way round the Dining Room and back into the Galley without anyone noticing and thereby winning his bet. I don't recall what happened to the salad, I only hope it got thrown away.

I also had to spend two weeks in the Provision Stores, two weeks in the Butcher's Shop which included a lot of freezer work. Then I spent four weeks as a Cook in the Galley. I remember being put on omelettes at breakfast. I was trying to make about seven omelettes at once, all different, and getting in a terrible mess, making too many simultaneously whilst the Waiters on the other side of the hot press screamed and yelled that they couldn't serve up such a mess and demanding another to be made. Eventually the Sous Chef had to come to my rescue.

It was during my time in the Galley that I experienced my first death at sea. As I have said, many youngsters had taken advantage of the 'ten pound pom' scheme offered by the Australian Government whereby you paid ten pounds per person for your voyage out, the balance of the fare being paid by the Australian Government. On arrival in Australia, these immigrants would be put in a transit camp until proper work and housing had been found. Their passports were kept by the government for two years after which time you were free to stay or go. However, should you wish to go home before the two years were up, you not only had to find the fare home but had to repay the government the balance of your fare out in order to repossess your passport. Not many had those sort of funds which was the main reason they were emigrating in the first place.

This often meant that the onus was on parents to travel out to Australia to visit their offspring. Voyages out to Australia were always full of laughter and joy as these retired folk looked forward to seeing their sons or daughters for the first time since they left. The atmosphere on voyages back a few months later was quite a different matter. Many elderly passengers were depressed with the cold realization that they would probably never see their children or grandchildren again as the fares were expensive and their years were advancing.

It was a lovely sunny morning about half way across the Indian Ocean and I had gone out on to the after end of C Deck between breakfast sittings to have a cigarette. As I was leaning over the rail, something came hurtling past me from above and landed in the sea. At first I thought someone had thrown garbage over and then to my horror I realised it was a body. I immediately threw a lifebuoy over near him to mark the spot and dashed to the nearest phone to call the Bridge. Immediately the alarm was raised and the ship started to go into a Williamson Turn which is a figure of eight to bring you back on your same course. Stopping a steam ship travelling at 28 knots is not like stopping a car at 30 mph, it takes much longer. About 20 minutes went by whilst we slowed and tuned and a boat lowered. The body of the passenger was recovered but unfortunately he was dead, probably the impact of hitting the water at that speed from that height rather than drowning. This gentleman was one such case as I had described above and according to his wife, had been so depressed since leaving Sydney, he just felt life was no longer worth living. All very well of course, but his wife was then doubly distraught.

Another evening I was put on carving and serving roast pork for the Tourist class dinner. Towards the end of the first sitting it was obvious that there was not going to be sufficient for second sitting as it had been popular during the first. I went to the Head Chef, George and informed him. Back then, a Head Chef's idea of supervision during service was to sit in his office in the Galley with a constant supply of Guinness. "We'll see how we go" was the response I got. This was encouraging as usually by that time of the evening , George could only manage an alcoholic fuelled grunt. I returned to the carving station and sure enough about half way through the second sitting we ran out of roast pork. I went back to the George to inform him. Most mortals would have panicked but not him. George calmly walked to the Garde Manger and removed a few trays of streaky bacon from the fridge, destined for breakfast the following morning. To my dismay, he poured gravy over and flashed the trays under the salamander and served them up. As I stood there agape, he turned to me and growled, "Bleeding pork isn't it?" Amazingly nobody complained.

I then spent a couple of weeks in the Laundry. Ship's laundries then were usually positioned right at the aft end just below the mooring deck, open in order to get some cool air when in the Tropics. We used to work just wearing a towel most of the time and it was hard graft constantly loading huge, ancient industrial washing machines with sheets, towels, napkins and tablecloths dragging them out and reloading into water extractors and finally into the tumble dryers, before feeding them through the callender to press them. They then had to be folded manually. This was constant from 6.00am until 8.00pm. It was physically exhausting, and due to the heat partly from the weather and partly from the laundry machinery, many cases of Allsopps lager were consumed in the course of a day.

One evening, my cabin mate, John informed me he had invited a girl back to the cabin that night and could I give him a couple of hours privacy? I was tired but thought it was unusual for John and so decided to find elsewhere to sleep. By the time the Crew Bar closed, I still had nowhere to sleep and not wishing to spoil John's evening, went back to the Laundry and lowered myself on the rope down into the lazarette where the sacks of soap powder were stowed. I went to sleep in my boiler suit and when I awoke at 6.00am, I was so stiff I could hardly move, let alone climb back up the rope. I reached my cabin and knocked gently on the door, not sure if the girl was still there. The door opened and John stood there with his toothbrush in his hand. To my query regarding the girl's presence he informed me that she had left at around 11.00pm. I could have throttled him.

I also spent time in the Linen Locker and also the Print Shop; a week with the Plumber; and a week with the Carpenter helping with minor repairs and taking soundings of the water tanks. A couple of days were also spent with the Chief Photographer developing photos and with the Shop Manager in the ship's shop. My time in the Print Shop was interesting as there were no computers then and type had to be set using the old typeset. Anyway, one morning in Melbourne, the Printer, Ken sat on his spectacles and broke them. Not having a spare pair, an appointment was made with an optician in Melbourne and off he went. However he was unable to get an appointment until the afternoon and so he spent the morning in a Melbourne bar whiling away the time. He had his eyes tested but there was insufficient time to have the lenses made up before sailing so they arranged to send them to Sydney by overnight courier. Inevitably in Sydney the package with the new spectacles arrived and was delivered on board by the Agent. The Printer put them on and then complained that they were no good, everything was blurred and he couldn't see a thing. The problem was that he had spent so long in the bar in Melbourne before his appointment he had got totally pie-eyed before having his eyes tested. Now he was trying them on first thing in the morning, completely sober, and so everything was blurred. For the next few months until the ship reached England again, Ken would spend the morning drinking crew rum until he got sozzled enough to see through his spectacles and start work in the afternoon. Well, that was his excuse anyway.

My final two weeks were spent with a week on the Bridge on the 8 to 12 Watch and a week in the Engine Room on the 12 to 4 Watch. On the Bridge I was under the charge of the Officer of the Watch, the Junior Second Officer. Entering or exiting port was an interesting time on the

Bridge as these were days before bow or stern thrusters and tugs had to be used in most ports. Also, the Captain did not have direct control of the ship's power from the Bridge as nowadays but had to rely on communication with the Engine Room for speed and propulsion forward or astern. However, at sea with nothing but miles of water to look at in every direction, it could become a bit boring for four hours at a time. During the evening watch it had to be totally dark on the Bridge. Forward of, and below the Bridge was the Stadium where passenger sports, etc, were held during the day as it was sheltered on four sides. Due to the confines of four and six berth cabins, couples found it difficult to have some privacy and the dark Stadium was a popular spot at night. On each Bridge wing was a large signalling lamp. Detecting movement and low sound down in the Stadium, we would give enough time for them to get into a compromising position and then hit the power which would floodlight the Stadium. Couples were caught like rabbits in the headlights ...literally! We would only leave them on for a few seconds and then switch off but the swearing and abuse which drifted up went on for some time.

The Engine Room was something else. Steam ships seem far more complicated and messy than the modern day diesel-engined ships. Large boilers, engines and other associated machinery took up much more space then and the noise was constant. I was under the charge of the Junior Second Engineer who probably wanted a mechanical idiot like me down there as much as I wanted to be there. Although I did not understand much about how everything worked, it was an experience to see the conditions the staff had to work under and I had a better appreciation of why Engineers have more than a few beers after finishing a Watch. One night I was sitting in the Control Room when the Junior Second Engineer told me to watch all these dials as he was nipping out. If anything moved, he informed me, not to touch anything but to let him know when he returned. I was terrified. What if the Bridge phoned down wanting a different speed or something? Fortunately, they didn't but I watched about a dozen gauges and dials with concentration. On his return I informed him that one of the gauges had moved about one third of the way round the dial. Showing concern, he asked me which, and I pointed to the specific gauge. It was the clock and he had been sitting on the toilet for 20 minutes.

CHAPTER 5

I was still 19 years old and the excitement of travel was still very raw. After departure from Le Havre, we had progressed to Lisbon and Las Palmas, then Bermuda, Barbados and Trinidad. There was usually a few hours off in each port but with our limited wage, there was not much you could do apart from walking as far as one could in the allotted time. Mind you walking to Sandy Lane Beach in Barbados for a few hours in the sun certainly beat the idea of sitting at a desk in London. In Trinidad however, the Crew Assistant Purser, Martin kindly invited me out for the day along with a couple of others. We had a car free of charge from Libby the Tour Agent who came with us and we drove over the mountains to Maracas Bay. What a place! I had not seen beaches like this before, apart from on film. During the day I was introduced and got very used to Planters Punches not realising quite how potent they could be. At 19, I was still testing the limits of alcohol I could sustain, sometimes with disastrous results.

The Assistant Pursers' accommodation was

up on the Stadium Deck, a couple below the Bridge and the parties up there were notorious. You were allowed to invite passengers to your accommodation only until a certain hour but as long as you were discreet, a blind eye was normally turned. However, every night the Assistant Pursers had two large bins of punch made up which stood at the end of their alleyway. One was a red wine punch and the other a sort of green crème de menthe punch. These were 'port and starboard' punches, not for any specific party but just to drink whilst getting changed into evening dress and in case anyone stopped by for a drink.

These Stadiums which I mention, on the forward part of each ship where sports were held, had folding wood and glass screens which could form a weather resistant area for activities but could be folded back to create open deck space. Unlike the Panama Canal where the canal dues are calculated on the gross tonnage of the vessel, the canal dues for the Suez are calculated on open deck space and so these were always folded right back for a Suez transit as the less enclosed space you could declare, the less the fees. Also unlike the Panama where there are three series of locks to pass through due to the difference in the level of the Atlantic and Pacific oceans, there are no locks in Suez as it is all on the one level, a channel through the desert. There are however the Bitter Lakes where the vessels congregate to go through the narrower channels in convoy. Sometimes this happened at night and all ships were required to have a Suez lamp right in the bow, like a large headlamp to keep the ship steering in the centre of the channel and not veer to the side and run aground.

Martin, the Assistant Purser used to keep an air pistol under his pillow. At around 4.00am when he would collapse on his bunk in full blue mess kit, he would remember that the light switch was over by the door. Rather than face the arduous task of stumbling back across to the door and turn out the light, and negotiate back to the bunk in the dark, it was easier to reach under the pillow for the air pistol and shoot the light bulb out of the deckhead. He became a good friend and after about six years at sea married the daughter of a wealthy Australian cattle farmer, went to university as a mature student and became a Barrister, soon afterwards migrating to Australia.

As a Cadet and having to share a cabin, inviting a girl back to the cabin was naturally a lot more difficult. For a start all junior Officers had to be away from the public eye by midnight, which I later found out was fairly generous. The general idea was that it did not look good to see the Officers drinking until the wee small hours and then looking bleary eyed the next morning at 8.00am on duty. Of course, there was a lot more than general enquiries at the

Bureau. Money was exchanged to different currencies, accounts collected, shore tours sold for the various ports, foreign stamps sold, lost property dealt with, crew wages calculated, official reports typed and just about any other thing you could think of. As well as this, documentation was handled for the various ports regarding Immigration, Customs and Health arrangements for passengers and crew for each port visited.

The Pursers Officers were of course in every shipping line notorious for making extra money over and above salary, much to the bitter envy of Officers in the Deck and Engine departments. Like every other faction in life where money and accounts were handled, there was always the opportunity of making that bit extra to fund the comforts in life, especially when going ashore in the various ports of call. As one rose in rank so the rewards increased. However for a Cadet this was yet to come. We did however have the Library books as a perk. There was a fine for anyone losing their library book and being unable to return it. We would sometimes take a walk along the deck mid-afternoon when many had fallen asleep with a book in their lap. A careful extraction of the book then meant we would lock it away and fine the passenger for losing the book. After disembarkation, the books were then returned to the shelves. What a wicked thing to do, but times were desperate.

When the ships went out to Australia via Suez

(or round South Africa if the Suez was closed), the voyage usually took four weeks including a stretch of seven days at sea between Dakar and Cape Town and nine days at sea from Durban to Fremantle. If they sailed via Panama, the voyage took six weeks as after emerging from the Western end of the Canal they would turn North and proceed up the West coast of the USA as far as Vancouver and then down to Australia via Hawaii, Fiji and New Zealand. On my first trip, after leaving Trinidad we called at Port Everglades, my first time in the USA. The Immigration formalities for passengers and crew were long and drawn out, the only difference being then that one visa was obtained for the whole crew list rather than now each crew member has to have their own; but that is more due to the constant crew changes that happen in US ports nowadays, and the fact that we are constantly sailing in and out of US ports. There were no crew changes in foreign ports back then, the entire crew was in transit through the USA.

The trip through the Panama Canal was exciting. Like most enjoyable things in life you always remember the first time! Though at the time I was not to know that I would transit the Panama more than a hundred times before I retired but it always carried a degree of excitement especially as the ships got larger. Always there would be a first voyage Cook amongst the Galley staff. The mechanical cog wheel tractors which pull the ships through the three sets of locks in Panama are known as mules. Inevitably, one of the more senior Cooks would instruct the new Cook to draw a bag of carrots from the stores and be at the Galley gunport door at 4.00am to feed the mules as we transited the Canal, this being the old and tested way of speeding up the Transit. They would fall for it every time.

From Panama, we called at Acapulco, then a small town with no docking facilities except for fishing boats, and large vessels had to anchor in the harbour and operate a tender service operated. We did not sail until 6.00am and several of the more experienced lads decided to show us some of the more well known brothels and bars of the area. It was a great night out on the town and we arrived back on board from La Huerta's and Rebecca's much the worse for wear at 5.00am, but far more experienced in life than the day before. We called at Los Angeles, San Francisco, Vancouver, Honolulu, Suva, Wellington and Auckland before entering the most beautiful harbour in the world...Sydney. Most of the ships could go under the bridge and dock round at Pyrmont, usually berth number 13 but occasionally at number 20. Only the Oriana and Canberra would dock at Circular Quay just before the bridge as they were too tall to pass under. Circular Quay was always a favourite as it was right in town at the bottom of Pitt

Street and George Street near the Manley ferries, but Pyrmont 13 had its attractions too, namely the Montgomery Hotel, better known as Montys where the ugliest of Aborigine whores hung out waiting for business with drunken sailors as they returned late at night.

The night prior to Wellington, however, there had been a series of parties which had kept me up until 6.00am. At 7.30 am, I was not really fit to work. However, the others got me dressed and up to the office but I was not in any state to do anything and all I wanted was to go back to bed. The Senior Assistant Purser was not too impressed, needless to say and told me I had to stay at the Bureau Reception desk until we sailed... as punishment. We sailed at Midnight. I had no breakfast, lunch or dinner and when Midnight arrived and I had been on the Desk for 16+ hours, all I wanted was my bunk. On arrival in Auckland, the Purser called me in to his office and introduced me to the Agent as well as a young lad of 17, Stuart, who was apparently hoping to join P & O as a Purser Cadet. I was told to show him around the ship and explain what the job and the training entailed. I asked him where he would like to see first as it was still only 7.30 am and cabins, etc., would be unavailable until people finished breakfast and went ashore. Stuart explained to me that he had seen over all the ships on many occasions so we went to my cabin and got heavily into the beers by 8.00am. That was the cementing of a lifelong friendship and our paths would cross many times.

Having arrived in Sydney that was the end of the main line voyage and the ship would empty out not only of passengers but cargo also. There were six hatches on most of these passenger ships which held baggage, cars and other cargo to be offloaded. Rather unusually we were only in Sydney for two days. Normally a ship would be berthed for about seven days as you were in the hands of the Australian waterside labour who like most dock labour at that time, were strongly unionised and notable for their lack of work output. With all their meal breaks, smokoes, shift changes and any other reason they could figure to stop work, even the simplest task took forever. Not to worry, I had to work the first day and would have the second day off. That night I had a reasonably early night and was up and about around 8.00am looking forward to seeing the sights of Sydney. Due to our short stay we were at Circular Quay and the main two streets of Sydney, George Street and Pitt Street were close by apparently. When I reached the end of the gangway, I was wondering where to go first and chatted to the Baggage Steward who walked the length of the quay with me. He suggested that as nothing would be open yet, we should have some breakfast. I should have known better. We went in to an establishment called The Island Trader at the end of the quay and ordered a couple of pints of 'breakfast.' Various other members of the crew also wandered in including the Bosun, Plumber, Carpenter, Printer and soon there was quite a crowd, increasing all the time as the morning wore on. Rounds of beer were coming in thick and fast and it became difficult to leave, as the pints were lining up. Morning became afternoon and afternoon became evening. Eventually at 8.00pm I had to be helped in getting up the gangway and back to my cabin by several of my benefactors. When I got up the next day with a mother of all hangovers, the ship was at sea and heading back north away from Australia. What a great day out I had in Australia, all I had seen was the bar at the end of the quay.

On a couple of occasions, the two of us Cadets had been put in front of the Purser for reprimand as the Deputy Purser was beginning to despair of us. The Purser, Big Jim, as he was known had a bit of a reputation for being liverish in the mornings and he used to have a flask of iced water delivered to his desk each day prior to his arrival, and from which he would gulp down glasses of the stuff in an effort to rehydrate himself. One morning, knowing we were to appear in front of him on his arrival in the office, I switched the flask of iced water for iced gin. He started into us and took a few hefty swallows. All of a sudden he went bright purple and made strange sounds as he dashed out for his cabin. We left his office and he did not bother to send for us again after he recovered. Fortunately he never found out who the culprit was.

When the ship arrived back in Tilbury, John was sent on leave for 10 days and told to return to Orcades as a Junior Assistant Purser. My fate was unknown to me at the time as I had burned the candle at both ends on several occasions and as I was still a probationary Cadet, I started to wonder. I was told to stay on the ship for the period it was in port and then go on leave when the rest of the crew returned for the next voyage. It didn't sound good. The day I went on leave however, which was the day the ship sailed again for Australia, I was told I was also being promoted to Junior Assistant Purser and instructed to join the Oriana in Southampton four weeks later. At least I was getting four weeks leave, John only got 10 days. But the main thing was my pay would go up to 38 pounds a month. I would be able to pay off my bar bill for which I'd had to borrow. I went home and the next week, sought out Fred, my mentor to regale him with tales of yore and to thank him for setting me on the path, not to righteousness of course, but nevertheless a path.

CHAPTER 6

The Oriana was our second largest ship, built in 1960 and the pride of the Orient line prior to the merge with P & O. She was 42,000 tons, carried 550 First Class passengers in the forward half of the ship and 1,800 tourist class in much the same amount of space in the after half. There was a crew of just over 900. Various barrier doors throughout the accommodation ensured that the Tourist Class passengers never managed to stray in to First Class and vice versa. As crew members we had various ways through from one to the other, some rather unofficial, through a couple of hatches in the Radio Office, through a conference room called the Red Carpet Room or through a machinery space down on D Deck. There was a way through the main galley, as well as through the crew quarters down on F Deck. There was a cinema where First Class used the upper circle and Tourist Class below in the stalls. There was a staircase connecting the two for emergency purposes but this was another route.

The ship was in dry dock in Southampton

for two weeks and alongside Berth 106 for one more, so a total of three altogether. I was the only male Junior Assisstant Purser during this time although there were two female Assistant Pursers as well. However, these were before the days of sexual equality and only male Assistants could be on duty overnight. I therefore had to stay on board every night while they were able to go off for a meal or to the cinema, disco or whatever. I did however receive an extra thirty shillings a night for the privilege of being called out several times. I had to allocate cabins for standby personnel, crew who were unable to access their own cabins, those who were only there for the dry dock and shore personnel and contractors who were working on specific projects. Of course, I was told that with the exception of Superintendents, everyone should share cabins. At that stage, most people were un-known to me and a degree of trust had to pre-vail. Everyone decided he was a Superintendent and nobody wanted to share a cabin. Arguments were commonplace and many got upset, some rightly so. You also had to be the keeper of the keys overnight in case of fire, flood or other emergency as at the end of the working day, most of the crew could go ashore for the evening so I ended up with keys to absolutely everything on board, bars, shops, freezers, galley refriger-ators, storerooms, safes and lockers. I was quite pleased after nearly three weeks to see the regular crew rejoin.

There was one 'Superintendent' who used to stay on whichever ship was in refit, be it Tilbury or Southampton and always had his wife, son and daughter stay as well. Naturally I had to give them two cabins. Nobody seemed to know exactly what he did but as he was there every refit, he seemed to be known by everyone, especially the Head Waiters in the Dining Room. During the day, you would see him walking around the ship with a boiler suit over his suit and a clipboard in his hand. At mealtimes he would appear with family in the Dining Room and at weekends they would go ashore as little work happened at weekends due to overtime. A few years later, when a Hull Superintendent and an Engineer Superintendent were having lunch, they discovered that he was neither and they summoned the Head Waiter. The Head Waiter thought that he belonged to one of them and gradually by process of elimination, it was discovered that he was nothing to do with the company at all. They were a homeless family, no job, they just lived on whichever ship happened to be in refit and had become so well known that it was just 'assumed' that he worked for the company in a management capacity and nobody felt comfortable to ask as they felt they should know.

On the first weekend when only a skeleton crew remained on board, it was quite lonely. I had just settled down to my dinner in the Tourist Class Dining Room when a whirlwind appeared. It was Stuart, the lad from New Zealand. He had managed to get a cheap passage on a cargo ship to the UK and had been accepted for training as a Purser Cadet, being sent down to Oriana for the weekend to assist with whatever was needed. I had just bought a case of Allsopps lager for the Saturday evening and needed assistance with that to start with. I had several jobs, including that of general dogsbody as there were no Purser Cadets on the Oriana. I assisted the Crew Assistant Purser with all matters crew, and if the Tourist Class Cashier had a line I would also open up and sell tours, change currency and generally helped anyone who was snowed under. One of the more senior of the Assistant Pursers was in charge of cabin changes and accommodation allocation. Larger cabins or cabins on a higher deck were always being requested. When a successful transaction had been completed, he very often took us up to the Plough Tavern, the First Class pool bar when the office closed at 6.00pm and we would have a couple of hours on the champagne cocktails to celebrate his windfall.

The Bureau was not open 24 hours a day as it is now. It used to close at 6.00pm and one Assistant Purser would be on call through the telephone exchange from 6.00pm until 8.00am. The phones on board these old ships were not automatic and had to go through the ship's switch-board. Four Telephone Operators covered the 24 hours in four x six hour shifts. They would act as a filter so that we would only be called out for something relatively important and not for some trivia which could wait for the Bureau to open, like checking for a pair of flip flops left inadvertently by the swimming pool. It is amazing what people class as important enough to call a person from their bed in the middle of the night. Again it was only the male Assistants who were on call at night, though our wage was the same. Our favourite telephone operator was nicknamed after the racehorse, Arkle. This was not because she looked like a horse, anything but. However she had never been known to refuse a jump!

Although the Bureau closed at 6.00pm, this did not mean that we had the evening off. The Entertainment staff then consisted of one Entertainment Officer and three Social Hostesses who would run quizzes, arts and crafts, etc. There were of course musicians playing dance music throughout the evening and of course, later in the evening, the inevitable disco. The main entertainment in the evening was either a Horse Race, a Frog Race, a Casino Night, or various themed nights involving dressing up, like a Fancy Dress Night, Island Night, Wild West Night or Ladies Night. Due to the small number of entertainment staff, the Pursers staff had to help out and it was a requirement that any operation involving cash had to be handled by the Pursers. This of course we did not mind as it was a licence to print money. Horse and Frog races were pretty similar involving a wooden structure which had to be wound or pulled but the betting system was the same, the winner for the evening inevitably being the Senior Assistant Purser. There were no Casinos on board then, only slot machines, no tables, and so a Casino Night would be arranged with various members of the crew running tables such as roulette, blackjack, crown and anchor, cock and hen, champagne dice, tombola, etc. The Assistant Pursers always ran the roulette, and two operated the cash desk. Whilst it did infringe on one's time, it also offered an opportunity to gain some extra income, so nobody minded. I had been used to this on my previous ship which was one class, but now on the Oriana, everything was doubled. Each event had to happen in First Class one night and then again in Tourist Class the next. There were very few nights when we were totally free so any dating usually had to be later on in the evening.

The great thing about now being a Junior Assistant Purser was that I had my own cabin, although it was sometimes not easy to access with a passenger in tow, particularly if she was from Tourist Class, as our accommodation was in First Class and just below the Bridge so running the gauntlet from the Masters at Arms and Senior Officers was normal. The other great thing about a two class ship was that you could have a girlfriend in the First Class as well as one in Tourist Class with the comfort of knowing they were not going to meet. Sometimes, after entertaining a lady from First Class in your cabin, you could feign exhaustion and after her departure get your mess kit back on and go down to the Tourist Disco to later return for a further session of entertainment, ensuring that you had remade the bed before going out. Dining for the Senior Officers was hosting a table of passengers in either the First Class or Tourist Class dining rooms. Dining for the Junior Officers was at Mess Tables in both dining rooms, usually at the back and out of sight of most passengers. Of course the First Class menu was far superior to the Tourist menu and so everyone would try and get a seat in the First Class. On Oriana there was also the Silver Grill, available to First Class passengers only and for a very small supplement. The idea was that Passengers from First Class could reserve a table any evening up until 2.00am and the only extra cost was 2/6d for smoked salmon and 5/- for caviar. The only Officers allowed in there were the Captain, Purser and Chief Engineer. They were supposedly to be entertaining passengers when they dined there but more usually it would be the three of them entertaining themselves after several rounds of cocktail parties had ensured they had missed dinner.

The actor, Archie Leech, British by birth and better known as Cary Grant was travelling on this one particular voyage and occupied S15, a beautiful apartment on the Stadium Deck. He had been in Europe on location, making a film and was returning to Los Angeles. He had a champagne reception to celebrate his wife's birthday in the First Class table tennis room. It was a grand affair and all thankfully went well. I was very nervous a few days later when I had to go and ring the door of his suite and ask him to sign the bill. The reason for my nerves were that I knew the Bartenders had ripped him off by serving a lesser quality champagne later in the party when invitees had already got well into it and were unlikely to notice. Fortunately, he had not noticed, was pleased with his party and put me entirely at ease, also adding a large gratuity for the staff. He was a delightful man and I felt proud to have spoken to him albeit for such a short conversation.

Another fairly regular traveller between UK and Australia was Spike Milligan. Naturally he travelled First Class and at times he would try and get on the public address system when there was nobody around. All of a sudden it would burst into life with Spike saying something like "What's the weather like in Tourist Class folks? Raining, I believe! It's lovely and sunny up here in First Class'. He once told me at the bar that he had been on tour in Port Said and on the return to the ship, their bus had passed what he thought were locals by the side of the road who were shouting, 'Baksheesh' to them. He then told me that it was only later on he had realised that they were Tourist Class passengers. He always liked to make fun of the First and Tourist Class distinction but with good humour.

The Assistant Pursers had their own un-official dining arrangements however. Around 5.00pm the First Class Maitre D'Hotel, David would come to the Bureau to enquire what we would like for dinner. It never mattered what was on the menu. After deciding on, for instance, smoked salmon, a fillet steak followed by crepes suzette and then stilton, it would be decided which one of our four cabins would be the host cabin. Whilst having our sundowners at the Plough Tavern from 6.00 to 8.00pm a Waiter, Wine Steward, and Buffet Boy would have been taken out from the First Class dining room to set things up for our dinner. We would then sit down to a five or six course meal with all the best wines from the list, a vintage port with the stilton and a fine cognac with the coffee. This happened most nights at sea. A year earlier I had been scrounging a bowl of soup in London every couple of days. Now I was dining like a Lord. I was still only just 20 years old!

CHAPTER 7

One of the Leading Hands (Petty Officers), John who worked as clerk for the Deputy Purser was off duty at lunchtime in Honolulu and we decided to go ashore together. We went to the Ilekai Hotel, one of Honolulu's finest in 1969 as it had a revolving bar at the top. This was still quite a novelty then. However we went to the Pool Bar and spent the afternoon swimming and drinking Vodka Gimlets. I was not used to cocktails, certainly not in the quantities we were downing them and by early evening we had moved on to Margueritas. We had far too many of these on top of all the vodkas and so around 8.00pm we decided to try something else. We moved on to Harvey Wallbangers. It seemed a good idea to visit the revolving bar at the top of the Hotel. By this stage it must have been obvious that we were struggling as hotel security was called as we awaited the elevator. We were told that we had to behave as they did not wish to be called to escort us down from there. I reassured them we were perfectly OK and there was nothing to worry about. At the top, the views were stunning, at least I think they were. Things were a little blurred. John ordered more Harveys and as I took my pineapple glass from him, it slipped through my fingers and smashed on the floor. What a waste of a Harvey Wallbanger! Security was called. We were both escorted by the scruff of the neck, down to the ground floor lobby and thrown out of the hotel. It was probably just as well as it was around 11.00pm and we were sailing at Midnight. Unfortunately no cab wanted to take us as they said we were drunk. What cheek! We started running, well, after a fashion, but it was obvious we would never make it on time. Fortunately Lady Luck was smiling upon us as two crew members from the ship's shop who had rented a car for the day came past and gave us a lift. I recall trying to make a stupendous effort to appear sober as we walked up the gangway about ten minutes before sailing.

When the ship arrived back in Southampton, I went on 10 days leave before returning for a Mediterranean cruising season. During this short leave the real Apollo 13 incident took place and I remember sitting up all night with my father as we waited to see whether the astronauts would make it back or not. This incident was nail biting as the whole world was enthralled. The movie with Tom Hanks stuck very much to the facts I am happy to say. For the Mediterranean cruising I was a cashier for the

Tourist Class as there was much more currency exchange. The Euro had not been introduced yet as the British Government had yet to hoodwink the British electorate into joining 'The Common Market'. Each cruise passenger needed a combination of pesetas, escudos, lire, drachma, francs, to name a few as the ports were different each voyage. At the time, Britain's Labour Government had introduced a fifty pound per person limit on foreign currency being taken out of the country. Each passenger had to have a currency card on which we had to record every transaction of currency exchange. This was a completely pointless piece of red tape, paying lip service to the Government's regulation and achieving nothing considering the amount of time it added to every transaction. There was quite a lot of money to be made on currency exchange as rates fluctuated daily. The Purser at the time had a Siamese cat called Brandy who was a real character. I have always liked cats and Brandy used to sit on my counter. Often when I had laid out the change for a passenger to pick up, when they weren't looking, Brandy would sweep this money straight back into my cash drawer.

There was always a substantial difference between the rates on board set by the Company at the start of the cruise and what banks ashore in the various ports were offering for sterling. Whilst the ship was in Lisbon, the other cashier and I mustered what sterling we could and borrowed sterling off both the First Barman and Shop Manager. I went ashore with around a hundred thousand pounds in cash stuffed into large pockets sewn into the lining of a duffel coat. It was a really hot day and a duffel coat looked seriously out of place let alone uncomfortable in the searing heat. I queued up at the foreign exchange teller at a Lisbon Bank sweating profusely. When my turn came, I asked to change some sterling to escudos and the teller who spoke no English asked how much. I wrote the amount on a piece of paper and thought she was going to faint. She went off to get the Manager. I explained to him that I needed it for a cruise ship and he nodded and the teller started to put the cash together. The trouble was, she was going to give me it all in 1000 escudo notes. The maximum denomination we took on board was 100 escudos. I tried to explain, but of course she did not understand. More sweat streamed down my face. I wrote on a piece of paper 1000 and crossed it out, writing 100 alongside it and ticking it. Ah! She understood. She then put it all together in 100 escudo notes but...it was all in mint condition, brand-spanking new notes. It had to be used notes as if we had bought them back from passengers after they had been ashore. The teller did not understand. The queue behind me got longer. More sweat streamed down my face. I took a note and screwed it up and then flattened it out so that it looked used. Ah! Once again success rained and she understood. The problem was she only had new notes. I decided I would just take my sterling back. She didn't understand. I took the new 100 escudo notes in the end. There was a mountain of them and I looked like the Michelin Man on arrival back at the ship, a rather sweaty and nervous Michelin Man in fact. A crisis meeting was held with the other cashier, First Barman and Shop Manager. We took the money up to my cabin and filled the bath in the bathroom next door with water. Then we put in ash tray contents and tea bags to make a revolting swirl. Into this we placed the money to make it look old and used and dried it on cotton lines with paper clips under the air conditioning in my cabin. This had to be the original method of money laundering! We were up all night doing this as we had to pay in to the Purser the next day. We got away with it and the four of us made a tidy sum but I often wondered if the stress of it all had been worth it.

Brandy, the Siamese cat was always around. We used to carry hares in the freezer as Jugged Hare was an item on the First Class dinner menu. A hare's coat can look a bit like that of a Siamese and one night someone nailed one of these hare skins to the inside of the Purser's cabin door whilst he was out socialising. Brandy had been kept in a cabin out of the way somewhere. Around 2.00am, the Purser, Brian, a short and rather rotund man from Melbourne who liked his alcohol rolled back to his cabin to retire for the night. Shutting his cabin door there was a scream which pierced the night. We were all called from our beds; Pursers Officers plus all the Senior Leading Hands, Chef, Second and Third Stewards, Chief Baker, Chief Butcher, First Barman, Shop Manager; We were all paraded in the First Class D Deck foyer. He yelled at us all demanding to know who had killed his cat. This was news to most of us and we all stood there, perplexed, except presumably the perpetrator of the crime. After 10 minutes of being shouted at, Brandy must have been released from wherever he was being held and trotted across the foyer heading for home, the Purser's cabin. The Purser was speechless, a mixture of relief that Brandy was safe and rage at his overreaction with some unknown person making such a fool of him. As we were dismissed, there was a lot of discussion as to who it could have been. It remained a closely guarded secret but there were quite a few people who had a grudge against Brian. Although we never found out, certainly the Chief Butcher, Malcolm was the prime suspect.

The Purser was very fond of Brandy and when he strolled into his office, he would pat his hands on his knees for Brandy to jump up on his lap. When we were in blue uniform, we occasionally would stroke Brandy's coat the wrong way and shake talcum powder in, before smoothing his coat out. Brandy would later walk into his master's office and leap up on to his lap with very satisfying results. There would be a huge cloud of talcum powder followed by a fit of coughing and the Purser would emerge from his office looking as if he had just taken part in a Homepride Flour TV ad and spluttering recriminations. Again, he suspected, but never managed to have anyone admit to it.

Due to my partying excess and other nightly exercise, it was not unusual for me to be late in the mornings. The Purser's Bureau ran across the width of the ship on A Deck so that the serving counters opened up forward-facing to serve First Class and aft-facing to serve Tourist Class. The only entrances were a door from each class on the port side both of which were in full view of Clive, the Senior Assistant Purser's desk, and he was always there. I did manage to overcome this obstacle by climbing over the serving counter of the First Class stamp sales window and then sneaking across to my desk whilst he wasn't looking. It took him ages to work it out as I always had an excuse that I was somewhere he hadn't thought of when he was looking for me. However he was very suspicious and it was only a matter of time. I had developed the art of this by running along the alleyway and diving across the counter. Of course it was easy when there were no passengers at the desk but when there were, the mail clerk, James, would see me coming and politely ask the people in the queue to take one step to their right as I rushed past them and took a dive over the counter. Some expressed surprise but after a while they got used to it and understood the reason. One day however, I believe Clive had been tipped off, as when I arrived on the deck the other side I found my face next to his ankles so that was the end of that. Punishment for things like bad timekeeping was usually to be 'banned off decks' for a week. This meant that you were confined to your cabin during off-duty time, only allowed to work and meals; no bars, no socializing, nothing. It was OK for a week but any more became very boring. Other misdemeanours meant being given an extra week of being Duty Assistant Purser at night and I once did a complete round the world trip being called out at night as well as working long hours during the day. September 1969 saw my 21st birthday in Auckland. Needless to say I was late as usual and had my time off cancelled. I had to work until the ship sailed which was Midnight. I did, however, have a party after we sailed which inevitably meant I was late the next morning too. Clive was becoming exasperated. However, my work was always up to date as I always worked late or when I officially had time off to ensure that my work deadlines never suffered. I suppose looking back, although I liked to party and enjoy myself I had enough responsibility to ensure that neither the ship, nor the passengers or crew ever suffered due to my folly. I guess it was the forerunner to flexitime...although nobody had actually come up with that term before.

My other recollection of Brandy was when we had to return passports to passengers after having collected them for certain Immigration formalities. The American crew and passenger lists had to be produced in a different format to everywhere else in the world and the car-bonated skins had to be duplicated on a Banda machine. This machine was a horror to work and used this peculiar-smelling purple spirit not unlike methylated spirits, which combined with the carbon produced the print. It was not terribly pleasant to us except for Brandy. For some reason the smell turned Brandy on and he sprayed, as tom cats tend to do when aroused. He sprayed all over the passenger passports. They stank of tomcat pee. The next day we all brought in our aftershave and whatever else we could find and as each passenger arrived to collect his/her passport, behind the scenes it was 'doctored' by being sprayed or doused in aftershave before being returned. Thanks a lot Brandy. You cost us a fortune.

One time on an outward voyage to Australia we arrived in Los Angeles at 6.00am. As there was always so much happening on a Los Angeles day, even I knew to have a relatively early night. Not so, one of my colleagues, Chris, who had partied the night away and by arrival in LA was still in standby mode and not in a position to do much. The public address system had a selection of buttons allowing announcements to be placed over First Class only, Tourist Class only, crew only, a combination of any two or the entire ship. Clive, the Senior Assistant Purser, realising Chris was probably not in a good state to liaise with Immigration or having anything to do with passports, put him in charge of the PA system. There were Immigration inspections going on for First Class, Tourist Class and crew in three different locations, mail collection in two different locations, Customs inspection in two locations, car rental reps and baggage forwarding agents available, and a host of other services. Prior to making any of these announcements it was very important to ensure the correct selection of buttons on the PA system. Often, whilst half way through one particular announcement, someone would come and thrust a piece of paper in your hand, putting you off your stride. Chris did not need much putting off that morning. He was leaning against the bulkhead and everywhere there was confusion as he was announcing for First Class to go to a Tourist Class location for Immigration and vice versa, and passengers were approaching the Desk saying they had to go somewhere they had never heard of. As the confusion accelerated and Chris's voice was becoming more slurred as he slipped further down the bulkhead, the final words to emerge over the entire ship as he threw in the towel and collapsed on the deck were "Ah, fuck it".

Prior to my final trip on Oriana as a Junior Assistant Purser, I had been becoming increasingly fed up with the fact that I was probably the lowest paid crew member on board and that included the 16 year old Deck/Bellboys when their overtime was taken into consideration. Officers did not receive overtime. We worked it, we worked for however many hours it took, but we were paid an annual salary and that was it. After seeing the commissions that the Shop staff earned, I thought perhaps a job in the ship's shops would be more to my liking, hopefully eventually becoming a Shop Manager. After all, I had seen the Shop Manager's Bentley in Southampton and the First Barman's air conditioned Daimler. When the ship arrived in Southampton I spoke with the Superintendent Shop Manager, an ex-Purser himself before taking a job in the office, and he reluctantly promised me he would speak with the Superintendent Purser, always referred to by his initials, CJD, another ex-Purser. I went on leave for my ten days and rejoined for a six month trip, not having any other choice. On the day of sailing the newly appointed Purser told me that CJD wanted to speak to me in the Purser's cabin at 2.00pm. I was thrilled as obviously he had been informed of my request. When I entered the Purser's cabin at 2.00pm my feet didn't touch the ground. He yelled. He shouted. He foamed at the mouth and I worried he was going to have a heart attack with the shade of purple his face had gone. I was told in no uncertain terms that I was an Officer and that was it. If I had wanted to become a Leading Hand (Petty Officer), I should have thought about that before, and there was no way that an Officer would be reappointed as a Leading Hand. I would have to sail on this voyage and he suggested I applied for long leave the next year and think things over. I left the cabin, shaking, as it was not what I had expected. Well, at least he had answered the question. It was 'No' apparently.

CHAPTER 8

This next trip on the Oriana took us out to Australia via South Africa as at that time the Suez Canal was closed. The Oriana's top speed was about 34 knots and the Commodore very often drove her at that; a fact which later in the ship's life would be attributed to the sad state of her engines. Whereas I had been used to nine days at sea from Durban to Fremantle, the Oriana did it in seven days. That meant that various tasks for arrival in Australia had to be done much faster.   After our arrival in Sydney we went off on a couple of Australian cruises but did not remain for the full season as we then sailed northbound for Vancouver from where we would do the first season of North American cruises. The Americans in general were not so aware of cruising. They had been well used to voyaging and transportion to which their US President Lines and Matson Lines would be testament. Vancouver in January is cold. The ship would spend three days there, storing and changing over the on board currency to US dollars. This would be a welcome break for the crew and some had already planned on skiing up in Whistler. One night at sea on the way north, and there were many of them, the Senior Second Officer, Les, on the 12 to 4 Watch decided to give a few of us a demonstration of how to ski as he had apparently taken ski holidays on several previous occasions. Those of us interested in the benefit of his experience were on the Bridge at 1.00am and for navigational reasons, the Wheelhouse was in total darkness. Les strapped a couple of long chart rulers to his feet to act as skis and the Bridge Seaman was sent to the cleaning locker to fetch two brooms for ski sticks. We all stood with him on the port Bridge wing while he explained the importance of bending knees, etc. The Helmsman was instructed to turn the wheel making the ship heel right over to starboard and creating a natural slope for Les to complete his demonstration by skiing from port to starboard Bridge wings via the Wheelhouse. Unfortunately for Les, just as he was reaching his top speed through the Wheelhouse, the Commodore chose that same moment to step out from the Chartroom to the Wheelhouse to check on the night orders before retiring for the night. The two collided in midflight and both went rolling around the Wheelhouse deck amongst the clatter of Les's makeshift ski equipment. There seemed to be a lot of shouting, all of it from an extremely irate Commodore as we spectators discreetly left the

Bridge wing via the outside ladder. Les was fairly sheepish at breakfast the next morning, informing us that further ski demonstrations had to be put on hold for the foreseeable future. He did not actually get to ski in Vancouver as the Commodore had him on double watches for the entire three days.

The Staff Captain, Peter, was the complete opposite to the Commodore. He was a delightful character and quite a showman. He would not have been out of place in an Old Time Music Hall. He was renowned for his rendition of a song called, 'The Hole in the Elephant's Bottom' which he delivered with great gusto at times when pressed by passengers who had heard it before and when the Commodore was not around. It was usually on a Fancy Dress or some such night and he would enter into the spirit of the evening by appearing later on when the Commodore had retired for the night, wearing black tails and a top hat. When support for his rendition reached its climax he would start, prancing from one end of his audience to the other, giving it his all and everyone was encouraged to join in the chorus. He was a marvellous entertainer and very much adored by passengers and crew alike. I never heard anyone ever say a bad word against him.

We did three cruises in all, the first one, out of Vancouver and heading for Panama, picking up other embarking passengers in San Francisco and Los Angeles, through the Canal and to several Caribbean islands. Then back through the Canal and dropping passengers off in the same ports on the return. This was a four week cruise round trip and we did two of these with a ten day cruise to Hawaii in between. In both Los Angeles and San Francisco on our voyage up from Australia, we were berthed across the pier from the Oronsay, another of P & O's ships who was outward bound from England to Australia. In Los Angles we heard that there was illness on board the Oronsay but no other details. In San Francisco the next day no visitors were allowed on to the Oronsay and we were told that a couple of passengers had been landed to hospital with a suspected but unconfirmed condition. As there was nothing concrete, the Oronsay was allowed to sail for Vancouver. She sailed at noon and the Oriana sailed some five hours later. By that time, the rumours were rife that the passengers who had been landed to hospital had typhoid. It was confirmed later that night once the Oronsay had left American waters. Two mornings later when we entered Vancouver harbour, there was the Oronsay in the middle of the harbour with the yellow quarantine flag flying. Several more passengers and crew had become ill after departure from San Francisco and the ship was quarantined in Vancouver. We berthed at the Centennial pier which was a cargo berth and way out of town.

We sailed a couple of days later on our first thirty day cruise to the Caribbean and on our return, the Oronsay was still there anchored in the middle of Vancouver harbour. We then sailed for a ten day cruise of the Hawaiian Islands and when we returned, she was still at anchor in the harbour with the yellow flag flying. She was there for six weeks in total, with all her passengers and crew quarantined during that time. She was allowed in to the Canadian Pacific Terminal from time to time only to land the sick to hospital ashore, and she would have to sail back out again to anchor. There was nothing anybody could do and it must have been extremely difficult for passengers who had to extend their voyage to Australia by an extra six weeks, especially those with work commitments. I can only imagine what the Purser's Bureau must have been like. They should have all been given a medal. Martin, the Assistant Purser from Orcades and of air pistol fame was aboard there and I spoke to him on the phone. I asked him what the passengers were doing and he said the majority appeared to be coming up to the Purser's Bureau to complain. He also told me that he and his fellow officers were all taking precautions against contracting typhoid by drinking beer rather than water until the test results were known. All passengers and crew had to be tested and it was eventually determined that an Indian galley worker was a carrier of the disease. It wasn't his fault of course, he didn't even know it. However, this almost became a Diplomatic Incident between Canada and the United States. It was alleged that the Americans knew full well that it was typhoid on board and of course should have impounded the ship in San Francisco. However, it was further alleged that they had deliberately not rushed to announce their confirmation of the medical tests on the patients until after the ship had sailed out of American waters. The Canadians of course had no choice but to impound the ship and the problem became theirs.

It was a Board of Trade requirement that each ship, depending on tonnage, number of passengers and crew should have so many certificated lifeboatmen amongst the crew and so from time to time training sessions were held. I was put forward and on our second visit to Vancouver, about twenty of us lined up on the outside deck under one of the boats for the practical. It was bitterly cold, raining and an icy wind chilling you to the bones. Surely the inspector would not send us out in a boat in these conditions? But of course he did and we rowed around the harbour for about an hour. I don't think I have ever been so cold in my life, but it served to remind us that getting into a lifeboat is not a pleasure cruise and you don't choose the conditions. I was pleased to pass however so that I did not have to do it again.

On our second four week cruise to the

Caribbean and back we were between Acapulco and Los Angeles when I was called out by the telephone exchange one night as I was the duty Assistant Purser. It was about 3.00am and the Senior Night Steward met me and explained that in a certain Emerald Deck cabin in the aft section a large Canadian passenger, very drunk was insisting on seeing the Captain. I went down and knocked on the door while the Night Stewards all waited around the corner at the end of the alleyway to see what would happen. As I entered, this mountain of a man asked me if I was the Captain. I assured him that I was not and he said he did not wish to speak with me, only the Captain. His wife discreetly explained to me that he was a reformed alcoholic, her husband that is, not the Captain, and he had not touched a drop in years. However, the proximity and temptation of so much liquor on board had proved too much and he had succumbed. He'd certainly made up for it that night. He was ex-RCMP and he wanted to complain directly to the Captain that there were no life jackets in the tenders going ashore in Acapulco. He was not prepared to speak with me and lifted me up by my monkey jacket and propelled me along the polished floor from the cabin door on my front to the end of the alley where the Night Stewards all helped me up and brushed me down. The cabin door slammed shut. There was no way I was going to contact the Captain or even the Purser at 3.00am so I decided to contact Bob, the Assistant Surgeon with whom I had been drinking until around 1.00am. Bob saw no problem at all when I explained the situation of his inebriation. Bob got dressed in his Mess kit, loaded a hypodermic which he put in his trouser pocket. Back at the end of the alley, Bob said it would probably be better if he went in alone to speak with him. We all agreed wholeheartedly. After being let in to the cabin there was quite a bit of shouting, the door opened and Bob came sailing along the alleyway, much the same as I had done. A quick conference was held and we again knocked on the door. As soon as the door opened, we all piled in, wrestling the passenger to the deck while Bob gave him the injection. This calmed him down and we placed him on his bunk to sleep it off. I did wonder what the outcome the next day would be but fortunately we never heard another peep.

The amount of alcohol being consumed was second to none and my life was a complete alcoholic haze. We were about to make our final Panama Canal transit and were due to arrive in Balboa at 10.00pm and remain overnight bunkering until 6.00am. Passenger ships are always given priority for daytime transits. I was supposed to meet the Pilot at 9.30pm and escort him to the Bridge which I completely forgot about and was given hell when I arrived to help sort the mail once I realised we were alongside the berth. I was told to go to bed and be up at

5.30am as I would be clearing the ship for the Canal transit. As I weaved my way towards my cabin, a chap I knew from our office in San Francisco, Al, who always wore Rupert Bear style trousers was sitting in the Stadium with a bottle of champagne and beckoned me over. Why not? I thought. I might as well have a night-cap, not that I needed one. I had just got to bed around midnight feeling a little the worse for wear when Rick, one of the Assistant Pursers came in and said we were going ashore with Ossie the Tour Agent who would show us some Panamanian night life. I told him there was no way I was going ashore as I was quite drunk, already in trouble for it and I had to be up at 5.30am. No way was I getting dressed again and going ashore.

I got dressed and off we went.

Ossie took us to several bars full of girls, which seems to be the only type of bars they have in Panama. No wonder all seafarers enjoy their Panama visits. We ended up at the Intercontinental Hotel where I fell in the swimming pool at 4.30am. We got back on board at 5.00am and the others helped me into my uniform. When the Officials arrived they saw the state I was in, as all I could manage in verbal communication was a grunt and they decided to complete the paperwork at Cristobal, the other end of the canal when hopefully I would be feeling better. And off we went, though I don't remember much of that particular transit. It had been a good night out though.

One of the problems Clive had identified with me was that I enjoyed a drink with many of the senior tradesmen like the Chief Baker, Chief Butcher, Chef, etc., but that was the way you learned apart from the fact that these old salts were seasoned sailors. Clive decided that the next time Ernie, the Chief Baker invited me for a drink, he would accompany me to ensure I left at a reasonable time in a state of sobriety. I informed Ernie and he duly invited the two of us a few days later. Ernie was the perfect host and when I helped Clive along the alleyway at about 3.00am, I was in not good, but far better shape than Clive. He decided to let me go it alone the next time as it had taken him a couple of days to recover.

It was during our final call in Port Everglades that the Senior Assistant Purser from the Queen Elizabeth, now docked as a tourist attraction there, similar to the Queen Mary in Long Beach, came on to see me with some personal effects of one of their Electricians who had died on board as a result of an accident. He wanted us to deliver the effects to the Board of Trade to which we gladly agreed. He asked us if we would like to go over and join him for a drink, and see round the ship later in the day when we had some time off. When we got off duty at 2.00pm we caught a cab over to the Queen Elizabeth, choosing to go in uniform as it would look more official. However, the ship was now under American flag and they would not let us on board to see the Cunard Officer. Eventually, we paid our $5 and joined the end of the guided tour. The tour took us through the cinema where we watched footage of her wartime role. When everyone in our party left the darkened cinema to make room for the next party we slid down in our seats and then escaped out the back. We had no idea where the Officer's cabin was but roamed the deserted alleys hoping to find him. Of course, it did not take the tour leader long to discover we had slipped away as being in uniform we stood out from the others and the alarm was raised and security sent on a mission. We suddenly found ourselves being chased up and down decks, along alleyways with no idea where we were going. Just as it looked as if all was lost as we had American security closing in from both ends of an alleyway on A Deck with no escape, a cabin door opened and the Senior Assistant Purser said, "Ah there you are, come in". We bolted inside and that was that. He gave us a complete tour of the ship after a few drinks as we explained how they had not allowed us on board to see him, during which time we spotted Security and tour guides alike, and gave them the benefit of the single finger salute.

When the Oriana arrived back in Southampton, I was due to proceed on leave after working the harbour shift as had been advised by CJD, the Superintendent Purser. The night before I went on leave, Clive, the Senior Assistant Purser, whom I had given the run around for the previous 18 months and had returned the favour in punishments such as being banned from bars, night duty, cancelled shore leave, etc., invited me up for a drink before dinner. Whilst we had a drink, he said to me that although I had been the bane of his life for the past three voyages with my hell raising, he had to admit that my work was always done and he could not find fault on that side. It was a veiled compliment and we parted on good terms. At this time there was a change in the evening uniform. Usually when we were in blue uniform, we would wear blue mess uniform and when in white uniform, the jacket would be white, as it still is. This was a shame as the blue mess kit was definitely the smartest uniform we had but as I mentioned earlier, we had to buy our own uniform and many of the Engineer Officers were unable to afford it. I went home to consider my future. A few weeks later, I received a letter confirming my promotion from Junior Assistant Purser to Assistant Purser and appointing me back to the Orcades, the ship I had been very fond of as a Cadet. I was overjoyed to be returning there, I wasn't done yet!

CHAPTER 9

Having a few weeks leave was terrific, though you did not really appreciate how tired you were until after being on leave for a couple of weeks. Working seven days a week, long hours and being on call during the night, took its toll without realisation at the time. However, one of the things I did realise was how distant I was becoming from the friends I had ashore who had regular nine to five Monday to Friday jobs. Whenever I suggested going out for a drink it was always met with that it had to be Friday or Saturday nights. Other nights were out of the question as they were working the next day. I couldn't believe it. I worked every day of the week and had a drink every night of the week. Not with all of them of course, but a fair number and we soon felt ourselves divided which often happens when life takes you on different paths.

The Purser on board decided who did which job, and I was delighted to see a Purser called Ken was on the Orcades when I returned. He had been the Purser of the Tourist Class on Oriana the year before and he was a friendly man, not like some of the others who used to look down their nose at you, not always bothering to even know your name. Although, most of them seemed to know my name as I had come to their attention not always for the best of reasons. I was appointed as Crew Assistant Purser with which I was very happy. The Crew Office was down in what used to be the old Tourist Bureau and it meant I could work independently and away from passengers. I had a female Junior Assistant to help with all the lists and documentation, a Cadet to help generally and a Writer (clerk) who kept all the overtime records and crew customs declarations.

Although a bit daunting at first, I soon got to grips with the job once I had overcome those few crew members who would always try it on with someone new. The Irish, of course would always try to convince you that they did not pay UK Income Tax. They had to of course, as they worked for a British company. However, they always tried it on nevertheless.

One thing every Crew Purser dreaded, whatever ship, whatever shipping line was calling in Fremantle due to the three stripe Customs officer who presided. His name was Tom Hardiman and he was notorious throughout the world, He was a bully and enjoyed putting the fear of God among the crew. The Form Five, as the Australian Crew Customs Declaration is known, required a crew member to declare everything he had in his possession which was deemed dutiable. For instance a transistor radio, a popular item in those days had to have the make, model no, serial no, Country of origin and value declared on the form. Sometimes you had to take an item apart to find the serial number. You can imagine the amount of work required prior to arrival in obtaining all this information from a crew of anything from 600 to 900, ensuring that every detail was recorded and the crewman's signature obtained.

Tom would sit in the Crew Office, demanding a constant supply of beer and sandwiches and make a list of those he wished to interview. I would then have to send for them to come to the office with whatever items he wished to check. Sometimes, a crew member might have a stereo in his cabin and the whole arrangement would have to be taken down and taken up to the office. He would never lower himself to visit the cabin for convenience, he got off on the power. One particular incident I recall was our Bureau Bellboy being selected to produce his transistor radio. He was a young lad of 16, and was eager to get on in life. He returned with his radio and Tom examined it. Whether it was the lad's fault in wrongly inverting two of the digits in the serial number or the typist incorrectly transposing the information on to the form, we never knew. However, the serial number was incorrect, although it was obvious that it was the same radio and a simple error made. Not so for Tom! He fined the lad fifty dollars for not being able to produce the radio declared and a further fifty dollars for producing a radio he had failed to declare. I tried my hardest to reason with him but he wasn't having any of it. We, the Assistant Pursers clubbed together and paid the 100 dollars as we felt so sorry for the lad, but what a bastard he was. On the few occasions I have visited Fremantle in recent years, I have often enquired of the Customs Officers if they ever knew him. They have always said, they knew OF him but he had long gone before they joined the service but they knew of his reputation and I used to tell them various tales of what he was like. Many said they had heard horrendous stories over the years. The ghost of Tom Hardiman still lurks in the passageways of Customs House.

We sailed at 5.00pm that evening, thankful to get away. We set off for Adelaide and the Bridge had warned us that there were rough seas in the Bight and that everything needed to be secured. Once outside the harbour, things did indeed get pretty rough and by 8.00pm the three of us Assistant Pursers were in my cabin having a drink but having difficulty moving around, the seas were so violent. At 2.00am things were so bad that the Captain called the entire crew to, without exception. An announcement was made to the passengers advising them to remain in their cabins and not to try and move round the ship.

Movement was so violent that top bunks were being ripped from the bulkheads and collapsing on to the occupants of the lower bunks beneath. The carpenters were making their way round the cabins effecting whatever emergency repairs they could followed by the two ship' Doctors who had to attend to injuries. The ship was being pooped at the aft end, the waves coming at us from two directions and they were crashing over the Laundry rail and the water finding its way down to the E and F Deck passenger accommodation. I was sent with three Waiters to the Laundry to see what we could do to limit the flooding. The Laundry was awash with sea water. Ironing presses ripped from the deck combined with a tangle of linen was being sent from one side of the laundry to the other as the ship rolled from one side to the other. As we tried to secure linen to build a bank at the Laundry entrance, sheets would wrap themselves round your ankles and whip your legs from under you, and submerging you, dragging you from one side to the other to the far bulkhead. The trick was then to get out of the way fast enough before an ironing press smashed into the area of bulkhead where you had been deposited only seconds before. Elf and Safety would have had 20 pink fits. We eventually managed to build a suitable bank of linen to within a couple of feet of the top of the doorway leaving us enough room to climb out. It hadn't stopped the water flooding the lower decks but had seriously reduced it. When one of the Waiters pointed out to me that the water was now within a couple of inches of an electrical fuse box, I decided it was time for us to leave and we climbed out.

In the alleyway running forward on D Deck, there was a line of crew all chaining buckets. The waves had not only invaded the Laundry but had also flooded the steering flat and we had no steering. The Captain was on the Bridge and holding the ship into the oncoming seas and steering to accomplish this by speeding one propeller slightly faster than the other thereby holding our position. Pretty fortunate we had two of them I suppose. The line of crew was a mixture of Deck Hands, Waiters, Cooks, Officers, Cabin Stewards; anyone not already on other duties, and we chained buckets of water along the line in the hope of emptying the steering flat. There was a pump for this purpose but it had ceased to work. The ship was rolling to an extent none of us had ever before experienced and it was quite terrifying. It would roll right over to one side to around 42 degrees and we would stand with one foot on the deck and one on the bulkhead. There the ship seemed to stop, poised as we stood in silence wondering whether it would keep going over and capsize or roll back. Of course, it did roll back to everyone's relief after what seemed like an eternity, but then went right over the other way. We kept at this for a couple of hours until the Engineers got the pump working.

I decided to have a walk round the rest of the ship. I say 'walk' but it was more of a 'stagger'. I went through the Galley where the Chef and the Cooks were trying valiantly to get stock pots off the ranges and on to the deck. The galley gunport door was bulging with the force of the sea outside and it looked as if the securing dogs would break off. Over the years they had become worn and should have been much tighter. A trash bin flew through the air from one side of the galley to the other narrowly missing a couple of Cooks, hitting a washbasin which completely disintegrated. Although the securing racks had been used, they were never designed for this sort of punishment and the deck was knee deep in broken crockery and glass. I went up a few decks and went through the Public Lounges where a grand piano was chasing several of the Ship's Musicians around the room as they tried to secure it. Large, heavy armchairs were being thrown through the air from one side of the ship to the other, such was the force of the storm, narrowly missing some of the Bar Waiters who were trying their best to harness them. Broken glass and bottles were everywhere.

The Beaufort Scale only goes up to Force 16 and it had been way off the scale during the night at its peak. As dawn broke, the Captain still had the ship hove to and headed in to the oncoming sea, but very gradually it started to abate. A Mayday signal had been sent out, as we still had no steering, and once it was daylight, the Royal Australian Air force sent out a couple of planes to look for us. They took a couple of photos which appeared on the front pages of the Western Australian newspaper the next day showing the ship completely hidden in the trough between waves. And this was when it was daylight and things were starting to calm down. Passengers were still told to stay in their cabins and the galley staff managed to cook sausages and make toast which were delivered to cabins by the Stewards along with tea and coffee. Around Noon, things had calmed down enough for the Captain to turn the ship round and head back to Fremantle. We arrived outside the harbour entrance at 7.30pm that evening and two tugs nudged alongside to guide us in to the berth, as we still had no steering. We would stay there for the next few days. When the clearance had been given, several passengers ran down the gangway and kissed the concrete apron. Customs were naturally first on board, even though we had not been anywhere apart from a near visit to Davy Jones' Locker. God, it was good to see Tom again!

From the moment we berthed, the Purser's Bureau was about 15 deep with passengers who were due to disembark in Adelaide, Melbourne or Sydney. They wanted to fly. They wanted to go by train. They wanted to go by road. They wanted to do anything but sail again. In 1970, flights from Perth were fairly limited and so the trains used to get booked up well in advance. Road was not really an option as it was 4,000 miles to Sydney. They were very reluctant to accept the fact that the limited flights and trains were all booked up, nor were they too happy that they would not receive any refund for their unused portion of passage. Thank goodness they were all Australian and not American who would have wanted to sue God.

We sailed a few days later after emergency inspections and repairs and the weather had returned to normal by then so we had a fairly uneventful trip to Sydney. We waved goodbye to Tom again. Fortunately the numbers of passengers decreased as we disembarked around the coast and we had just enough crockery and glass to get to Sydney. However, we had to purchase more in Sydney as well as replacement bar stores and numerous other items smashed beyond repair. We started our Australian cruises out of Sydney. It was usual to have seven days in Sydney at the end of a voyage and prior to cruising as the ship would have to store, change over to Australian currency and in those days, Heaven forbid, Management used to give consideration to the crew having a break. Things are a lot different nowadays unfortunately. However, due to our delay in Fremantle, we would only have three days. Still, a day off would be most welcome. On the second day, it was my 'day' off and I worked the morning. Even if you were the Crew Assistant Purser, you still had to take your turn attending to passengers in the Bureau during port splits and afternoons at sea. After lunch, I handed my safe keys in to one of the other Assistant Pursers and was about to go ashore.

There was a man at the Desk who turned to me and asked me if I was the Personnel Officer. I mumbled that I was, assuming he was from P & O Sydney. He informed me that one of our crew, an Engine Room Greaser had been arrested the previous night for urinating in the street and needed someone to pay his fine so he could be released. So much for my afternoon off. I went and got some money and we set out for the Police Station. En route, I asked him where Les was, the usual chap from the office who dealt with crew matters. I became worried when he said he did not know who he was. It turned out that he was nothing to do with our company but an opal dealer who happened to be in the Police Station that morning making an enquiry when the crew member was taken through after his court appearance. In desperation, he had asked this man to contact the personnel guy on the Orcades to come and get him out as he had no money for his fine. This Good Samaritan did exactly that. When I got to the Police Station, they deliberately took their time in researching the case and then informed me that he had just left and was on his way out to Long Bay Jail. I was going to return to the ship but the Good Samaritan wanted to see it through and justice served. He drove me out to Long Bay Jail which is quite a way out of Sydney. We were not allowed to park anywhere near and I had a long walk through several security gates to get in. Eventually I reached the desk and enquired about my crewman. I was told that he had just arrived and was being checked in. I asked if that was necessary as I had the money for the fine, so could I not just hand the money over in exchange for a receipt and take the crewman with me? Nothing in life is that easy is it? I was told that once the checking in process had started, it had to be completed and this would take a couple of hours. Once completed, the fine could be paid and the checking out process could be started. I was locked in a room with no windows whilst all this went on. Eventually I managed to retrieve him several hours later, and he was naturally very relieved to see me. All the way back to Sydney, he kept explaining that he had not urinated in public and that it was a case of mistaken identity. Everybody is always innocent of course. Who knows whether he was or not? I was not in a good mood as I had spent my entire 'time off' getting him out of jail. However, it certainly did my reputation with the Deck and Engine Ratings no harm.

Australian cruising was everybody's favourite. The ship was full of young Australians. The men only wanted beer as long as it was ice cold and there was an endless supply. The girls however wanted something else and we were only too willing to supply it. I had mentioned before that these older ships had no bow or stern thrusters like the modern ships and had to rely on tugs for arrivals and departures. There was an exclusive club called The Sydney Bridge Club. This all sounded as tame as a sophisticated game of cards but could not have been more different. From the normal P & O berth, Pyrmont 13, it would take about 20 minutes from the time the last line was let go to the funnel passing under the Sydney Harbour Bridge. To become a member of this club, you had to pick up one of the newly embarked girls, once the last line had been let go and get her into bed before the funnel was under the Bridge. Of course, we did have a bit of an advantage here, in that the Deck and Engine Officers were all on standby for sailing for the first half hour or so after departure. At Embarkation, which was handled by the Sydney Office staff, one of us would be present in the terminal as liaison. We would have invitation cards already written out except for name and cabin, to a sail away party in the Assistant Pursers accommodation just prior to sailing. I always took the Bureau Bellboy with me to the Terminal and kept an eye on those being processed. When an attractive girl came through, and unattached, I could easily spot her name and cabin number and enter it on one of the invitations. The Bell-boy was dispatched on board quickly so that by the time she got to her cabin a party invitation was already there waiting for her. The rest was pretty straightforward.

CHAPTER 10

Cruising out of Sydney as a base port was incredible. As I mentioned earlier the passengers were all young Australians and New Zealanders, the lads all a bit untamed but there for the beer. The girls were all, well mostly gorgeous, in their early twenties and had come on the cruise for a good time. We young Officers also in our early twenties were only too eager to oblige. We had a captive audience, so to speak and the rule about having to be away from public areas by Midnight worked in our favour. Once the Officers all had to disappear there was nothing for the girls to hang around for ...so they came with us. We took it in terms to host the Midnight party. Booze was so cheap anyway, and we had several ways of obtaining it without payment, not that we needed that much. We had all had a skin full during the evening and by the time we reached our cabins, drinking was not the main item on the agenda. Within half an hour everyone had paired off and gone to a cabin.

Whenever we arrived in Sydney between cruises, we alternated between having a one night stay and having a two night stay. Sometimes, we had even longer, and it was when we had two days off each, I used to pal up with the ship's Surgeon, Paul and we would take off for the Hawkesbury River for two days. I had a girlfriend, Diane who lived out at Bobbin Head on the river. She would come and collect the two of us and Paul's girlfriend of the moment, and we would rent a cabin cruiser for the two days. It would be two days of total relaxation on the river, enjoying ourselves in every way imaginable. It was a great way to unwind after two whole weeks of...well doing much the same thing really.

As Crew Assistant Purser, one of my tasks was to prepare all the documentation for and then attend the Master's loggings at 11.00am most mornings at sea. This was the disciplinary session for members of the crew who had not abided by the Articles of Agreement in some form by either being late for work, being drunk at work, holding social intercourse whilst not in the execution of their duty, being caught in a passenger area whilst not on duty and a whole host of 'offences'. The 'holding of social intercourse whilst not in the execution of duty' usually meant 'chatting up a female whilst off duty'. The offence itself caused much confusion amongst the lower ranks and when a charge of this sort was read out, was often met with a strong denial of, 'I never touched her Guv, honest'. Defendants had to appear on the starboard Bridge wing at 11.00am on days at sea and would be seen individually in the Chartroom. The seaman would be ordered in and told to stand on a mat while the charge was read out. At that point he was asked if he had anything to say and I would have to record his exact utterance for the Official Log Book. Most had nothing to say, but on the odd occasion, someone would impart to the Captain what he could do with his job, his ship and all who sailed in her. The Bridge wing was accessed by a series of outside companionways which led up at the side of the open decks. Again, most seamen would make their way quietly and unobtrusively up there ten minutes beforehand but occasionally the sunbathing passengers would be treated to the sight of the Master At Arms dragging a drunken and belligerent crew member up these stairways, handcuffed and effing and blinding all the way. He was told to appear before the Master and before the Master he would appear. The largest number I had to prepare in one morning was 54 ...after a particularly enjoyable stay in Sydney.

These days it is all too easy and costs the various shipping companies a ridiculous amount of money. A crew member can just sign a 'Leave Own Will' form, pay his own air fare and leave at the next port, Immigration permitting. It usually means that the ship must sail short staffed until the replacement arrives which can be several weeks, depending on recruitment, medicals and visas. And of course the company has to pay the flight for the replacement. Sometimes, the crew member leaving has already withdrawn what cash he is owed and feigns having no money for his fare which means the company has to pay, as by this time the crew member has refused to work. However, back in the sixties, etc. air travel was limited and very expensive to say the least. The Captain of Orcades used to take a much tougher line. The crew member had signed to serve the Master until the ship returned to UK and therefore to stop working was an infringement of that agreement. When one day, one of the Bellboys decided to stop working, the Captain decided that it impeded the progress of the ship. The Bellboy thought he would be logged by the Master and discharged in Sydney, being eventually picked up by another British Merchant vessel travelling back to UK and taken on board as a Distressed British Seaman, his food being paid for by the Company. The Captain raised a civil charge ashore and the Bellboy was arrested by the Sydney Water Police and taken to Magistrate's Court that morning. As the Crew Purser, I had to attend as a witness to attest that he had reneged on his Agreement with the Master and to keep him on board was detrimental to the progress of the ship. I don't think the Bellboy had realised the Master's power or at least thought he would take

the offence to such a level. However, he did realise when the Magistrate gave him six months in
the notorious Long Bay Jail. It certainly served
as a deterrent to others as once the word went
round, nobody else stopped working.

After about four months of cruising out of
Sydney, it was time to return to the UK as the
Australian summer was starting to wane and by
the time we reached the UK it would be spring
and many of the ships would be ready to start
the Mediterranean cruising season. Fremantle
was our last Australian port and we nearly always sailed at 5.00pm. In that port there was a
bar on the dock, called The First and Last. This
referred to the fact that it was the first bar to
grab a beer after arriving on Australian soil and
also the last before leaving. Naturally, it was a
favourite with the crew, particularly the British
Deck and Engine ratings. Many a time at sailing,
the Bosun and Second Bosun would have to go
over to the bar and physically drag their charges
back on board.

Taffy, one of the Assistant Barman was no
such trouble. He had woken from his siesta and
suddenly remembered that he had not phoned
his wife. He jumped into his boiler suit and a pair
of carpet slippers and dashed down the gangway to the bank of public call phones round the
side of the terminal building. The last view of
the dock in Fremantle as the tugs pulled us out
was of a frantic Taffy running down the dock.

Too late, Taffy had missed the ship. He would report to the Agent who made arrangements for him to fly to the next port and rejoin there. He was met by the Agent and accommodated until the ship arrived, put on a disciplinary charge for missing the ship, fined for the offence, a forfeiture of wages for missed work, and ordered to have all the expenses incurred in his rejoining the vessel deducted from his wages. This type of occurrence was not that uncommon, but in this particular case our next port was Durban...nine days away. As the ship drew alongside in Durban, there was Taffy waiting expectantly still dressed in his old boiler suit and carpet slippers, having spent a week at the Seaman's Mission. At his disciplinary hearing on the Bridge, when asked if he had anything to say, he told the Captain that it was the most expensive phone call he had ever made, and he hoped his wife would appreciate it.

Another of the Assistant Barman, Kevin, known as Whispering Jack because of his quiet Irish brogue had been on the Canberra previously as a Bar Steward. Kevin had met with a girl from the Tourist end of Canberra and they were in bed in her cabin. The girl shared the cabin with her mother and they had not been expecting the mother to return as early as she did. When they heard the key go in the door, Kevin shot out of bed and hid in the shower while the girl quickly shoved all his clothes under the bed.

The mother entered and the girl pretended to be asleep. To Kevin's horror, the mother decided to stay instead of going out again and went to bed. After leaving a suitable period of time for the mother to fall asleep, Kevin crept from the shower. He was searching for his uniform when the mother stirred and Kevin leapt out of the cabin into the alleyway, closing the door behind him. He was now standing stark naked in the main alleyway on C Deck in the after end of the ship. Kevin's cabin was in crew quarters in the forward section of the ship. There was only one thing for it. Cupping his modesty in his hands, Kevin streaked the length of the Canberra, through Tourist Class, then First Class and into crew quarters and back to his cabin without getting caught. As far as we know, Kevin still holds the record for the fastest undiscovered streak on the Canberra. Sir Roger Bannister would have been proud of him.

As we approached the UK things started to get very busy in the Crew Office as we readied ourselves for the crew pay off. There was only so much you could do until the crew's final overtime for the voyage was in, the last few days being estimated. Once that was in, then the Portage Bill became the nucleus of all activity as final earnings, Income Tax, National Insurance, Graduated Contributions, total deductions and net pay due were all calculated and the respective returns to government agencies and to the company finalised and cross balanced. Bearing in mind that we were still on pounds, shillings and pence then, there were neither computers nor calculators. A Ready Reckoner (book of tables) and an Addo X adding machine were the only tools available so around the clock calculating for about 110 hours on the trot was the norm. In Lisbon, a representative from the Pay Department in London would join to ensure there were no glaring cock-ups and in Rotterdam, prior to the final leg up the Thames Estuary to Tilbury, we all used to say a prayer for clear weather. The dread of fog in Rotterdam could mean a delayed sailing which would involve arriving in Tilbury after midnight and an extra day's pay for the entire crew. When everything went smoothly however, there was a tremendous feeling of satisfaction to see the finale of your six months hard work resulting in all the crew taking off to cause havoc on British Rail from Tilbury Riverside to Fenchurch Street. I felt sorry for any regular rail passengers who made the mistake of catching an afternoon train on a day a ship docked.

As Crew Purser, I had to remain on board for a couple of days to tidy things up and then I was told I had to attend our London Office for three days to do a decimal currency course as a few months later UK was about to change from 12 pence to a shilling and 20 shillings to a pound to a straightforward 100 new pence to the pound.

Why I had to spend three days of my leave learning this I was not sure as we were always doing money exchange to currencies already in decimal and whilst a ship was cruising out of Australia, the entire ship changed over to Australian currency anyway. However, it appeared that I needed to be shown how to calculate the wages in decimal from the start of the voyage, even though the changeover would not be for a further couple of months and of course all the rates of pay were new. Even so, after spending two days on board after everyone else had gone home and then spending three days in the London office, I was only getting five days leave instead of ten. I had worked seven days a week for the past six months and was going back for another five month voyage. Five days leave hardly seemed generous in eleven months. Still that was the system. Leave was earned at nine days a month so anything owed was carried forward to a time when you would put in for long leave and take a few months.

CHAPTER 11

By this time in 1971, the Orcades was no longer able to call at ports in the USA as she no longer was able to comply with the US Coastguard's ever changing fire regulations. Nearly all the P & O ships had been upgraded to comply, but this was a costly business and for old ships like Orcades and Himalaya nearing their retirement, it was not worth the outlay. It made more sense to avoid the USA and stick to the Australian run via South Africa or Suez. This was no great hardship as far as I was concerned as it meant we did not have to go through all the Immigration requirements for the USA.

During the first few weeks of the voyage I spent many of the sea days on the outward leg to Sydney holding seminars for the crew to explain how the changeover to decimal currency would affect them. I took a lot of trouble over this, having only a dozen or so at a time so that they would not feel intimidated asking what might seem a silly question in front of others. I also mixed the departments so that no area of the ship was inconvenienced and held them during working hours in order to get the attendance. The ship would actually go over to Australian currency in Sydney prior to the April change over in UK and would go back to sterling for the voyage home after the changeover, so no one was going to be affected until that time. The supply of decimal coinage had already been placed on board prior to our departure from the UK. The crew who would be involved in retail sales like Shops and Bars listened intently, the others fairly half-heartedly as they felt it did not really involve them, at least, until I mentioned about their pay.

Once we reached Sydney, the ship was in port for seven days with no passengers whilst cargo was discharged and the ship was stored. Our first cruise was to be a 28 day Cherry Blossom cruise up to Japan and Hong Kong. This meant three days off each in Sydney. The next cruise would see us spend three days in Yokohama, two days in Kobe, a day in Nagasaki, three days in Hong Kong and two days in Singapore before returning to Fremantle and back round the South Australian coast. That meant that I would be able to catch up with Tom the Customs Officer again. However this promised quite a bit of time off for all the crew and of course that meant they needed money. Crew members were advanced wages every two weeks and I used to time it so that it was just prior to a decent port. However it was also essential not to allow anyone to run into debt, which was something many of them had difficulty in understanding. Most wanted the maximum they could get and failed to understand when I told them they were in debt or only had about ten pounds left. Cash advances were held in the Crew Recreation Room and I used to go up there with the money in a tin box with my assistant who would collect the signatures...and the two Masters at Arms who would sit either side of me. When disappointment showed on a crew members face I would always tell him to come and see me in the office afterwards and I would explain exactly where his money had gone, and if I had made a mistake, then I would rectify it. Most times this pacified a situation as the crew member would be sure I had made a mistake. I would end up with an enormous queue outside the office which would take me until around 9.00pm to clear. I did make an error on two occasions and was as good as my word. However, many of them had forgotten they were sending money home each month by allotment or that they had to pay off their uniform; a rail ticket; a fine; a forfeiture, and never realized how much their tax and insurance would be. On one occasion, an Engine Room rating did take a swing at me. Fortunately he was quite drunk and I put my head back as his fist sailed past me. By the time I had locked the cash box he was already unconscious on the deck where one of the Master at Arms had floored him. Overtime for the crew kicked in after four hours of work on a Saturday and the whole of Sunday. The Purser's Department had to work at weekends for obvious reasons but the Deck and Engine crew only had to do basic watchkeeping and emergency duties so on weekends at sea they had plenty of time to while away. This, most of them did quite effectively by drinking and so as a Crew Purser you soon learned not to pay an advance of wages just before or on a weekend.

The galley staff was always busy and did not have time to stand in line. For that reason I would pay them out separately from the Bakery after the main payout in the Recreation Room. By this time it was usually around 5.30pm and the whole place was a bustle getting ready to serve the First Sitting Dinner at 6.00pm. The Bakery was a self-contained section of the Galley that had a steel grill which could be opened during service for the Waiters to collect desserts, etc. The Chief Baker was a small, middle-aged man called Jack, and I soon learned not to schedule cash advances on a day when rum babas were on the dinner menu. The babas only had a mere whiff of rum about them as the most of the rum had already disappeared down Jack's throat while they were in early stages of preparation. In any catering establishment there is always rivalry between Cooks and Waiters and ships are certainly no exception. Filled with

Dutch courage (or Crew Rum in Jack's case), he would go outside the Bakery and pick a fight with the biggest Waiter around, for no real reason. The Waiter not wanting to get in too much trouble would pick Jack up and dump him in one of the large bread bins where he would lay, unable to get out by himself with his legs waving around until one of the junior Bakers rescued him. However, he never learned. Sometimes, the fight would escalate to a full scale John Wayne style saloon punch up and we would have to close the steel grill, locking ourselves and the money in the Bakery until the Masters at Arms had sorted it out. Then we could open up again and carry on paying as if nothing had happened. The Third Stewards were in charge of what was called Press Duty which was to ensure that moderate peace reigned between the Waiters and Cooks during service. One evening just prior to service, I was paying out money from the Bakery when I noticed one of the Waiters pick up about six dinner plates from a stack and creep up behind Rod, one of the Third Stewards. He had a grudge against him for some reason and was going to fix him once and for all. Before I could warn him, the Waiter brought the plates crashing down on the back of his head and Rod sank to his knees in front of the Hot Press, a small trickle of blood starting from the wound and trickling down the back of his neck. Now Rod was a big fellow, nicknamed Big Mary as he always called everyone Mary. Any other mortal would have been knocked out cold but not Big Mary. He wavered a bit and shook his head to clear it. Then to the Waiter's horror he got back on to his feet and turned round. The Waiter stood there with his mouth open, rooted to the spot, unable to believe that this man was not unconscious. Big Mary brought his fist up in a giant swing and caught the Waiter's upper jaw. He left the deck like a rocket at Cape Canaveral and landed somewhere over the Cook's side of the Hot Press. When Big Mary looked at his fist the Waiter's two front incisor teeth were sticking out of his fist. He still has the scars to this day.

Generally if you treated the crew with respect and showed concern for their welfare, they would reward you back in their own way. Let's face it, everyone was away from home for long periods, might have problems with wives, girlfriends, children, elderly parents, etc. with nobody to speak to about their problems. There was a Welfare Leading Hand who was like an Agony Aunt and ran the crew shop and entertainment but his powers were limited. Most of the crew who had a problem ended up in my office as problems always seemed to require finance to solve them. I seemed to be the Ultimate Agony Aunt. Nevertheless, although lending a sympathetic ear often did the trick, you were still bound by limitations as to how much you could help and occasionally there was bad feeling. I learned not to walk on the outside unlit deck areas on my own after dark as well as keeping my cabin door locked at night, I often used to sleep with a brass fire nozzle under my pillow.

It was during this voyage that Ken, the Purser, and 'Ginlips', the Chief Officer came up with a plan to save the company money by having crew paint passenger cabins. Apparently it cost fifty pounds to have the shipyard work force paint a passenger cabin in dry dock and so their idea was to have a crew member who wanted to earn extra money during the long boring sea evenings, paint one of the spare passenger cabins for fifteen pounds. To prove he could paint, however, before being let loose with a paint brush, he would have to paint a crew cabin, for which he would be paid the number of overtime hours it had taken him. This would be called the 'Paint and Save Club'. It would be open to all crew members including Officers, thereby giving many passenger and crew cabins a facelift, saving the company money and offering crew a chance to earn a bit of extra cash, and as a bonus it might keep them away from the bar for a few nights. After all, on this voyage we would be spending many days in Sydney as well as going to Japan and Hong Kong. I was particularly enthralled with this as I too found it to be quite a good source of extra income by just paying myself out under various guises. It did backfire on us at the end of the voyage when the Purser and Chief Officer were hauled over the coals for not getting the Management go ahead for the scheme, and I got into trouble for paying out the crew in cash and not adding it to wages for taxation purposes. None of us had actually thought of that, and I had to spend two days of my precious leave in the Pay Department of our London Office working it all backwards to produce a tax return.

My first time in Japan and the Far East was enthralling. Mind you, in Japan, you had to be careful as everything was so expensive and even a beer could set you back a tidy sum. You soon learned never to run a tab but pay round by round. Also I used to have our Agent write the name of the ship and dock in Japanese and duplicate several hundred so that any crew member going ashore took one of these and could show a taxi driver and find the correct dock. All passengers and crew had to take a Japanese shore pass with them, stamped by the Immigration on arrival in that particular port. All passes had to be collected in prior to sailing...and the Immigration checked them. If one was missing, the ship did not sail until it was produced.

In Kobe, Dick, The Senior Assistant Purser (SAP) and I decided to go trout fishing in the mountains overlooking Kobe. We spent a pleasant morning, catching several but throwing them back as was the requirement. On the way back to the ship we decided to stop off at an English Pub called the King's Head for a couple of pints. Around Noon, Dick informed me that he had to go as he might have to play soccer for the crew team and if he was not back by 1.00pm, he was playing soccer. 1.00pm came and he was not back so I was just about to leave when Gordon, a Scottish Radio Officer arrived and said he was glad he had caught me as Dick had sent him to tell me he was definitely playing soccer. Gordon asked me to have one more seeing as he had just arrived and so I did. Some eight hours later, we were still there. We got back to the ship by taxi around 10.00pm and then I had the lovely job of checking off the 600 odd crew passes so the ship could sail at Midnight. How I did it, I don't know but by 11.30pm we had 100% in and sailed on time.

We arrived in Hong Kong, and berthed at the Ocean Terminal, right in the middle of Kowloon for three days. The fashion in those days was to have a suit made by the tailors there, plus anything else you might fancy, trousers, shirts, whatever. They would make anything you wanted within the time limit of the ship's stay. The quality, of course not exactly Savile Row but still good value for the various times most crew members needed to wear a suit. Mostly for court appearances and funerals I always thought. This arrangement was one of the Crew Purser's perks. Two tailors were chosen by the Crew Purser, usually Jimmy Chang and Anchors and they would set up shop in the Crew Recreation room. There, crew members would choose their cloth, style and have their measurements taken. A couple of days later the tailors would return with the suits and once the crew member was satisfied he would be given a coloured card with his name and the suit price on and would come to see me in the office. I would have him sign the advance, and stamp the back of his card so that he could collect his suit. Prior to sailing the tailors would come to see me with their stack of cards, we would agree the total and I would pay them the cash less the generous discount which had been agreed beforehand. It was a lucrative arrangement.

Many of the crew kept parrots in their cabins and/or tanks with tropical fish. I did have a tank of tropical fish which had been given to me by the Maitre D'Hotel on the Oriana. One night during rough weather, I was awoken to the sound of running water and switching on the light saw the glass in the tank had cracked and the water was spurting all over the cabin with the pressure. I managed to save all my fish in a pint beer glass and had to go and wake the Chief Baker, Danny, whom I knew had his own tank, and ask him if I could board my fish with his until I could purchase another tank. Singapore, our next port was a haven for fish. They had salt water fish, cold water fish, tropical fish, every sort of tank and equipment you could imagine and for very reasonable prices. I returned from my trip ashore with an enormous aquarium style tank and had to have the carpenter remove my built in couch settee to accommodate the tank. However, it was wonderful, very restful and was the envy of many on board.

Any livestock of this nature had to be recorded on a crew member's customs declaration and on arrival in every Australian and New Zealand port, every parrot and fish had to be sighted by the Agriculture Officer. I would have to accompany the Officer and many a time we would have to sit there counting about 50 fish in a tank while they were swimming around. However, should a fish die between ports, the body would have to be kept until the next port. I know the Australasians are very protective of their environment but this was bureaucracy at its height. I was very fortunate on the Orcades that we had a great Captain, Ralph, who took a shine to me and several times a week on a sea day he would phone me down in the Office around noon and ask if I was busy. Even if I was, I would say no as you could never be too busy for a Captain. He would request that I go up and on entering his cabin, he would indicate his drinks cabinet and suggest I pour two gin and tonics. He would talk about any subject but would inevitably come round to the fact that he felt that it was I who controlled the crew morale as I held the purse strings. Obviously word spread back to him from people like the Bosun and the Chief Steward that I was very fair when it came to dealing with the crew and looking after their financial affairs. In his eyes I could do no wrong which as it turned out was quite lucky at times.

CHAPTER 12

One of our regular ports on these cruises out of Sydney was Noumea in French Caledonia. It is a lovely island and in those days there was no dock for cruise ships so we had to anchor out in the harbour and use the lifeboats to tender passengers and crew ashore. There was, and as far as I know still is, a ruling that you can't arrive or sail in the hours of darkness and so we would remain overnight and sail at 6.00am, sometimes later after a good 24 + hour stay. This was of course very popular with the crew as it meant they could go ashore after serving dinner and we always hoped that enough would have returned in time and in an acceptable state to serve breakfast. On this one occasion, it was around Midnight when a couple of tours had returned and there was quite a queue on the dock, the tenders gradually reducing the line but it was taking a while due to one of the tenders having broken down with engine problems. Crew always had to wait until the passengers had been ferried and then they could board the tenders. Several Waiters, four of them in fact including two brothers from London had been out for a few too many drinks and were in high spirits. Some of the passengers were quite slow in boarding the tenders so these good minded souls decided to speed things up a bit by helping the passengers into the tenders. Unfortunately, in the state they were in they forgot to check that there was a tender alongside and assisted several passengers into the water. Also, even more unfortunately was the fact that one of the 'passengers' that they assisted into the water happened to be the Chief of the Secret Police who was standing near and not in uniform when he was 'assisted'. Chaos reigned and soon there were police cars all over the place as passengers were retrieved from the water and our four crew members were cuffed and driven away. I did not actually hear about this incident until the next morning when the Staff Captain visited my office with the names and told me the two of us would have to go ashore with their Seaman's Books and translate their statements into French. On arrival at the police station we saw our four errant shipmates locked in a space under the stairs. They were unable to lie down or stand up and were having to crouch in the small space where they had been held for the past nine hours. They did, however look fairly pleased to see us. The Staff Captain and I spent most of the day at the station, doing translations. However, at around 2.00pm another crew member, a friend of theirs who was a Utility Steward and not very bright, turned up at the Police station and demanded to see his friends. On being told that it was not possible, this idiot decided to take a swing at the French Gendarme behind the desk. This Gendarme was very agile considering his size, and easily demonstrated this by swinging himself over the counter and knocking the Utility Steward out cold. And then there were five!

At 5.00pm we were told we would have to sail without them as their case would not come up in court for another couple of days and so the Staff Captain and I returned to the ship having left their Seaman's Books with the Police so that after the court case they would be able to fly to Sydney and rejoin the ship. Several days later we heard that their case had been heard and all five of them had been sentenced to six months hard labour. There was shock amongst the crew and during future calls in Noumea crew were very well-behaved. The ship returned to England, went back to Sydney and returned again to Southampton. The crew had been paid off and I was still there the next day preparing to go on leave myself the next morning. It was 6.00pm some eight months after the incident and I was about to lock the office when this smart looking lad came in and asked if he could speak to me. I did not recognise him at first as he had a really short haircut but it was one of the brothers who had recently returned after his hard labour in

Noumea and had come to the ship to enquire after his gear and balance of wages. I explained to him that it had been landed months ago to the Board of Trade Office in Southampton when the ship had first arrived back and he and the others would have to pick it up from there after 9.00am the next day. Neither of us was in any hurry so I offered him a beer and we sat down while he related his experiences. He assured me he was now a changed person and how much he had regretted his folly. 'Never again', he kept saying to me. He explained that they and others had spent their six months building a nice new dock in Noumea at which ships could now dock alongside without having to tender. After completion of their sentences, they had returned to the UK separately as DBS (Distressed British Seaman) on one of several cargo ships which were returning to England. Sure enough, when we next visited Noumea there was a brand new dock there and every time I call there, I am reminded of the guys that built it and what dreadful toil it must have been.

During the final call in Sydney, we had to change the ship's working currency back from Australian dollars to sterling, but this would be the first time that any of the crew had seen the new British coinage. The changeover all went smoothly with one exception...the Radio Office. The Chief Radio Officer was an Irishman by the name of Willie an he had the devil of a time trying to understand the fact that there were now only 100 pennies to the pound rather than 240. One evening, Dick, the SAP and I went up to the radio Office to try and explain it to Willie to make his life easier. Willie was in the middle of calling home at the time and so we waited until he had finished his call. We had no wish to eavesdrop but the first part of the call was being made before we realised it was private and made a discreet exit. However, the beginning of the call went thus,

Willie : "Who is that speaking ?"

Patrick: "This is Patrick, Dad"

Willie: "I want to speak to my eldest son, Michael"

Patrick: "But this is Patrick...I'm your oldest son"

Willie: "Can you put Michael on the phone?"

Patrick: "But you don't have a son called Michael"

Willie: "Well put Patrick on then"

Patrick: "This IS Patrick"

At that point we left the Radio Office having abandoned all hope.

On the voyage home, it was Charlie, the Baggage Steward's birthday. Like anywhere else, any excuse for a celebration was always welcome but after the fourth day of birthday celebration, the Purser mentioned to Allan, the Crew Third Steward, and I discreetly that he thought perhaps the Baggage Steward's birthday should now come to an end. We went down to his cabin where Charlie was passed out on his bunk, stark naked and face down, totally out for the count. We tried to rouse him by first of all shaking him and then a jug of cold water. Not a flicker. At that moment, Tony the Second Steward arrived. Tony and his older brother Ken were both very large men from London's East End. They had a reputation of being villains and everyone respected this. After explaining the situation, Tony said there was no problem, he would rouse him and told us to stand well back. He grabbed a toothbrush from a beaker by the basin and rammed it handle first into Charlie's anal cavity; still not a flicker. Tony took out his lighter and ignited the bristle part of the brush which crackled and flamed, burning down the handle like a fuse. We all stood and watched from the doorway with morbid fascination. As the flame reached its destination, there was a scream and in one jack-knife style movement, Charlie was up and standing. Not ready for work admittedly but he was up. He couldn't actually walk or sit down for three days but I felt sure it was a birthday he would remember.

The day before we arrived in Lisbon when the Pay Department representative would fly out to meet the ship, I sent out the 'shock sheets'. These were a carbon copy of a seaman's account of wages for the voyage, an advance copy of his wage slip which would all too often, show him how little pay he had left to receive and wondering how he would get home. I would then have an open office for a few hours so that I could deal with any queries and either explain it to the individual or on the very rare occasion correct a mistake. Therefore it was to my horror when the Bosun walked into my office and informed me he had the entire Deck Department outside my office refusing to work and up in arms about their overtime. He informed me in very basic terms that I had made a complete fuck up of their overtime. I explained that the record of hours was kept by the Third Mate, and not by me. I could only go by the number of hours he gave me. The Bosun stated that the hours were fine but it was the rate at which it was paid that was wrong.

How could I have made such an error? I couldn't believe it. I told him to bring the first man in and asked him to point out the problem. He explained that 5/3d per hour was totally wrong, it was only half the rate he should be paid. I breathed a huge sigh of relief. It showed how much attention the Deck Department had given to the seminars I had gone to all the trouble with regarding decimal currency. I explained to him that it was not 5/3d per hour but 53p! The Bosun was silent and looking rather sheepish as I told him I was not wasting my time explaining to them all...yet again...about decimal currency. As he was as much to blame as anybody, he could take them all away and explain it to them himself. He apologized profusely and went off to deal with it.

We were the first ship to do a decimal currency pay off and it seemed worth a small celebration afterwards. The Chief Steward, Billy, a jovial character by nature but definitely not to be crossed, weighed in at around 350 lbs. Big Billy, as he was known, was from Bethnal Green and before coming away to sea had been an amateur wrestler. The local pub in Tilbury was 'The World's End', and as it was near to Tilbury Riverside Station where the crew would be causing havoc waiting for the London train, we caught the small ferry across the river to Gravesend, where several pubs there tended to cater for a certain clientele normally only allowed in if you had a 6" knife scar somewhere visible. However, I had Big Billy with me plus the East End brothers, Tony and Ken. The four of us sat at a table and I went to the Bar to get the first round. The rest of the clientele were mainly dockers who had been in there for most of the day, having little else to do. Ken got the second round in. Now, Ken had a bit of a stammer, not badly so, but at times it was a bit more noticeable. The Man Mountain, Tony went to get the third round and whilst he was waiting for the pints to be poured, one of the dockers nudged him and laughingly asked him if he had heard that guy with the stammer. He then proceeded to do an imitation which obviously the docker thought was rather amusing. Tony smiled at him and took a long pull at his cigarette to get the red end glowing. Still smiling, he informed the docker that he had heard the guy with the stammer and that it was in fact his brother. As realisation dawned on the docker's face, with one swift movement Tony shoved his lighted cigarette up the docker's left nostril and pinched his nostrils together. There was a scream to start with which lapsed into silence as the docker passed out on the floor of the pub. Tony calmly picked up the drinks and brought them back to the table and the conversation carried on as if nothing had happened.

My parents had moved down to a small town in the New Forest by this stage and as it happened lived quite close to where the Purser (Ken) and his delightful wife Jackie lived in Sway. Also not far away in Brockenhurst lived the Captain (Ralph) and his wife Helen. Although leaves were short we often met up for a pint in one of the local New Forest pubs. One afternoon at home our phone rang and my father answered it. He passed the phone to me mouthing that it was for me and when I asked who it was, he told me it was Ralph. Ralph? Who the hell was Ralph? I took the phone and the voice confirmed it was Ralph. I realised it was the Captain of the Orcades and he expected me to call him Ralph when away from the ship. He informed me he and his wife were having a dinner party the next week and wondered if I would like to join them. "Thank you very much Sir", I said to Ralph, I would be delighted. When I went to their house he graciously introduced me to his friends as a colleague officer who 'works with me'. What an absolute gentleman. He could have said works under me or for me or reports to me but no, he told them I worked with him and was one of his most trusted officers. What a wonderful man he was and deserved every respect either I or anyone could give him.

The ships did not have mortuaries, as they do now. Inevitably there would be deaths amongst passengers and occasionally amongst crew but the bodies were buried at sea after a post mortem. The body would be sewn up in a canvas body bag and weighted. At a suitable hour of the evening, the ship would stop and the Captain, Senior Officers and next of kin would attend a burial service in the gunport, culminating in the canvas body bag covered in a flag being gently slid into the deep. The Bosun would be in charge of this and a dress rehearsal held prior to the actual service. It was not unusual however for the body to actually disappear into the sea during the rehearsal and sometimes another bag had to be hurriedly filled with pumpkins, marrows and potatoes. This would then be buried at sea at the service when the real body was already lying on the ocean floor some miles back.

Only if foul play was suspected, did a body have to be kept until the next port. This could be as much as a week away and so a freezer would have to be emptied or at least cleared to allow a suitably large space between the body and the meat cartons. Alan, the Chief Butcher was a practical joker at the best of times and on one such occasion he had a dead body in the freezer. The metal stretcher was just inside the door and a sheet over the corpse. The Goan Assistant Butcher did not like bodies and did his best to avoid going into that freezer at the time. However, Alan sent him in to fetch a box of kidneys needed to defrost in time for breakfast the next day. In spite of the Assistant's protests he was told to fetch the box. He reluctantly stepped over the stretcher to reach the stow on the other side where the box of kidneys were, shielding his eyes from the corpse on the stretcher. Alan followed him in to the freezer and said to the Goan that he was making such a fuss as a corpse couldn't do anything, it just lay there. He then gently pulled the sheet back about ten inches, saying that this particular man had been rather ugly.

Now, we used to carry a few pigs' heads to decorate the buffets and Alan had slipped in to the freezer earlier and placed one of these under the sheet. The Goan stared wide eyed as Alan spoke of the ugly facial features and revealed the pig's head. The Goan screamed, dropping the box of kidneys as he dashed for the door. The poor man took several days to recover from shock.

CHAPTER 13

I was particularly looking forward to my ten days leave this time, well eight after I had tidied up the cash after pay off and overseen an Indian crew change; this especially after only having about three days the previous leave. It was therefore a pretty devastating blow when we learned on our arrival that there was no Assistant Purser on leave to take over from us while the ship was in port for the ten days. We would have to split leave between Dick, the SAP, David one of the Junior Assistants, and myself. We would have to do three days each. Dick lived in Whitby in North Yorkshire so it was agreed he would go home for six days and then return. I had to stay for the first two anyway so it made sense that I would do the first three and have 6 days off after that. David who lived in Surrey would go home for three days, return to take over from me for three days and have another three days leave when Dick returned. That meant we had 6 days each instead of ten but not very satisfactory really and a typical example of how the Management were unable to control their staff levels. There was always an excuse of course. Usually it was the fact that an unusual number had left the company which had come as a surprise. Perhaps they had got pissed off with not getting their leave.

As I was the first one standing by, I had to take over what was called the 'Harbour Float' from the Purser, the rest of the ship's cash having been transferred to the bank on arrival. Ken, the Purser was taking long leave, unfortunately for us and he handed me the keys to the safe with a five thousand pound float for emergency use. I did not check it immediately as I was busy getting the balance of the crew cash off to the bank so by the time the dust had settled, it was Saturday morning and I thought I had better check the Harbour Float. To my relief, it was all there, the whole five thousand pounds. However, it was there in the form of one cheque...for five thousand pounds...from the Purser who had cashed himself the cheque so he had some cash to go on leave with. It was Saturday and the banks were closed until Monday morning so we just had to muddle through; Ken's idea of a sense of humour.

We set off again a couple of weeks later to do a series of six, fortnightly cruises in the Mediterranean from Southampton and it promised a whole load of new ports for me. I had handed over the job of Crew Purser to another Assistant Purser, David and was now one of the two Cashiers, selling foreign currencies and shore tours.

The newly joined Cashier was Stuart, my friend from New Zealand. I did not enjoy the job as much as the Crew job, but it was a change, and it also meant more money to make on the currency exchange. The newly-joined Purser, Dennis was a small man with the accompanying complex. He was very much by the book, totally devoid of any sense of humour and pretty much disliked without exception.

As cash handlers we were supposed to balance our safes twice a week but for practical purposes, it was usually done once a week without problem. We all worked on an unwritten system whereby if you balanced down, you made up the difference from your pocket. If you balanced up, you put it in your pocket. Most times, this worked pretty well. All except for one Junior Assistant Purser on the Arcadia, Tony, who had been a fellow Cadet with me training in London. Sometimes, passengers who had laundry bills to pay were not very forthcoming at the desk to settle them and it meant knocking on cabin doors the night before docking to collect the money. 'I was going to come by in the morning before we got off', was an all-too-common excuse. Sure you were! Anyway, Tony very often felt it was too much bother to traipse round the decks knocking on doors, as he preferred the idea of a drink or two after work, so he was constantly having to write a cheque to balance his safe. He eventually resigned after a couple of years explaining his reason for leaving that he really could not afford to work for the company any longer.

With Purser Dennis, he liked to check our safe balances early morning before we opened up for business. After all, this was a company regulation. This meant balancing after we closed for the day and then having him check our safes at 7.00am. One particular time we were en route between Lisbon and Madeira and due to a particular currency transaction, we were temporarily a thousand pounds short between the three of us. This was because we had done that at the bank in Lisbon and had 1000 escudo notes. This was a larger denomination than the maximum 100 notes we accepted. We had the notes but could not produce them and we were going to have to change them to smaller denominations in Madeira. We decided to make Dick, the Senior Assistant Purser's safe correct and he would be the first to have the Purser check. Stuart and I were each five hundred pounds short. Dead on 7.00am the next morning, Stuart and I appeared to be finishing off so Dennis checked Dick's safe. He counted every bundle of notes, making a thorough job of it. Having finished, he started off across towards me when Dick called him back to sign his cash day book. As he leant over the desk, a bundle of 100 x 5 pound notes came flying through the air to me which I caught and placed in the safe. Dennis then counted all the money in my safe including the airborne bundle which he had just counted in Dick's safe. Finding everything in order, he set off to count Stuart's. I had to call Dennis back to sign my balance sheet and as he leant over to sign I hurled the same bundle of notes over to Stuart who placed the money in his own safe. Dennis then counted Stuart's safe including the same bundle for a third time, so everything worked out well. We had got away with making some cash and Dennis was happy that he had checked the balances as per the company's regulations.

Dennis had an extremely annoying habit of sitting at his desk and shouting, 'Somebody', when he wanted an errand run. Whoever was passing his door was supposed to go in and see what he wanted. One day he did this and the answer came back, 'Fuck off'. Dennis, pretty nonplussed with this, shouted back, 'Who said that?' Inevitably, the answer came back, 'Somebody'. We never found out who it was, as they skedaddled pretty smartish before Dennis could get out of the door, but it was always thought to be one of the Cabin Stewards.

During the summer months, there was always more activity on the crew change front as a crew member could be discharged from the ship giving 48 hours notice prior to a UK port. As we were in and out of Southampton every 14 days, this could be a nightmare for the Crew Purser. Being summer, it was holiday season and many of the crew were very transient and not necessarily P & O regulars. One of the problems was keeping them out of the passenger bars, particularly on the last night, especially the Disco as it was fairly dark. One night, as Duty Assistant Purser I was called by the Staff Captain and Chief Steward to go to the Disco with them as a few of the Deck Ratings were in there with some female passengers, drinking and dancing. We soon identified about five of them dancing on the floor and decided our best ploy was to stop the music to cause the least disturbance. One of them left voluntarily and the Staff Captain, Jock, and Chief Steward, Big Billy argued with two more gradually easing them towards one of the exits. I led the other two to an exit on to the deck the other side to try and reason with them. On gaining the outside deck, the three of us were alone and they decided the best thing would be to throw me over the side. As they picked me up, I managed to grab the railings as I gazed down at the turbulence being caused by the propellers as we were right at the aft end of C Deck. They were trying to release my grip on the railing when suddenly Big Billy appeared from the Disco. He had come to look for me. The two of them released me and went to deal with Big Billy whilst I climbed back inboard, quite shaken from my near death experience. As they approached him, Big Billy took off his mess jacket and put his fists up. I am not sure what they thought they might achieve as Big Billy knocked out one and then the other. They were then dragged off to the brig for the night before being handed to the shore authorities the next day. Thank God for Big Billy.

Now Big Billy had only just returned from cargo ships. The system in those days was that Deck and Engine Officers alternated between passenger and cargo ships. Upon promotion to the next rank up, you were invariably appointed to a cargo ship for a few trips to gain experience and seniority before returning to a passenger ship. When the next promotion was due it was back to a cargo ship again. For obvious reasons this did not happen with Purser's Officers with the exception of Chief Stewards. On being promoted to Chief Steward, you went to a cargo ship and then back to a passenger ship where unless otherwise requested, you remained.

Now Big Billy had just finished his time on cargo ships and used to enjoy relating a couple of his experiences whilst there. It would seem that on the first voyage, an electrician had turned off the oil feed to the bearings on the main engine whilst he effected a repair. This was all very well, but he unfortunately forgot to turn it back on again. The ship was ploughing across the Indian Ocean and the officers were having dinner in the wardroom. Suddenly there was the most dreadful screeching noise and the ship bounced through the water like a kangaroo before coming to a grinding halt. Everyone looked at each other, speechless, until Hedley, the Chief Engineer said, 'Goodness we've stopped, and immediately sent the Steward to his cabin to fetch his fishing rod! Once received, he went out on to the deck and cast his line. A few minutes later, Ralph, the Second Engineer came bursting into the wardroom, covered in soot and oil from head to foot, asking where the Chief was as the engines had completely seized. Big Billy told the incredulous Ralph that he was out on deck fishing. Ralph stormed out to find him and appraise him of the situation but Hedley reassured him that if that was the case, there was nothing that could be done but to wait for a deep sea tug to arrive which would take days...and in the meantime there was probably some good fishing to be had.

Not surprisingly, after the vessel had been towed across the ocean to a repair yard, the Chief Engineer did not return for the following voyage but was replaced by Harry who was army crazy. He had done his National Service in the army and in his own mind had never really left. On joining the ship as Chief Engineer, he decided to muster all his Engineering Officers in the foyer to introduce himself. They all arrived in the foyer and were mildly surprised when he had them all line up in order of rank. They were a lot more than mildly surprised when he suddenly stood to attention and in true sergeant major fashion yelled at them, 'Engineers!

Engineers 'shun!' They were still staring at him blankly wondering if he had just escaped from somewhere secure, when he tossed each of them a brown paper parcel and ordered them to their cabins, change and back on the double. They all scampered off, returning a few minutes later wearing camouflaged boiler suits! Harry didn't stay long either apparently.

Apart from his cargo ship tales, Big Billy was a crafty old sod. His right hand man, the Second Steward had to work from a desk in his own cabin and Big Billy would spend his working hours sitting in an armchair in the Second Steward's cabin. That meant anyone phoning Big Billy in the Chief Steward's cabin would receive no reply and therefore phone the Second Steward's cabin. The Second Steward would then be charged with the task as the caller had not been able to get the Chief Steward. Thereby, Billy sat there all day doing nothing whilst the Second Steward ran round like a blue arsed fly. If the Second Steward's phone rang whilst he was out, Billy would let it ring. After all, it was the Second Steward they wanted, not him.

Occasionally though Big Billy would stir himself into action. In Tenerife one time just prior to sailing, a Utility Steward had returned from ashore having sampled more than he should of the local brew and was making a spectacle of himself in the main foyer in front of the Bureau and the passengers. The Purser sent for Big Billy. He marched along the alleyway and stood in front of the Steward gently persuading him to move from the foyer into the alleyway. Once there, the firescreen door closed and there was more shouting from the Steward and then a loud bang which was the Steward's head colliding with the door. The door then opened and the Steward reappeared in a half-nelson with Big Billy marching him back to the crew quarters where he was guided to the crew mess room. Unfortunately he must have slipped on the top stair and he fell head first down two flights of almost vertical ladder.

A few days later whilst inspecting the food in the crew mess room one evening, this same Steward was ranting, holding a knife and announcing that he was going to kill the Chief Steward. Word must have reached Big Billy, as to the Steward's horror, Big Billy suddenly appeared. He told me to come with him to be a witness and he took the Steward behind the hot press where a large pan of water was boiling. He quietly informed him that if he had any more trouble from him, he would put his head in the pot and tell the Purser that the had ship rolled, he slipped and the water scalded him. There were five more months left of the voyage and not one squeak was heard from the Steward again.

CHAPTER 14

At the end of the Mediterranean season, once again we would be Australia bound. I looked forward to my leave but due to a departmental restructure, it was decided to make an Assistant Purser in charge of the food and beverage costing reporting to the Catering Deputy, previously done by a Petty Officer. This did make sense as it prepared you to a certain extent for the higher rank later on. However, as I had been chosen as the one to be appointed on the Orcades, I had to spend three days of my precious leave in the Head Office in London yet again. The job itself was interesting and different and carried quite a bit of freedom especially when it came to split afternoon shifts in the passenger Bureau and port duty. I was exempt from both of these as on sea days I had to help oversee deck buffets and in port I was on the dock checking the tallies on the stores being loaded. This job suited me down to the ground as I had my own office, and was able to work my own routines.

Prior to sailing from a British port the Board of Trade would usually hold a Boat Drill on sailing morning and prior to passenger embarkation. Why it had to be sailing morning I shall never know, when everyone is busy trying to get the ship ready for passengers and departure. This was commonly known as Board of Trade Sports amongst the crew. I am not diminishing the importance of this safety drill, but I never saw why it couldn't be done the afternoon before .But hey, we are talking Government officials here, so that would explain it. Not all lifeboats had engines then, some had Fleming gear which consisted of a number of handles attached to the prop shaft and were propelled back and forth by the operating crew but some had oars. The boat that I was in charge of had this antiquated propulsion system and during the exercise in the harbour, a launch had passed creating a wash which had spun the lifeboat. Some of the Indians lost control of their oars and as I had the steering oar at the stern (in place of a rudder), it took me up in the air. I was holding on to this great long oar for dear life and it swung me out of the boat and dangled me over the water. The Indian crew were all very concerned and instead of trying to get the boat pointing in the right direction, were all trying to grab my legs to pull me back inboard. It was like a Charlie Chaplin movie. We eventually got sorted and brought the boat alongside the vertical iron ladder going up to the dock. When I reached the top, exhausted from my ordeal, a BOT inspector looked at me and said, "Where are you going? You're not finished yet".   To which I replied, "You might not be, but I bloody well am".

A good friend of mine, Robbo, who had been in the group of Cadets six months after I started had just joined the ship and had the cabin next to mine. Unfortunately we still had Dennis, the Purser. I always recall one day an elderly lady coming to the desk to enquire if we had a knitting pattern handed in to the lost property. Unfortunately we hadn't. Apparently she must have fallen asleep on deck in a steamer chair and the pattern must have either blown away or she left it behind and one of the Deck Stewards probably thought it was rubbish and disposed of it. We did, however, acknowledge that it was a bit of a blow for the old lady. Dennis, however was not letting this go that lightly and at 6.00pm when the Desk closed for the evening all the Purser's Officers and the Deck Stewards were summoned to the Bureau and given a twenty minute lecture on the difficulties of completing a piece of knitting without the pattern.

As I mentioned before the drinking and partying was to such an extent that I must have done several round the world trips in my early twenties that I did not even know I'd been on. An overnight stay in port was always a recipe for trouble and I seem to recall on more than one occasion waking up in the morning in a strange bed in a strange city and thinking where the hell am I? Not only what time does the ship sail? But what ship am I on? And, who exactly is this girl in bed next to me?   We set off from Sydney on what was called a Fire Dragon cruise. This would take us round the Southern Australian coast to Melbourne and Fremantle (great to catch Tom again!) and up to Penang, Port Swettenham (now called Port Kelang) and back to Australia.

We sailed from Melbourne at Midnight. Now in the Crew Office there were two safes normally used by the Crew Purser but on Australian Cruises one of these two safes was given over to the Bank of New South Wales to use as they would put on board two bankers to handle the currency exchange much to our disdain, and they would operate from a hatch in the Crew Office which had at one time been the Passenger Bureau for the Tourist end when the ship had been First and Tourist Class. Around 1.00am, one of the Nightwatchmen checked the door to the Crew Office and found it open with nobody there. The safe which was given to the use of the Bank was also open and nothing in it. The alarm was raised and we were all called from our beds.

Poor Robbo, he was the Crew Purser at the time although of course it had nothing to do with him. The Australian police were notified and a team of them boarded in Albany to investigate. There were all sorts of theories buzzing around. One was that the robbery had taken place in Melbourne and the money taken ashore prior to sailing. The Coastguard had found a life ring with a flashing light on it just outside the harbour and so another theory was that the money could have been dumped over the side with the marker to be picked up by a smaller craft or the life ring could just be a decoy. So, nobody knew whether the money was still on board or not. Arrival Fremantle saw rummage crews come on board and tear the ship apart, air conditioning trunking, behind bulkheads, deckheads, everywhere, but not a trace. Passengers were allowed ashore but had their bags searched on the gangway but the crew was not allowed ashore. The police stayed with us all the way to Singapore and naturally we all had to make statements as most of us would have held the keys to this safe at some stage. The Australian C.I.D. even sent off a crew list to their counterparts in UK to enquire about criminal records for anyone among the crew. Naturally the information was confidential and we could not be privy to it but one of the C.I.D. Officers did say to us that if we knew just who we were working with, we wouldn't be able to sleep at night. I don't recall how much money went missing, but I don't think it was ever found or the culprits discovered. However, allegedly an examination of the safe lock showed that only a couple of tumblers were working and the lock could easily have been picked with a hairgrip. Anyway, the bank's insurance prevented the Bank of NSW travelling after that.

On sea days when I was not summoned to the Captain's cabin for a lunchtime drink, several of us used to head for the Tavern Bar by one of the swimming pools. Dick the SAP, Robbo and I used to gather up there to be joined later by Mike the Junior Second Officer, when he was relieved of his watch at Noon. We were usually ahead by a couple of beers when Mike joined us and so usually left before him. Mike was very much a ladies' man and had usually sorted out his chosen prey from amongst the young female passengers early on in the cruise. One of the sacred times of day was the afternoon siesta from around 1.30pm to 4.30pm. I say sacred as without this we would never have managed to keep going through the all-too-short nights. Many a time I would have just dropped off to recover from the night before when my door would barge open and Mike would enter with about four young girls and announce they had come for a party. I would be unable to get out of bed as I always slept naked and would have to sit up in bed reluctantly while Mike poured us all drinks from my supply and put the music on. Of course there was method in his madness as after one drink, he would then disappear to his own cabin on the next deck up with his chosen companion for the afternoon leaving me sitting in bed and having to entertain the others, until I had to ask them to go at around 4.00pm so that I could get ready again for work, having had no sleep, only more drinks. He later became a Captain and is still a good friend but to this day, I have never forgiven him.

On one of our many fortnightly cruises out of Sydney, we had arrived in Lautoka in Fiji when the auxiliary circulating system broke. A large pipe had burst in the Engine Room through age and corrosion and was not easy to fix. This affected just about everything on board. There was no flush water for the toilets, no fresh water with which to shower, no air conditioning and no refrigeration. There was also no steam in the Galley so cooking was out of the question. To add to all this, it was blazing hot in Lautoka and the ship being of steel construction heated up like a pan on a stove. The poor Engineers struggled in all this heat in an already baking Engine Room to repair the problem. There was not much we could do to help so the obvious answer was to go ashore to a local bar and rehydrate ourselves there. Mike was off watch at Noon and so off we went. This bar had a 'Poke-a-box' game whereby every time you had a drink you had a free go at this and if you won...another free drink. We had been about to go around 4.00pm but kept winning free drinks and returned to the ship a bit late. It was announced that the local sugar factory had helped out by encasing this broken pipe in a huge cement box and now it was a case of it setting before we would be able to test it.

That meant staying overnight and all the next day in Lautoka. We were serving buffet on deck for the passengers for breakfast, lunch and dinner and were quickly running out of cold food. Freezer doors remained closed to preserve the inside temperature. It was impossible to sleep inside the ship and so just about all the passengers and crew dragged mattresses up on deck and slept in the open air and mosquitoes. Once again, thank goodness the passengers were all Australian rather than British or American, and treated the whole thing as an adventure. At 6.00pm the next evening, however, with tests completed we sailed from Lautoka for an over-night sail to Suva the other side of Fiji. With obvious relief, the air conditioning was working and the ship gradually cooling down, toilets were flushing, and we were able to serve the passengers a regular dinner. All was well...until we came through the breakwater entering Suva harbour the next morning when the cement box gave and everything went again. We glided alongside the wharf in Suva successfully without power and thanked our lucky stars that we were back in port and not drifting helplessly at sea. There had not been sufficient time to cook off raw food for more buffets and so feeding everyone was going to be a problem.

It was decided by the Ship Management that the passengers would have to eat ashore and so arrangements were made with the two largest hotels in Suva, the Tradewinds and the Intercontinental to lay on buffets at lunch and dinner. Everyone was given two vouchers and those that had lunch at one would have dinner at the other. The Purser, Dennis decided that the Maitre D', Tony and I should go to the buffets and ensure that there were no problems. We arrived at the Intercontinental and inspected their excellent buffet and then accepted the Management's invitation to complimentary drinks at the bar. At around 6.00pm, we decided we had better have a look at the buffet at the Tradewinds and jumped in a cab. Their buffet also was excellent and once again we accepted their invitation to use the bar. We eventually arrived back at the ship about midnight to find the Purser waiting for us on the gangway, having been waiting for several hours for me to report back to him. He was relieved to hear all had gone well, but not best pleased when he realised how we had spent most of our time. We sailed the next morning back to Sydney as a temporary replacement piece of piping had been found in Suva and we were back in business.

In Singapore we were changing some of the Indian crew as it was only a short flight to Bombay and cheaper than doing it in London. The outgoing crew members left the ship to be accommodated in a Singapore hostel so that the incoming crew could embark straight into their ship cabins and start work. One outgoing crew member's suitcase had apparently gone missing and Robbo was told by Dennis to 'find it'. As I happened to be standing nearby, I was told to help him. We decided to start at the hostel where the outgoing crew were having a party with the duty-free booze they had taken off the ship. Robbo and I were invited to join in which we did. I cannot recall whether the suitcase was ever found but to the best of my recollection I believe we had a terrific night out in Singapore, having to feed Dennis a load of bullshit on our return.

Among the newly joined Indian crew, there was one white face. It was Stuart from New Zealand, now an Assistant Purser. He had just finished being Crew Purser on Canberra and was taking a long leave to visit his family in NZ. He could not afford the return flight so had managed to get himself on the charter flight from London to Bombay with the Canberra's Indian crew change. In Bombay, he had visited Goa and then managed to get himself a seat on the charter flight from Bombay to Singapore with the new crew joining the Orcades. From Singapore, he travelled with us to Sydney as a passenger, the company only charging him the victualing rate. From Sydney he purchased a flight to Auckland. Amazing then what you had to do to get home as if you lived outside UK or India, it was totally down to you. Needless to say, we had a lot of fun back to Sydney, only adding to Dennis's woes.

Charlie, Phil's Assistant Barman from Northern Ireland had been well impressed in Hong Kong by the new TV sets for sale as they were in colour. We did not have colour TV in the UK at that time and so Charlie decided to splash out on one in Hong Kong so that he could impress his friends at home in Northern Ireland. After he had taken it home at the end of the voyage and returned after ten days for the next trip, we enquired how the colour TV had gone down. Charlie explained that on the Saturday lunchtime he had been in his local pub and invited all his mates back to his house to watch the soccer match...in colour. Charlie had supplied sandwiches and copious amounts of Guinness as two o'clock neared for the start of the match. The TV was switched on and to his horror it was all in black and white and he had to suffer all the rubbishing he received. He was convinced that the TV was a dud and that the salesman in Hong Kong, knowing he worked on a ship had deliberately sold him a black and white TV. It had not occurred to him that there was nothing wrong with the TV but until the UK started broadcasting in colour, the TV would only show in black and white.

Whilst in Singapore previously I had been fascinated with the trishaws and thinking that if I had one of these back in UK, I could earn some extra money when I took a long leave. I spoke to the providore whilst we were storing and he said he would see what he could do. After the stores were finished, he phoned me to say he had got a freight one for sale and could I get over to his office? I took a cab there and paid the money, eight pounds, and the owner put brand new motorbike tyres on it. There were no passenger seats as it was a freight carrier but it was heavier and more robust so I would be able to fix my own seats on to it. The providore asked me how I was going to get it back to the ship. I hadn't thought about that and so I decided to ride it. I did not know the way as it was right across Singapore and every time I stopped to ask directions, everyone thought I had stolen it and wouldn't tell me. I eventually arrived at the security gate and they obviously thought the same thing. I produced the paperwork and my ID and they reluctantly let me through after phoning to check with the providore that I really had purchased it. I still had no idea how I was going to get this on board. On arrival at the ship's side, Dick the SAP brought the Purser's staff down to see it and I was busy giving them rides along the dock when Dennis appeared. He had gone into the Bureau and finding the office deserted had started to search, not at all impressed when he arrived at the gangway to see all his staff down on the dock riding in a trishaw. Dick got the blame for that. Fortunately the Bosun, Robbie was in the Main Bar having a drink with Doug, the First Barman and between us all we managed to haul it in through the gunport and down into the Stores area where it remained parked on No.3 Hatch cover at F Deck level.

About a week later I was on Storeroom rounds with the Captain and Purser. We entered No. 3 Hatch where the main meat freezer was and the Butcher held the door open for the Captain. The Captain told him to shut the door as he had really come down to see my trishaw. He got on the front of it and told me to ride him round as he had heard about it and wanted to be my first passenger. Dennis stood there agape as I rode the Captain round the hatch three times. Afterwards, he told me he would settle his fare by buying me a beer in the main bar. We left Dennis there still with his mouth open.

Dick, the SAP and I had a favourite watering hole called the Riverina bar. It was hatch only service to the Stewards and so fairly enclosed and we enjoyed the company of Phil the senior Bartender and his assistant Charlie, he of the coloured TV fame. Phil and Charlie had already come to the attention of the powers that be as they had a pair of canaries behind the bar. On the outward voyage to Australia, one canary had laid an egg and was sitting on it to hatch it. When we had been in Fremantle there were only two canaries and all would have been well if there had still have been two when we departed our last Australian port. However, the egg hatched between Adelaide and Melbourne. This caused huge interest amongst the passengers as well as the crew and the two bartenders received Lord knows how many birth congratulation cards. The Australian Agriculture officers were completely thrown by this turn of events, having not had this situation before and ever higher authority had to be consulted throughout the day in Melbourne until finally a bureaucrat made a decision and all was well. We departed Melbourne with three canaries all fully documented.

The ship's Plumber was called Wimpy. Nobody ever knew how good a plumber he was as he never actually did anything. If there was a leaking tap, Wimpy would pat it with his spanner and say that it was a job for dry dock and we would have to live with it for the time being. On most days at sea, the Captain conducted inspections of various areas including passenger cabins, public rooms, galleys and crew quarters. Each day the inspecting officers would meet the Captain at 11.00am in the main foyer where he would decide who would go where and with whom. At precisely 11.00am Wimpy also would be hurrying across the main foyer with a sweat on carrying his bag of tools, ensuring he was noticed by the Captain who would acknowledge him and then comment on how hard working the Plumber was as he was always in a hurry whenever he saw him. The reason Wimpy had a sweat on was because he had spent the morning drinking beer in the Print shop and had just come up three decks quickly in order to reach the foyer in time for the Captain to notice him. Wimpy was in a hurry across the foyer at that time because the Petty Officers' Bar opened at 11.00am and Wimpy always liked to be the first one there.

One of the bonuses I had with being in charge of the storing was that we nearly always arrived in Sydney on a Sunday and there was no storing on a Sunday due to the exorbitant rates of overtime for the waterside workers. John, my friend from Oriana, he of the Ilekai Hotel incident had given me the phone number of his girlfriend Judith in Sydney and explained that she had a twin sister. I gave her a call. Although I spoke to Janet and explained who I was, it turned out not to be very convenient as they were in the middle of a family row involving her sister. I gave the whole idea a miss. However a couple of weeks later, I was summoned to the gangway one afternoon as someone was asking for me. It was Judith, John's girlfriend, a gorgeous blonde about 23 years old. She had come to apologise for not being able to come to the phone. She came on board for a drink and ended up staying the night. That was the start of a great relationship. She would always come to the ship as soon as it docked in

Sydney and as it was a Sunday with no storing, spend most of the day and night in bed going at it like rabbits. The only interruptions were phone calls from good old Dennis. Knowing I wasn't storing, he felt he would use me as his messenger boy and no sooner had I got undressed and got down to serious business with Judith, than I would be summoned to his office, given some mundane errand to perform and then back up to bed again with Judith. I needed the 14 day cruise to recover from a four day stay in Sydney.

There was one night I had been out and about a little early and by the time it was 11.00pm, I was clearly the worse for wear. I was trying to return to my cabin but was faced with a mountain to climb to the Officer's quarters in the form of a staircase. I was attired in my mess kit and was on hands and knees making progress of one stair at a time when two Officers realising my predicament came either side and picked me up under the arms and carried me up the stairs. As we were about to enter the Officer's quarters, Dick the SAP came through the door and went, "Oh my God, let me have him, I'll take care of him". The two Officers told him not to worry, that I had obviously had a good night out and they would just stick me on my bunk and let me sleep it off. Dick was flapping round like an old hen. The next thing I remember was about 7.00am and I came to on my bunk still in mess kit but feeling like death. I showered and shaved and put on fresh uniform in an effort to rejoin the human race and went down to the Bureau. The reception I got from Dick was fairly frosty as he related the story of my being put to bed. Apparently the two Good Samaritan Officers who had helped me in my predicament had been the Captain and the Staff Captain.

Dennis always had the knack of appearing at the least convenient of moments. Dick and I had just left Dennis's office at 4.30pm after receiving a reprimand for drinking behind bars. We had a ten minute lecture and a stern warning. At 6.00pm, Dick suggested we went for a pint behind the bar in the Riverina Room. I looked at him incredulously as if he was mad. However Dick assured me that Dennis was busy in his office with an enormous pile of passenger questionnaires which would take him forever. Reluctantly I agreed and we headed up the stairs. We had just raised our glasses to our mouths for the first sip when Dennis appeared at the hatch behind Dick. We were immediately summoned to his office where an even bigger reprimand was issued and we were both banned from the use of passenger facilities for two weeks.

We were not the only ones to fall foul of Dennis, mind you. Robbo, forever the party animal had really gone to town over Christmas attending every Christmas party with great gusto. He hadn't been to bed apart from the occasional nap for an hour and was able to hold his liquor well. Unfortunately what came to the attention of Dennis was that Robbo was still in his mess kit even at daytime parties on day three of the Christmas celebrations. On day four, I was just getting ready for work after my siesta when Robbo appeared in my cabin looking very spruce, clean shaven and in an immaculate set of white uniform, starched and pressed. He asked me to pour him a gin and tonic which I did as I could tell he was rattled. He told me that at 4.30 pm it was 'the big one' as he put it. Dennis had sent for him. Some 30 minutes later Robbo reappeared for the other half, looking a little pale and apparently Dennis had really let rip.

In Capetown on our way back to Southampton, my father had asked me to contact a business acquaintance of his to pick up some cash that he owed him. I was busy storing in the morning and the businessman, Larry called to see me around 11.00am. He was on his way to the races and asked me what time I finished and if I would like to bring a friend. He would send a car at 2.00pm. I had just finished getting changed when I bumped into Robbo who was thinking of going ashore. Knowing he liked the horses, I invited him and we went off to meet our transport. We were both taken aback when this chauffeur driven Daimler arrived and we leapt in the back. On arrival at the racecourse, the chauffeur pointed us in the right direction and gave us the required buttons to enter the private box area. We had a great afternoon, moderately successful on the betting front but making full use of the complimentary bar in the private box. After the races, we bade a grateful farewell and had agreed to meet one of the company Agents, John and go back to his house for supper. After a great and of course boozy evening we suddenly noticed it was 11.00pm and the ship sailed at Midnight. John leapt into his Mini and off we went, although John was in no fit state to drive. We roared into the docks and were trying to ascertain which road took us to the berth where the Orcades was. We could see the ship but couldn't get to it. Suddenly we hit a kerb across the road and the Mini took off, breaking the front axle as it landed. There was nobody around and we were despairing as it was ten to midnight. A flat bed truck appeared driven by a young couple and we flagged them down. They did not know the way either and we went to a series of dead ends before finally screeching to a halt by the ship. The gangway had gone and the ship was already making headway, about ten feet off the dock. The side gunport at dock level was still open where the gangway had been and we both took a running jump. Fortunately we both landed in the gunport rather than the water and dashed straight for our cabins, tearing off our clothes and putting uniform on. The Bridge had seen two people jump and suspected they were crew but the light was dim. By the time the Master at Arms checked on our cabins, Robbo and I were sitting in my cabin in uniform having a quiet beer where we said we had been for the previous couple of hours. Had we missed, it probably would have been the sack for both of us as the next port was Dakar in Senegal, seven days away and only a few days before the crew payoff. Robbo was Crew Purser.

CHAPTER 15

As we neared the end of the voyage, the prospect of another five months with Dennis was not an attractive one and many of the Petty Officers, whom he really used to ride, had already requested to take their leave so that they would get a change of ship away from him. Dennis was scheduled to return but sometimes the company moved in mysterious ways. Dick, the SAP and Robbo had already decided they could not take another six months of him and had requested long leave. I was tempted also as I had only had short leaves for the past couple of years and was feeling the need for a longer break, even if only to get rid of some of the alcohol from my body. However, the thought of taking a long leave in February really did not appeal and so I decided I would bite the bullet and return for one more so that I could start a long leave in the summer. As it turned out, the company started to panic when they realised the number of senior Petty Officers they would have to find replacements for and decided it was a lot easier to replace Dennis. So Dennis, against his will, proceeded on leave. To our joy, his replacement was Ken, the previous Purser who had finished his leave and was waiting for a ship. Both Dick and Robbo wished they had stayed but it was too late.

Always on sailing day from the UK, the Management would catch the train from London, wearing their bowler hats and clutching their briefcases to attend the ship for a Management inspection. They would tour the ship in the presence of the Senior Officers, have a sumptuous lunch and then disappear back on the train prior to sailing so they would not be late home. On each occasion, on completion of the inspection all the Officers would have to appear in the Ballroom, forming a square round the dance floor by department and the Management would come round and shake hands. This would be followed by a short speech of encouragement telling us what a fine job we were all doing. However, on this occasion, it was more in the form of a reprimand as if we were to blame for the aging ship and all the breakdowns and problems we had endured on the previous voyage. I can remember the exact words of that speech in 1972 when we were told in no uncertain terms that 'a lot of money had been spent getting this ship back into working order, and it was YOUR job to keep it that way'. Whilst they all adjourned to the bar to wet their whistles, someone switched all the bowler hats around , so that

at sailing while they were all on the dock waving
the ship off, there were many Laurel and Hardy
lookalikes, some with hats perched on top of
their heads and others with them down over
their eyes. We sailed at 4.30pm that afternoon
for Australia. I am not quite sure what all the
money had been spent on as by 6.00pm, some 90
minutes into a five month voyage we had broken
down.

We were not actually dead in the water but
problems with a turbine had slowed us to a
speed of around 10 knots. We made it to Las Palmas albeit three days late. The normal length of
voyage from Las Palmas to Capetown was seven
days and we managed it in 12. We limped round
to Durban where a new turbine was waiting having been flown by cargo plane from England. We
remained there for two days whilst it was fitted,
which I found quite convenient as I had another
girlfriend there, also a Diane, a previous passenger returning from Australia on whom I was rather keen. We couldn't go at full speed, the ship
I mean, not the girlfriend and I, as the turbine
had to settle in and so our normal nine days at
sea took 13. However, we did manage to catch
Tom from Customs when we arrived in Fremantle. Round the Australian coast we charged to
Sydney. To bring us back on schedule they had
cancelled the first of our 14 day cruises and cut
down our seven day stay in Sydney to 32 hours.
We had to store from the moment we docked,

without a break, right through the night until we sailed. About two hours prior to sailing, we had received most of what we had ordered with the exception of the 60,000 fresh eggs. I enquired about these and the supplier said he thought we had received them in Melbourne. I assured him we hadn't. He disappeared to make an urgent phone call. We waited expectantly. We had to sail at 4.30pm as we were off to the Far East again on a four week cruise and top speed was required. At 4.10pm, the egg truck which had obviously been loaded in a hurry came screaming down to the dock amidst all the streamers and crowds who had turned up to wish a Bon Voyage. The driver swung his wheel in a sweeping arc and half the eggs fell off one side of the truck. The crowd cheered. It could have gone in to the Guinness Book of Records as the world's largest omelette cooked at Pyrmont 13. As the tugs pulled the ship off the berth, the Dockers were throwing cases of eggs to us in the gunport and we managed to have just enough to reach the first Japanese port which was Yokohama.

We always had to be careful to load minimum supplies in Japan as they were pretty crafty. They would quote you a price in say January, a couple of months before you arrived so that you could plan your loading programme. Prices were always much more expensive in Japan. However, when you arrived, you would suddenly discover that the price had doubled over the previous couple of weeks and it was easy to be caught out where you had no choice but to take the supplies and bite the bullet. However, experience taught you to be wary where Japan was concerned. Japan came and went fairly uneventfully and we arrived in Hong Kong for our three day stay. I had recalled that an old friend in the same house as me at school had gone to work for the Bank of Hong Kong and Shanghai, and had mentioned that at some stage he might be stationed there. The last time I had seen him was in 1967/8 when he was working as a trainee for the bank in London and I had been training as a Purser Cadet. It was our second day in Hong Kong and we were storing. The Ocean Terminal in Hong Kong where we were docked had a bar on the top floor called the Mermaid Tavern where you could get a pint of ice cold English lager and I had just had a couple in between storing junks and was on my way back down, when I noticed a small branch of the Bank of HK and Shanghai. I went in and in my best pidgin Chinese asked the clerk if he knew my friend. His eyes lit up and he said he worked in the Kowloon branch ten minutes away. He got him on the phone and we agreed to meet that evening when James had finished work.

We covered many bars and restaurants in the Nathan Road that night and were vaguely aware at some stage of a convoy of fire engines rushing down the street presumably to attend a fire somewhere. We were sailing the next day at Noon and James had said it was a shame as I could have used his sports car during the day while he was at work, and on the Queen's official birthday, they were all going out on a junk for a party and I was invited. Sadly I had to decline all these invitations as we would be at sea. We bade farewell and I arrived back on board at 6.30am and was getting in to my uniform for my boss's 7.30am meeting when the Maitre D', Tony arrived at my cabin for his usual gin heart-starter at 7.15am. As he was thinking out loud he happened to wonder when we would now be sailing. I looked at him blankly as he explained about the Boiler Room catching fire the previous evening when a shore welder's torch had caught some loose oil and the entire Boiler Room had burned out. We were going nowhere until it had been completely rewired. We attended the meeting and the latest was that we would be there for at least another seven days. Now I knew where the fire engines had been going to the previous evening whilst I was drinking in Nathan Road. I was thrilled and immediately phoned my friend to say that I would now be available for all the social events he had mentioned.

I had the time of my life. The only work I had to do was to take on a few more stores for our extended stay in Hong Kong. The other Purser's Officers were not so lucky of course. They were inundated with passengers all demanding to be flown back to Sydney as they could not spare the extra time off work. The foyer in front of the Bureau was about twenty deep for the first several days. I would wander into the back of the Bureau and ask if anybody wanted anything from ashore. I would then retreat hurriedly under a hail of telephone directories and airline guides which were being hurled in my direction. Eventually of course, the party was over and after ten glorious days in Hong Kong, we sailed for Singapore with a newly wired Boiler Room. Once again I kept thinking about the speech telling us a lot of money had been spent getting the ship in working order and wondering how the sequel speech would be delivered.

When we got back to Sydney, another of our 14 day cruises had been cancelled to bring us back on schedule again and we were to do a three week cruise to Tahiti. I had never been to Tahiti before and was hoping to get a bit of time off as we were only going to be there for a day. At least that was the plan. When you enter the harbour in Papeete, you have to swing hard round to port to progress to the dock. However, as we entered, there was a blackout and we just went straight on without any steering power and up onto a sandbank. Eventually, after several hours tugs were able to pull us off, the electrical system was repaired and we docked. Fortunately there was no damage but we would have underwater surveys done to reaffirm this, a Lloyd's surveyor flown in, before we could sail. We would be there for three days. I had a wonderful time, hiring a jeep for two days and driving round the island, clockwise one day and anticlockwise the next. Once again, I had enquired in the Purser's Office if anyone wanted anything ashore as they were busy with passengers and only getting an hour or so off. My enquiry was met with much the same reaction as it had in Hong Kong.

The last night we were in Sydney before the ship sailed back for the UK, Judith had casually mentioned that her boyfriend was not very happy about her coming down to visit me. Christ! I wasn't surprised. She had never mentioned him before. I asked her why she had told him and she said that she felt she had to. I still didn't understand why. Anyway when we returned on board after going ashore for a meal we went to bed and I did not give it another thought. At this point, I must mention that one of my duties was to be in charge of the crew mess rooms. Dougie, the Senior Mess Man was a giant of a guy and I used to give him a bottle of scotch each week to make sure there were no complaints about the crew food. It was a system I found worked well. That last morning in Sydney, I was woken by a hammering on my door at 6.00am. Judith was still asleep and so I dragged myself out of bed and wrapped a towel round me. It was Dougie. I thought perhaps there was a problem in the mess, the Crew Cook had over-slept and there was no breakfast for the crew or some disaster like that. However it was worse than I thought. He immediately asked me if I had a 'bird' in my cabin. When I admitted that I was not alone, he enquired if her name was Judith. When I admitted that it was, he suggested I got her out of there immediately as her boy-friend was on board and looking for me. He told me that he had found his way on board and came down the mess room and had been asking for 'the fruit and veg Officer'. Dougie said that he had immediately twigged as to who the guy was looking for and had sent him right up forward in the crew quarters round the Plumbers and Car-penters cabins whilst he came up to warn me. I promised Dougie an extra two bottles of scotch. When I asked him how big he was, he confessed that he was massive, much bigger than himself. I promised Dougie a third bottle if he would stay on the stairs for five minutes and do whatever it took to ensure he never made it to the top.

In a most gentlemanly manner, I hauled Ju-dith out of bed and told her to get dressed and get off home. She was shaking as we said our fond farewells for the next few months. She wasn't the only one. I decided to wear my boiler suit so that I could be mistaken for an Engineer, Laun-dryman, Carpenter, anything but a fruit and veg officer. I decided to keep away from the office and my cabin and considered the inside of the funnel to be a reasonably safe place. I had to get through until 11.00am when we sailed. I reported to my boss, the Deputy Purser at 7.30am and appraised him of the situation. He suggested I stayed down in the provision stores until after we sailed. I went down to see Arfon, the storekeeper who built a 'hollow' in a stow of cereal boxes and walled me in after handing me a fire nozzle to use for protection if all else failed. When the engines started rumbling at 11.00am, I felt a huge sigh of relief. Mind you, as I emerged back into the public arena again, various people stopped me to ask if I had seen my 'friend' who had been asking all over the ship for me. Robbie, the Second Steward even wound me up by saying he must have been the guy who paid his passage round to Melbourne just before we sailed. I knew he was having me on but I could not be 100% sure and kept a very low profile until we had left the last Australian port.

A friend of mine, Cliff once told me about a time when he had arrived in Fremantle outward bound from Europe. They had on board one of the Sitmar ships an elderly lady travelling alone. She must have had some sort of dementia unfortunately and she was refused entry into Australia. She knew nobody in Australia, what on earth she was doing travelling out there, nobody knew. That meant that they were going to have to carry her all the way round to Sydney when the ship would empty out, keep her on board for the cruising season and take her back to Europe some months later. On the other side of the pier was a ship from another line, the Achille Lauro heading homeward bound to Europe. Just before that ship sailed he collected the little old lady and told her to accompany him. He escorted her with luggage on to the other ship and sat her down while he got her a cup of tea. He told her to stay where she was and zipped off just before the ship sailed back to Europe. A few days later, he received a message from the Achille Lauro which read simply, 'Thanks for the present'.

Ken, the Purser had done his National Service in the RAF and a 'banjo' is a fairly common expression to military men, meaning a sandwich. However, it is not always familiar to non-military men and the Night Steward was no exception. So, when the Purser decided to have a quiet night in with a book, and he decided about midnight he fancied a sandwich, asking the Night Steward to get him a banjo did not seem untoward. The Steward racking his brains, remembered that Charlie, the Assistant Barman played the banjo and knowing we were all still behind the bar after it had shut came and knocked on the door. He asked Charlie if he could fetch his banjo from his cabin and take it to the Purser's cabin as the Purser was having a party and wanted to play the banjo. Charlie duly obliged. He knocked on the door and when the Purser answered it, Charlie was standing there strumming away 'When I'm cleaning windows' by George Formby. Seeing the perplexed look on the Purser's face and the fact that there was no party going on, Charlie held out the banjo to the Purser, mumbling that the Night Steward had asked him to fetch it. Light eventually dawned on the two of them and the Purser invited Charlie in for a beer while they had a good laugh about it.

With all our mechanical problems during the previous months, there was no telling what would happen next and our arrival date back in the UK was anyone's guess. This made it particularly hard for the Crew Purser as he needed to get ahead but had no idea what date to pay the crew up to. Eventually we limped in to Southampton and after deliberation, the powers that be decided that after the scheduled Mediterranean cruises, the ship would go to the breaker's yard in Taiwan. I was due for long leave as I had literally only had 11 days leave in nearly three years and had 248 days owing to me. I left the ship, not realising just how knackered I was until I had been on leave for a couple of weeks and then just deflated.

The Captain, Ralph was unfairly blamed for all the problems the ship had and was forced to take early retirement. He naturally felt very bitter about it as it affected his pension badly. Typical of Management of course, they needed a scapegoat to absolve themselves of any blame, the

Teflon on their shoulders ensuring nothing would stick to them. I felt very sorry for Ralph for the way he was treated and it served as a warning to all of us that behind the false smiles and camaraderie, the Management could never be trusted. Ralph moved up to the Isle of Skye to be near family but every year for the rest of his life he included a three page handwritten letter to me with his Christmas card.

So it was with mixed feelings that I finally left the Orcades for pastures new. I had been due for promotion to SAP for a while but you had to be in the right place at the right time. In other words you had to be on leave and available and not already working the other side of the world and I had been passed over several times because of this. It was around this time that with the gradual demise of line voyages that the British India Steam Navigation Company came up for sale, and was purchased by P & O. They used to have the East African run out to Mombasa but had now trimmed their fleet down to two ships, the Uganda and the Nevasa, after the Kenya and Devonia had gone to the scrapyard. The Uganda and Nevasa had had been converted to educational cruise ships. However, these two small ships came to us with enough Senior Officers to man an armada, and I needed to be available if I was not to be passed over further. I had made great friends for life on the Oracdes and certainly had a whale of a time but nothing lasts forever and it was time to move on. After all it was mid-July in 1972, I was 23 years old, and I had 248 days paid leave to look forward to...or so I thought.

CHAPTER 16

I departed with several vans of stuff I had collected over the past years, one of them refrigerated of course as being on the Purser's staff, many 'gifts' of meat and other things came our way. Booze could not be taken off due to Customs regulations but sides of beef from Australia, lamb from New Zealand, cases of avocados and kingclip fish from Capetown had all been properly butchered and packed on board and ready for offloading. I had installed quite a few large chest freezers in my parent's garage especially for the purpose. My convoy left the ship after late in the evening when the docks were quiet and I could offload all my booty in the dark without my parents' nosy neighbours taking an interest. My parents weren't too happy to see an enormous fish tank arrive in their small abode which had to be set up straight away to take the exotic fish I had collected on my travels.

I settled in to a well-earned leave after buying a sports car, taking an extended driving trip through Europe and ending up in Javea down on the Spanish Costa Blanca where one of the Barman, Des from the Orcades had sold his house in Torquay and bought a bar, and didn't intend going back to sea. I made the most of my time off but in September decided it was time to head back to England. After a few days back home I decided to go and see a girlfriend for the weekend over in Brighton. It was a Friday and I set off around 11.00am taking the coast road through Southampton on my way to Brighton. I had packed a few clothes in a suitcase plus some underwear that she had left in the washing machine the last time she had stayed, and stuck the case in the boot. As I was about to leave, I decided to take a couple of T-bone steaks out of the freezer for that evening's dinner, wrapping them in a coat to ensure they did not defrost too quickly in the sun.

As I drove through Southampton at lunchtime, I noticed that the Oriana was in Berth 106 on a one day turnround between Mediterranean cruises. I knew my friend, Dick, the SAP from the Orcades was on there as Senior Assistant Purser and decided to pop on and see him for a beer at lunchtime. I drove in through one of the lesser used dock gates and parked up. We did not have long, a couple of beers, a quick chat and off I went again on my way to Brighton. I drove out through the main dock gate at the end of Herbert Walker Avenue and was randomly stopped by the police who wanted to know who I was and where I had been. I explained that I worked for P & O, was on leave and had just dropped in on the Oriana to see a friend. The policeman then asked me if I had taken anything off the ship and of course I replied that I hadn't. Seeing my coat stuffed behind the driver's seat, he picked it up and out fell two T-bone steaks. It didn't look good. I was told to pull over and asked to explain where the steaks had come from if they had not come from a ship, and why they were concealed in a coat. I tried to explain that they had come off a ship originally but not that particular ship. 'Which ship?' he wanted to know. It was one of those times where the more you try to explain a perfectly innocent situation, the worse it gets.

He pondered my explanation for a while and then asked me if I had anything else in the car. Completely forgetting about the suitcase in the boot I replied no, but of course he wanted to look. As I lifted the boot lid, there was the suitcase and I knew I was in trouble when he told me to bring it in to the office. Asking me what was in it, I explained that it was just some overnight gear for my weekend in Brighton. He asked me to open in it which I did. I could have died of embarrassment as right on the top were my girlfriend's pair of black skimpy panties, a black suspender belt and a bra. He held them up admiringly, looked at me and said, "This your overnight gear for Brighton is it, Sir?" He was enjoying every minute of my discomfort as I stammered that I could explain. He told me he had seen enough and did not want me to explain; he wanted me to put the case back in the car, drive away and have a 'very nice weekend in Brighton'! I tried to tell him that I would really like to explain but he was having none of it, and I had to get into the car and drive away while the going was good but to this day I am still frustrated that he had not let me explain and must have thought I was a transvestite.

I had only had half of my leave at the end of October when I received my next assignment. I received the promotion for which I was overdue and on joining the Orsova in November I would be Senior Assistant Purser. The Orcades, Orsova and Oronsay were all sister ships in size, though different in layout within. Although the Orcades had been turned into a one class ship for the immigrant run, the Orsova, Oronsay and the larger one Oriana, all inherited from the Orient line were still First and Tourist Class.

CHAPTER 17

Prior to joining the Orsova, I had to do what was called a 'standby' on the Chusan in Tilbury. The regular crew on returning to UK would all go on 10 days leave and someone who had just been on leave would take care of everything on board in their absence, before they returned for the next voyage. The Chusan was thankfully in wet dock, but the Himalaya was around the corner in the dry dock at the same time. The Himalaya would be sailing the day before the Chusan. Allan, the Second Steward, Arthur (Gypsy), the Head Waiter, and I were all leaving the Chusan that morning when the regular crew had returned. The Himalaya had already manoeuvred round to the landing stage by Tibury Riverside Station in readiness to embark her passengers from the boat train, and she was due to sail at Noon with the tide for a season of 14 day cruises out of Australia.

The three of us left the Chusan for the short walk to Tilbury Riverside station at 11.00am. The next train to London was at 12.15am. We headed for the buffet on the station as we felt we deserved a beer in managing to get away from Chusan without too much hassle. Gypsy, however, decided he would quickly visit the main bar on the Himalaya, so long as there were no Customs around to grab another bottle of scotch and 200 cigarettes. We already had our allowance from the Chusan but Gypsy thought he would get a second lot from the Himalaya. Allan and I warned him not to go anywhere near the Himalaya as we had heard that one of the two Head Waiters had walked off after a row and they were desperately trying to find some-one before the ship sailed. Gypsy registered this information, but reassured us he wasn't going anywhere near the Dining Rooms, only a quick visit to the main bar to obtain his lifesavers, the entrance to which was right beside the top of the bottom gangway. We told him we would wait for him in the station buffet.

At Noon, the gangways were landed and the Himalaya drifted out to the middle of the Thames to start her river transit to the estu-ary. We were concerned as Gypsy had still not appeared and we thought he must be talking to someone he knew. As we watched, we suddenly noticed Gypsy waving frantically to us from the rail on one of the upper decks and asking Allan to give his relatives a phone to explain what had happened. It would appear that on en-tering the main bar on the Himalaya, he had bumped into the Shore Chief Steward respon-

189

sible for the manning. Although Gypsy was not the answer to his dreams, he would fill the slot and he was escorted straight away to the Crew Office to sign the ship's Articles. Gypsy had to immediately start work by dealing with all the passengers who wanted to change their sitting and table, of which he had no previous input. We caught the train to London and on to home. Gypsy returned eight months later.

The Orsova arrived in Southampton at the end of her series of Mediterranean cruises. I joined her at the start of a three week dry dock and she was then programmed to go on a Christmas cruise followed by a Round the World Voyage. Unbeknown to me at the time there had been some health issues during the previous couple of cruises, the cause of which, unknown at the time but on investigation during the dry dock turned out to be a contaminated fresh water tank. Once the source was known, all the European crew who had proceeded on leave were contacted by their GPs to be checked out for related disease before either returning or going to another ship.

Nearly all the Purser's staff was going on long leave and so there was a brand new team of Junior Assistant Pursers with little to no experience amongst them. The lad I appointed as the Crew Assistant Purser was the most experienced with two weeks of sea time! This did not look good and I started to feel I had been dealt a bum hand. The Indian Crew from Goa were all working through the dry dock and were ordered by the Head Office to supply a stool test to ensure they had not contracted a disease borne from the contaminated water tank. A simple enough task one would have thought; there were 260 of them and a medical team from ashore arrived on board to collect the samples. They all, to a man refused point blank on the grounds of racism. They felt that because they were Asian, they were being singled out as the cause of the problem. Of course, this was not the case at all, they were being checked for their own good but they would not believe the fact that the European crew was also being checked by their GPs at home. Of course, most of them being the gentle folk they are would have gladly complied but in most situations such as this there were about a dozen troublemakers, dare I say shit-stirrers, who threatened the others. Not so much threatening the men themselves but their families back home in Goa.

A few days later, an unfortunate and unrelated incident occurred when one of the Goan crew died. He had been depressed apparently and drank himself stupid. He then asphyxiated by choking on his own vomit. The newly appointed Assistant Surgeon, Peter had to attend to him but pronounced him dead at the scene. I was sitting by myself in the Dining Room just about to start my dinner when he arrived and asked if he could join me. Glad of some company, he sat down and started to describe the incident by telling me how he had given the man mouth to mouth resuscitation and had to suck the vomit from the man's throat. He completed the description by saying that it had very nearly made him sick as well. I sat there with the first forkful of food in my mouth which I was unable to chew or swallow. That was the end of the meal for me before it had even started and I sat there and watched him tuck in totally oblivious to what he had just done to my stomach.

I had taken over from an SAP called Mike. He gave me a good handover but of course all this came up after the main body of crew had left including all the Senior Officers and I found myself as a newly promoted two stripe Officer having to deal with the Senior Management ashore with what was nothing less than mutiny. The situation dragged on during the first of the three week layover with my having to muster all the Goan crew at 4.00pm each afternoon in the First Class Ballroom where representatives from the P & O management and the Indian Seaman's union tried to convince them to do the stool test as required by Public Health. It was pointed out to them that as a condition of their contract in signing the ship's Articles of Agreement that they would agree to any medical tests demanded by any Country's Public Health Authority and that by refusing, they were in breach of the agreement. As I mentioned earlier, most would have complied without fuss but were being intimidated. Eventually, well into the second week, the 260 crew were given an ultimatum, twenty four hours to decide whether to comply, or dismissal from the ship and from future company service.

The next day at 4.00pm we all met again and there was no change in decision. They all refused and were then informed that their employment would be terminated. After the meeting I was called aside by the Superintendent Purser from the Office and told that I and my team had until 9.00am the next morning to have all their wages, Seaman's Books, baggage lists, etc. ready for departure to Heathrow. I stood there aghast. That meant my entire team, around six inexperienced Junior Assistant Pursers and myself working through the night until 9.00am. I voiced my views, in as positive a way as I could and was told as the Canberra was in the next berth on an overnight stay between cruises, he would send all their Purser's Officers over to report to me to assist and that I could work them all through the night as well. The Canberra's Officers must have been thrilled to receive this news just as they were about to finish for the day and were looking forward to a rare night ashore in Southampton. They turned up around 6.00pm not in the best of moods and I put them all to work along with my Orsova staff. Meanwhile the

Goan crew having been fired were in no mood for co-operation and were drinking heavily. We had to have them sign that they agreed with their overtime hours and the cash advances they had received. I was horrified to see that the records for such were incomplete due to inefficiency of the previous Crew Purser and we just had to take the crewman's word in order to get everything done for 9.00am.

When the deadline arrived, and a fleet of buses turned up on the dock to convey the 260 to Heathrow airport where an Air India plane had been chartered, we had just finished and I thanked the Canberra crew for all their help and they went back there to prepare for embarkation for their Christmas cruise, having worked for 24 hours without a break already and then having to appear all smiling to welcome their new passengers. To cap all this, word had naturally got around to the other vessels and as well as our 260 Goan crew all protesting on the dock and refusing to board the buses, there were the 320 Goan crew from Canberra and around 80 who were left from the Orcades which was waiting to depart for the breaker's yard in Taiwan. There must have been almost a thousand protesters in all when the media arrived. Southern TV who had their offices in the old Southampton rail terminus certainly did not wish to miss out on such a scoop and were interviewing crew on the dock. The police arrived and gradually each bus was loaded with protesting crew and as each one filled it was driven off to the airport until all 260 had been dispatched. Once that was complete, the others drifted back to the Canberra and Orcades, the TV cameras went away and peace reigned once again. I often wonder how the poor bus drivers managed but I am sure once they were away from the docks and speeding up the A30, things would have calmed down as they contemplated their future. I am convinced that most of them thought that the company's threat would not be carried out.

Back in the Bureau on the Orsova, we contemplated our lot. The crew accommodation was a complete mess, the way the crew had left it, and there were no crew to clean it up. We had a few British Cooks left in the Galley so food could be prepared but nobody to serve, dishwash or do all the hundreds of other jobs normally associated with a ship's major refit. We organized food as a buffet and used disposable paper plates and plastic cutlery to overcome that hurdle but the whole ship was a shambles with dockyard work going on but no crew to support anything such as garbage removal, laundry, etc. The Management arrived for meetings on board and we waited for confirmation that the scheduled Christmas cruise would be cancelled. There was no way they would be able to muster a new Goan crew and fly them from Bombay in time; the cruise was due to depart in six days. We waited in anticipation for the announcement. We were correct in one aspect that they could not get a new Goan crew in time for the Christmas cruise but unbelievably, the decision was that the Christmas cruise would still go ahead as planned but with First Class passengers only. This meant around 500 in the First Class accommodation and with the normal compliment of British Waiters and Cabin Stewards, this would suffice. As a bonus for these 500 passengers, they would not be restricted to just the First Class half of the ship but be able to spread themselves throughout the Tourist public decks and bars also.

Then the bombshell was dropped. Extra British crew would be joining to handle many of the duties normally done by the Goan crew. They would be accommodated in the Tourist passenger accommodation and eat in the Tourist Dining Room. The notices for jobs had already gone out to the various Shipping Federations around the Country for crew. I knew then that I would have to give the poor Crew Assistant Purser some help, the poor lad had only two weeks experience and that was two weeks more than the others. It was stressed however that these extra British crew would only be joining for the 16 day Christmas cruise and be paid off at the end as the ship would be in Southampton for five days and a new Goan crew would have been mustered and be waiting to join on arrival and settle in before the ship departed on her scheduled Round the World voyage. Now getting temporary crew for a couple of weeks is always dodgy as they are not exactly dedicated to the job, the ship or the Company but getting them a few days prior to Christmas spelled out Disaster with a capital D.

The next day they started arriving from Glasgow, Belfast, Liverpool and London. They arrived with no luggage, no uniform, but several had remembered to bring their guitars and harmonicas. Many had come for a singsong and to have a wonderful Christmas, but certainly not to work. I was starting to think that I did not like being a Senior Assistant Purser and I certainly did not like being on the Orsova. Amid the general confusion of the registered crew joining, we were getting all sorts of people turn up looking for jobs. For instance, school teachers arriving on board and asking for the Personnel Manager, to which I would reluctantly admit as I was assisting the Crew Purser. One man explained to me that he was a school teacher and normally taught geography but the schools were on holiday and he heard we were looking for crew. He told me he had done a bit of cooking so he got signed on as an Assistant Grill Cook. I had no British rate of pay for that position as it was normally filled by an Asian and I only had a rate in rupees but we came to an agreement and I sent him off to report to the Chef. There were several such instances and we had school teachers from everywhere working in the Galley and Laundry.

Eventually sailing day arrived. We were well understaffed still and the ship looked a shambles but the First Class end did not look too bad and we hoped we could get away with it.

No, we couldn't! The First Class passengers embarked and off we went to the Canaries. We were sailing with all European crew, what a mistake. In hindsight, the cruise should have been cancelled completely. Hardly any of them had any uniform and what they had didn't fit. The 'first class' service in the Dining Room was farcical. Long haired, unshaven men with ear-rings and tattoos with a jacket which wouldn't do up so hairy chests were on display was the norm. One such steward would announce at the table, "hands up for soup". One passenger asked for baked jacket potatoes and did get them...delivered by hand, literally one in each! The Maitre D', Tony from the Orcades, was swallowing Valium by the handful.

The cruise progressed from one nightmare to the other. As the complaints multiplied, the Purser's offices were inundated. The Orsova had two Bureaux, one on A Deck for First Class and one directly beneath it on B Deck for Tourist Class. They were connected by a spiral staircase within, and my desk was in the First Class one at the top of this interconnecting spiral. I was constantly being called to the desk to deal with irate passengers; we had to keep both the First and Tourist facilities manned even though we had First Class passengers only. The Purser, Dennis, with whom I had sailed on Orcades, could often be seen in his office with his head in his hands in utter despair. Every night when we closed, we then all had to continue working on the crew's wages as we had 16 days to complete a full pay off when normally we would have months. The Asian crew accommodation remained in the mess that the Goan crew had left it and the Tourist Passenger cabins now being used by the extra British crew were not much better. Much of the upholstery and drapery which had been taken from the Tourist Accommodation for dry-cleaning lay in heaps at one end of the Tourist Dining Room, the other end being used as a crew mess.

By the end of the first week, the passengers had formed a deputation and daily meetings were held with the Captain and the Purser, who had to admit reluctantly that service and conditions were not as they would wish (to put it mildly) and in tandem with the Shore Management, various concessions were made such as complimentary wine at Dinner and a free bar. This however did not deter the usual tactics of some passengers who contacted the media about the 'ship from Hell' and the TV cameras were on the dock once again when the ship arrived back in Southampton. Most of us had averaged 21 hours a day during this cruise from Hell and we finally finished everything at 5.00am, an hour before the Southampton pilot boarded. We disembarked the passengers and paid off the crew, signing back on the regular British crew who would sail on the world voyage. It was the

4th January 1973 and I had never felt so knackered in all my life. I decided that I could not do the world voyage, I needed the rest of my accrued leave and so I phoned my Personnel Officer in London. 'Impossible' was his reply, he was short staffed, nobody to replace me and I would just have to do it. I reminded him that I still had four months accrued leave due, it was now Monday lunchtime and the ship was due to sail at 7.00pm on the Friday evening. I would stay until then but at 6.30pm on the Friday, I would no longer be on board. He told me he would visit me in Southampton the next day on the Tuesday. That night I slept for 12 hours but did not feel any better.

Where on earth was this useless union(masking itself as an association) we had been made to join and who were only interested in our subscriptions and the lot of the Navigation and Technical Officers?

It had just been announced that they could not muster a new crew from Goa in time but a B.I.S.N.Co crew from Calcutta would join for the world voyage. These were very loyal people but their standards and working practices were far different to that of P & O Goans. They were also Hindu as opposed to the Goans who were Christian which meant their diet was different and they required their own Galley. A space was found and quickly converted within three days. However, they were unfamiliar with P & O ships and different standards and the prognosis did not look good.

It was Noon and Tommy the Purser's Personnel Director arrived, came in to the Bureau and stared through me and several others. We must have resembled zombies from another planet as he did not recognise any of us. He asked one of the Assistant Pursers where he could find me, whilst standing looking at me. When the gobsmacked Assistant pointed me out, he was incredulous. "My God", he said to me, "I knew it had been bad, but I hadn't realised it had been THAT bad. I WILL replace you somehow", he said to me. We had lunch and he told me he would promote someone and have them here for Thursday, the day before sailing and I said I would stay until the Friday evening until just before the ship sailed. Rob, my replacement arrived at lunchtime on the Thursday and we started to hand over. I was quite embarrassed by the state of things and kept apologising to him as I am sure he felt I must have been a complete incompetent to have let things get in such a mess. Friday, 6.30pm arrived and I was just collecting my gear and dropped by the Dining Room to say goodbye to the Maitre D' and wish him luck. He was just about to start his Waiter's briefing prior to Dinner and came out to see me. He informed me that there was 15 minutes to go prior to the Welcome Sailing Night Dinner at the start of a 90 day world trip and four of his Indian waiters did not have shoes and six of them did not have trousers! I wished him the best of luck as another handful of Valium disappeared down his throat. I dashed down the gangway to my rental car and watched as the Orsova slipped her moorings and sailed off.

I was in the old docks and had only about twenty miles to drive to the New Forest but I was falling asleep by the time I reached the dock gates. The Canberra was in the new docks for a few days prior to sailing on her world trip and I just drove in to the new docks and boarded her. I called out the duty Assistant Purser and he gave me an inside cabin for the night. I slept from 7.30 that night and woke at 11.00am the next morning. I drove home and went back to bed. It took me several weeks to recover from that nightmare trip and I started to think about my future. I wasn't sure any more that this was the life I wanted.

CHAPTER 18

My parents put me up for a few nights but they did not have room in their small flat so I moved in with two ex school friends in Bournemouth. John was working as a waiter part time at a nearby steak restaurant and bouncer at a local nightclub on Fridays and Saturdays. Tony was working for a guy who tarmacked driveways, and so to supplement my leave pay, I tarmacked driveways too. It was hard work as the art is to work quickly before it sets. One person usually has to keep the shovels hot over a fire and rotate them to the shovellers. I always tried to get that job but so did the others. We all had to share one room in this flat, our old public school would have been so proud to witness the prominent careers for which they had prepared us.

I went for interviews with Marks and Spencers Management but the Manager was so rude to me asking me why I had bothered applying when (a) I did not have a university degree, and (b) I wasn't Jewish. I replied that it had not stipulated that in the qualification requirements and why did he bother giving me an interview if that was the case. I felt like asking him if he could tell by the shape of my nose or did he want me to drop my trousers. We parted company with mutual disrespect for each other, and I have always felt a grudge against M & S since, due to his attitude. I also applied for various jobs with ship supply firms but the best that was offered was twelve pounds a week plus luncheon vouchers. Forget it. Then somebody told me about the NAAFI and they were looking for trainees to become District Managers so I applied. I realised that if accepted, training in UK would have to be endured before getting a posting abroad, but certainly an appointment in Germany or Singapore, Cyprus or Hong Kong looked quite appealing. I applied and was granted an interview in London. The interview was conducted by three elderly gentlemen and at the end of the interview I was asked if I had any questions. I asked what the promotion prospects were from District Manager. This flummoxed them completely as they all looked at each other as if I had landed from the moon and eventually one said that nobody had ever asked that before. Surely if you were applying for the job of a District Manager, that was it. My disappointment must have shown as I explained that at the age of 24, I really did not want to have reached the pinnacle of my career with another 40 years of doing the same thing. A few days later a letter arrived offering me the job but for the reasons explained above, I wrote a letter back to them, thanking them, declining and explaining my reasons. They wrote back and said that should I ever change my mind, there would always be a vacancy. I still have the letter and might contact them one day.

However, I was now out of applications, still tarmacking and running out of leave. Then, one morning the letter arrived with my next appointment. I have already mentioned that the days of the long sea voyage were coming to a close with the demise of the Queens Mary and Elizabeth, and other companies not just British but the French, Italian and Dutch lines were suffering too. Although the ships were being redeployed for cruising rather than transport, it was obvious that cargo holds were not required and ideally the space could be put to better use. A shift in social structure was indicating that different classes were outdated and that a ship should be all one class where the passengers could roam the entire ship and not just half of it. Additionally, we were reaching the stage where everyone wanted en suite and not a hike down the corridor to use communal bathrooms. Many Companies including P & O tried to convert their existing ships to one class which worked only to a degree, as it was very obvious to everybody, which had originally been the First and Tourist sections. P & O had made an initial move in the right direction by commissioning a ship to be purpose-built for holiday cruising, although the keel had originally been laid as a car ferry. The build had not gone far and so was easily altered. It was to be a small ship to carry only 730 passengers and would be built exclusively for the American market. The Americans were behind as far as cruising was concerned and the British, Italians and Dutch saw the potential to replace the main line voyages and add to the holiday cruising which had been enjoyed by Europeans and Australians for years.

Thus, in the summer of 1972, the MV Spirit of London was launched in Italy and after a brief call in Southampton and a transatlantic repositioning, she arrived in what would be her home port of Los Angeles. This would be the first time that P & O had based a ship abroad, and away from the UK, although she was still registered in Britain. The crew who had first sailed on her from Italy was now becoming time expired and my new appointment was to fly to Los Angeles to replace David, the Senior Assistant Purser. I thought about this and decided that as it was something totally different to what I had done before and as my attempts at other ventures had failed, I might as well give it a try. There were a couple of uniform changes for this new venture. For a start, we no longer had to wear the blue reefer jacket at all times, just for formal occasions and in cold weather. Instead, we would wear shirts with epaulette slides like airline pilots wear. This was a huge improvement and a welcome one. The other was a change in the white uniform. Instead of the starched long white trousers and four button jacket with white shirt and black tie, this would now be shorts with long socks and an open neck short sleeve shirt. This was the best of the lot as it was so comfortable and with having to fly back and forth eased the amount of luggage you had to take.

I had only done short flights within Europe before and so this was my first long haul flight, twelve hours with British Caledonia from Gatwick to Los Angeles. On arrival, the 11 of us were met and driven to the Imperial 400 Motel for a one night stay before joining the ship. Vouchers for dinner and breakfast were handed to us for the Hobby Nobby coffee house, five minutes' walk down the road. When we arrived at the ship the next morning, I started to have misgivings, it seemed so small compared to the ships I had been used to. The interior was spotless, being new and appeared to be all plastic and neon, which of course in true American style, it was. However, I soon met up with some familiar faces. There was David, whom I was to relieve and Stuart the Assistant Purser from New Zealand with whom I had first come into contact in Auckland when I was a Cadet, and Lorraine one of the two female Assistant Pursers whom I had known on the Orcades. There were also a number of bar staff from the Orcades, Phil, now the

Bar Services Manager, Andy, Kevin (Whispering Jack) and several others.

After the formalities of joining, I was amazed to find that apart from the Purser and his two Deputies, whom I did not know, the actual Bureau staff consisted of only four of us. The 'Desk', normally a series of shuttered windows in most Bureaux was just a fixed construction outside of the main inside office in the foyer, totally open with zero security. The male Assistant who was the Cashier and one female Assistant worked on the Desk and dealt with the passengers while I and the other female Assistant manned the inside office. I discovered that as SAP and in charge of running the Office and desk, I was also the Crew Purser, yet again. I also was in charge of cabin complaints/changes and to put it in a nutshell, the four of us would be jacks of all trades as there was nobody else. Our cabins were minute and right at the aft end. The Spirit of London was a diesel ship as opposed to the usual steam ships and was far noisier with a lot more vibration. Diesel engines are far more economical, not only in fuel but in staff deployment and this was going to be the way forward. However, I wasn't looking forward to all the complaints from passengers regarding the noise and vibration. 'I must be right over the engine!' was a stock comment from many, who were totally unaware that 'most' of the passenger cabins were 'right over the engine' as the 'engine' was no small affair.

David and Stuart were both leaving and I had what was called a 'party cruise' as a handover with them. This was a short three day cruise from Los Angeles, calling at one port just over the US/Mexican border, Ensenada and return to Los Angeles. I couldn't believe it, I had never done anything less than 14 days previously. However, I was told this was not a 'normal' cruise, and that the usual cruise was either seven or 10 days to Mexico, always returning to Los Angeles. It all sounded rather boring, but not so this first party cruise. They were right, it wasn't 'normal' in several aspects as it had been marketed as a 'gay' cruise and advertised in all the San Francisco gay magazines. Embarkation that afternoon was a something else. I was no stranger to the gay fraternity as in those days, merchant ships were a haven for those of that persuasion dating back to the years when it was illegal. Many of the friends I had made at sea were gay and I found their friendship and loyalty were second to none. However, at embarkation, this endless parade of flamboyant black leather mincing up the gangway was indeed a sight to behold. The gay members of the crew were in paradise.

I had not met this particular Purser, Mike, before and he had been busy during the day. That first evening I obviously went for a few drinks. I was not used to jet lag, nor the larger American spirit measures and at the conclusion of the evening, I had drunk far too much. I slipped on the stairs on the way down to the main foyer and landed on my back on the bottom stair just as the Purser was about to start ascent. Stuart and John, the two Assistants, also on handover introduced me to him. I did have the feeling though that I had not caused a very good first impression.

The next morning, there were about 30 guys at the desk all requesting a cabin change. I mistakenly thought it was due to noisy cabins and was trying to explain that the few empty ones I had were no quieter than the ones they already had. However, this was not the case, they had all either fallen out with or become bored with their partners and had met someone else. They would insist on all talking at once until I blew a lifejacket whistle and obtained silence. I took the first one and said, 'Right, who were you with last night? With him? OK, who do you want to share with tonight? This man? OK! You take that cabin. Now who do you want to share with?' Eventually I got them all paired off and happy with their partners for the next night. It was different, I must admit, but I was glad to start the seven and 10 day cruises. These were down to Puerto Vallarta, Mazatlan, Manzanillo and Acapulco. It did become a bit boring like a bus route and not what I was used to. These were all new ports for me apart from Acapulco and of course were all in Mexico. The resort in Manzanillo was where Dudley Moore had made the film '10' with Bo Derek. Unfortunately for us, Bo was no longer there.

One of the main changes was the entertainment. This had always been a bit of an afterthought on ships that were transportation and apart from the few fun nights, consisted mostly of dancing and somewhere to show a movie. The ships had started to actually have a dedicated cinema and a projectionist whereas previously films had to be shown on deck on an evening when the weather permitted and the movie projected on to a bedsheet. There was always a break between reels and it had been the job of the Deck Cadets to run the movie. The Entertainment staff had never been professional and usually consisted of an Entertainment Officer who was a relic of the RNR Stores and Supply and a couple of Social Hostesses who were invariably ex Assistant Pursers who had become bored with the endless typing. However, now, for the American cruise market, entertainment had to be racked up a notch. The Entertainment Officer was now to be renamed the Cruise Director. This was a terribly misleading title as it suggested that he was the most senior person on board the ship and that everything from the stem to the stern came under him. Of course this was not the case, he was basically in charge of the Entertainment and Activity programme. There were however more in the way of professional entertainers on board, crooners, magicians, comedians and jugglers and cabaret artists. Many of the Entertainment Officers employed by P & O hailed from Butlins holiday camps in the UK, known as Redcoats. Brian, the Cruise Director was no exception. Allegedly he had joined the Orsova as a Musician during a break from Butlins, decided he liked it and became an Assistant Entertainment Officer on the Canberra. When the Spirit of London was announced, he saw the direction he wanted to go and persuaded the company that he was the right man to be the first Cruise Director. He was right in many ways and from that day on he would only go onwards and upwards, though he did not mind who got trampled upon in his quest to reach the top.

The next couple of months passed quite quickly and we were about to change to our summer itinerary which was Alaska. The old Arcadia and Oronsay had done one off cruises to Alaska but never a full four month season as we were about to do. I had seen photos of Alaska and it looked beautiful and although we would miss the sun and beaches of Mexico, the change of scenery and new adventure would be welcome. During the few days lay-over in Los Angeles, we changed a large number of the Goan crew. The new crew to arrive was due in to LAX at 6.00pm one evening and I and Bill, the Goan Supervisor, whom I knew from Oriana, had to go to the airport and escort them to the ship. Bill had been a pilot with the Royal Indian Air Force during the war and was a handsome man, never short of a fan club of middle aged American ladies. He had been visited by many of these during the day and apart from feeling tired from his exertions, had also had a fair amount to drink. We waited at the airport and the incoming flight was delayed more and more. We decided to wait in one of the bars. Of course, we were in uniform, which as I said before tended to resemble that of pilots. By the time the flight arrived, we had been waiting in the bar for three hours and many passengers were tut-tutting, seeing us keep ordering rounds of drinks but none of them were bold enough to approach us directly. As we got up to leave, I said to Bill, "Come on then Bill, if we have got to fly that jumbo out tonight, we had better go and sober up". There were gasps all round as we tottered out. Of course there was a Security gathering outside the bar waiting for us. We were grabbed and they demanded to know which airline we worked for. I told them to fuck off and mind their own business as we did not work for an airline. They did not like it but accepted it once they realised who we were. However, we were lucky a formal complaint was not made and that was the end of it.

Los Angeles would still be our home port for the 14 day Alaskan cruises and we sailed up to San Francisco and Victoria before going on to the Alaskan ports of Ketchikan, Juneau and

Skagway. We stopped at Vancouver on the return to Los Angeles as we would have to slot in two foreign ports (foreign to the USA, that is) so that we did not contravene the Jones Act, a thoroughly outdated Act which never gets high enough on any Administration's agenda for re-examination during the four years prior to their next election. It was rightly put in place many years ago to protect American flag ships by preventing vessels of foreign flag carrying passengers between two American ports. This was fine at the introduction but over the past 30 years it is hopelessly outdated when the use of ships has altered so dramatically, and apart from anything else, America no longer has any passenger ships. The USA is so advanced in some worldly issues but dreadfully behind in others. Our first entry into Vancouver harbour in June 1973 was to a welcome I had never witnessed before or since. It seemed that the entire Canadian population had come down to the harbour and cars were lined both sides of the channel leading up to the Lion's Gate Bridge, tooting and cheering. In the harbour a fire launch sprayed coloured jets of water and the entire area was a cacophony of noise and colour. It was and still is one of the most beautiful and friendly cities in the world, in spite of being nicknamed Hongcouver over recent years, and they were glad of the business cruise ships would bring to the city. In each of the Alaskan ports we were also given a large welcome with open invitation to attend a ceremony at the Chamber of Commerce followed by...drinks of course.

In order to comply with the Jones Act, we called each cruise at Alert bay on Vancouver Island. The vessel anchored out and we ran a tender service for passengers to go ashore. Most of them spent 10 minutes ashore, realised there was nothing there and returned on the next tender. However, the local Indian tribe decided to make a point by abducting the Staff Captain, Dickie who was in charge of the Shore Party and taking him off to their camp in the jungle. From there, they issued a demand that if we wanted him back, we would have to guarantee that on future calls we would sell tickets to the passengers to attend tribal dance demonstrations and to purchase handicrafts. Personally, I was all for sending a message back telling them to sod off and they could keep him. However, the Captain decided on a more diplomatic approach and agreed...so we got him back... and had to sell tickets.

In most of the Alaskan ports, there were just dirt roads and bars with pool tables, certainly not the extended list of activities there are today so a run ashore usually meant heading for one of the local bars for a game of pool. There certainly weren't the endless rows of jewelry shops and other commercial ventures which have conspired to ruin the atmosphere and local beauty of Alaska that have been allowed to set up to the greed of the Councillors who have permitted it. The Yukon and White Star railroad was still running all the way to Whitehorse in Canada in 1973 as a method of transportation, as well as the tourist train which ran up to Lake Bennett and back. Skagway was where the gold prospectors set out on the trail of 1898 in the Gold Rush and remains of the trail are still there and can be followed by ardent hikers.

One of my tasks was to have the Captain sign all the port papers for each arrival and he took great delight in winding me up and seeing my discomfort. He was known as Black Mac and he would growl at me to come up straightaway when I phoned him to enquire when would be a convenient time. I would have all the papers typed and neatly placed in a folder, not forgetting my cap when I entered his office. Staring at the health declaration he would enquire what he was signing. He knew damn well what it was of course, sign it and throw it across the room for me to take a flying leap and catch it before it hit the deck. Meanwhile he would sign the next one and toss it the other way to have me dashing from one side to the other catching pieces of paper. It must have evidently appealed to his sense of humour. Before taking my leave, he would always ask me a question to which he knew I would not know the answer. One time he asked me how many cases of Allsopps lager were remaining on board for the crew, and another time, he asked me when the Chief Engineer had obtained his lifeboat certificate. He knew I would not have the answers to hand, but I would admit as such and inform him I would find out and let him know. One day, Phil, the Bar Manager asked me to get his statement of the Captain's cocktail party signed, seeing as I was going up for a signing session. I innocently thought it was merely a case of collecting a signature. Not so. "What's all this?" he barked at me. I explained. "How much does it work out per head?" I did not have a clue but said I would find out. When I returned the document to the Bar Manager, I irritably told him what had happened and not to ask me to get things signed again. The next cruise, however, Phil asked me to get the next one signed and informed me it had worked out at 21 cents per head. I was reluctant to accept this challenge but saw a way of getting my own back. When he came to the document, Black Mac growled, "How much does this work out per head?"   I stood there smugly and firmly answered, "21 cents   per   head,   Sir". "How much does it normally work out at?" he barked. I deflated and told him I would find out. He was always one ahead which I suppose was why he was in the position he was, but I didn't appreciate the way he got his kicks.

One of my duties each port arrival was to

meet the Pilot at the gunport door as often the local Agent, Customs and Immigration Officers would board at the same time. This would enable them to have a free breakfast on board as well as claiming their complimentary spirits and cigarettes which most ports demand for a speedy clearance allowing passengers to go ashore in a timely manner. The Kalassi Deck Tindal, Baberjan was quite a character and would often make comment on my red and bleary look at about 6.00am when I had only had about two hours sleep after a night of partying. When I would appear, he would take one look and wave a finger at me. With his limited English he would say, 'Too much no good! Plenty all right!' However his words were wasted on me.

By the start of the Alaskan season, the Purser had gone on leave and we had a Deputy from the Canberra transfer over for his first time as Senior Purser. Dickie was quite a character but did like his liquor and our morning meetings at 8.30am each day were spent getting him out of bed, into the shower and then dressed in readiness for the Captain's meeting at 9.00am. This did not bother the two Deputy Pursers or I too much as he was very supportive of all we did, although as I found out later, he did have a forked tongue.

I was due for leave and my replacement was going to be Mike, the SAP whom I had relieved on the Orsova. The Assistant Purser John and his wife Pipyn were also leaving so we had a

75% change in Los Angeles, though I would stay on for three days up to Victoria on Vancouver Island and disembark there. For the three days up the coast it was party, party, party. We had made very good friends with Paul, the agent in Victoria and he and his wife were coming on a cruise the day I was disembarking. However, his brother Lorne would accommodate me overnight and take me to the airport the next morning.

The President of P & O North America was travelling with his wife and daughter. The daughter was very attractive and Mike, my relief, John, the newly joined AP and I were competing for her attention. We were convinced Mike had succeeded but apparently not, or so he claimed. In the cold light of day, we all three decided it was best not to draw that sort of attention to her father.

As I had mentioned we had three days of partying up the coast and by the time I came to disembark in Victoria I was ready for a rest. When the ship sailed at 9.00pm, and I left with Lorne, I could think of nothing better than a good night's sleep before my 6.00am flight from Victoria to Vancouver the next morning. We got to Lorne's house at around 10.00pm and as we entered all the lights came on...a surprise party in my honour. All his family and friends were there and so we had another night of booze and dancing until 4.00am when I gratefully sank into bed. I cannot describe how I felt an hour later when I had to get up to go to the airport. I made the puddle jumper which rattled over to Vancouver airport and boarded the Air Canada flight to Heathrow. What I hadn't realised was that it was a Vancouver to Frankfurt flight (via Heathrow) which had a German soccer team on board and all their supporters. To further enhance the situation, the German team had just had an unbeaten season and it was celebrations all the way for the next nine hours in which they insisted I took part by drinking beer after beer and joining in all the Oompah-pah songs. I staggered off the plane and slept for about three days.

CHAPTER 19

After a couple of weeks of enjoying the British summer, I was sent for by the Head Office. I was rather taken aback to find that Dickie, the Purser had put a comment on my appraisal that I wasn't very good at getting up in the mornings. Talk about pots and kettles! However, as he had not discussed this salient point with me, not surprisingly, before I went on leave, it was ignored and I was told I was to return to the Spirit of London at the beginning of September as Deputy Purser in charge of Accommodation and Bars. I was astounded as I was still only 24 years old. I was also extremely nervous as I felt I had only been Senior Assistant Purser for about six months and I was getting promoted again. However, the pay increase was quite substantial, but it did concern me that my knowledge in that area was fairly limited. Fortunately, the Second Steward, Harry, was excellent and took the trouble to teach me the ropes and we became firm friends. Harry had been on the Canberra for many years and hailed from Dublin. He was always smartly dressed and carried the respect of everyone who answered to him. The Bar staff were British on the Spirit but the Cabin Stewards and Dining staff were all from Goa. This had mixed reception with American passengers but the Indian crew had never seen so much money in tips in their lives and after a twelve month contract on that ship, they went home the equivalent of millionaires. However, this did not make it easy for them when on their next contract they had to go back to one of the regular ships for a mere pittance.

During this contract on the Spirit, I was brought in by the Purser to the inner sanctum, so to speak. It appeared that the Chief Customs Officer in Mazatlan had allegedly blackmailed Mike the Purser into bringing him down half a dozen bottles of deluxe Champagne and cognac each week, from Los Angeles which he would pay for. His threat if that did not happen was to delay the disembarkation of passengers and crew in Mazatlan causing much inconvenience and complaint. It was no odds to us so agreement was made and as I was in charge of the bar orders and supplies, I would buy these extra bottles in cash and the Purser would sort out the sale. This all worked well until as so often happens, greed came into it. It seemed that the Customs Officer had quite a few contacts with the local restaurants and the amount being brought down escalated each week. The week before I went on leave, we were carrying almost 300 cases of booze down to Mazatlan. At 8.00pm when we were alongside, the Purser would go up on deck and turn off the lights that shone out over the water on the port side. We two Deputy Pursers would then go down to the storing deck and open the gunport and lay out the rollers. A boat with no lights would arrive alongside and we would roll all the cases along to the boat. It was a quick and well executed operation, usually over in about 20 minutes, when the little boat almost sinking it was so low in the water, would disappear into the darkness, and we would put the rollers away and close the door and disappear from the scene. The Purser would turn the outside lights back on and then meet with the Customs Officer to conclude the business side. We would receive our remuneration from him later on.

During this second cruising season down to Mexico, we were certainly not alone. Sitmar, the Italian cruise line was also present with their Fairwind and Fairsea. These two old ships were ex Cunard's Corinthia and Sylvania which had been up for sale for ages, double berthed at 101 in Southampton until finally being sold to Sitmar and deployed for cruising in Mexico. We later discovered that the Italians were easily surpassing us in their trading. We would always play second fiddle to the Italians in this area, they are the masters of all skulduggery.

There was however one ship, the Island Princess, owned by Princess Cruises who were in direct competition to ourselves and a P & O management team from UK travelling on an inspection visit of the Spirit of London decided to visit the ship whilst both were in port. The Captain, Purser, Chief Engineer and I went along with the P & O management to have a look. We were met by the Italian Purser who showed us round. It was roughly the same size as the Spirit, slightly larger but with only 680 passengers. However, it was far more luxurious for the time and made the Spirit of London look totally inferior. P & O never liked competition and little did we know at the time but within a few months they had bought the competition, not only the one ship Princess Cruises owned, the Island Princess, but Princess Cruises Inc, as well.

When I flew back from LA on leave the next week, I looked forward to a comfortable leave. However, this was not to be. The very next week after I had left, they all got caught by the Staff Captain who had been tipped off by a rating in the Deck Department. The Purser was flown back to London, met at Heathrow by Company Officials and taken to the head office for interrogation. I had just bought a small apartment in Brighton and was not yet on the telephone. After a couple of weeks, my phone was connected and I started to phone round friends advising them of my new number. I also received a letter from the Head Office advising me that they were going to be making some changes on the Spirit of London and that as I had been there recently, they would like my input, and I was to attend on a certain day. A colleague appraised me of what had happened on the ship and passed my number to Mike the Purser who phoned me the night before I had to go to London. I told him about the letter and he briefed me on what it was all about. We were on the phone for a long time whilst he told me how much they knew and what they would ask me. Unfortunately he had not been able to get hold of the other Deputy Purser, Alan so neither of us knew what he had said.

I attended the Head Office as scheduled and feigned surprise when I was shown in to a boardroom with a panel of five executives all sitting behind the table, the chairman of which was Black Mac, the ex Captain of the Spirit. I was quizzed for about two hours and at the end, I was told to proceed on leave until contacted, while further people were questioned and more investigation held. I was warned however that my job was in jeopardy and I was lucky not to be spending twenty years in a Mexican jail for infringing Mexican Customs regulations. I replied that I did not see how that could be since it was the Chief Customs Officer that we were selling to and on his instigation. I stated that the only oversight I could see was that we had used the company property, i.e. the ship as a method of transportation for this venture and in hindsight we should have paid the company cargo dues. I was then told to catch the train to Southampton to the office there where the Hotel Services was based. When I arrived I found the Purser, Mike and the other Deputy, Alan already there and the three of us were ushered in to the office of the Deputy Superintendent Purser...Eric the Axe who took great delight in driving it home that our jobs were on the line and that as we had all been hand-picked for that particular ship we had betrayed the hand that fed us.

I heard nothing from the Office for the next few months. It was the winter of 1974 and Britain was on a three day week due to the miners' strike, except companies involved in animal feed. I got myself a job at a local factory that was still on five days a week as it made large paper bags for animal feed. I had to stand at the end of a machine which fed a large roll of paper in at one end, cut it, folded it, glued it and stitched it and shot it out at me at the other end. I was the 'taker offer' and would catch the bags as they emerged and hand them to a stacker. I worked nine hours a day for five days a week at this and received twenty six pounds a week which included a bonus of 4p per thousand sacks a day in excess of the 80,000 we were expected to do. It was the most boring job I have ever done and I used to get through it daydreaming about a good night out in San Francisco at the Red Garter Club or a previous cruise out of Sydney where sex was in abundance.

Andy, one of the Barmen on the Spirit of London, whom I had also known on Orcades, had left the ships, after marrying Jenny, one of the Beauty Salon girls and had taken a tenancy on a pub in Wells in Somerset. It was February in the UK and it was cold. I had first met Andy when he was a Bar steward on the Chitral when I was a Cadet in training and we had to spend an overnight on the ship whilst attending a sales meeting. We admired him for making the break from the sea and settling down to a 'normal' life ashore and to start a family. It had been about eight months since he had left and as Phil, the Bar Manager was on leave, we decided to take a trip to Somerset one Saturday morning to see how he was faring.

We arrived not too far from Wells at about 1.00pm at a place called Wookey Hole and decided to have a pub lunch. At around 2.00pm we decided not to visit him straight away as he would shortly be closing and no doubt looking forward to his couple of hours rest. However we were left with the problem of what to do for a few hours. Wookey Hole was quite famous for its caves, not quite so well known as nearby Cheddar, but still caves of substantial sizes had been discovered and for a moderate entrance fee, you could take the guided tour. It was bitterly cold and so off we went on the tour. There were about 25 in the group and we had reached the innermost cave named the Witch's Cavern. The cavern was completely full of water with a sand peninsula in the middle on which we were all standing. The guide informed us he would switch off the lights and point with a laser pointer to a fern overhead by a craggy rock in the ceiling which through a trick of light had the appearance of a witch's face which was why this particular cavern was so named.

We stood in the dark looking up to where the laser pointer was indicating. Now someone in the group took advantage of this moment to pass wind, extremely silently, I might add but to an almost choking degree. I have no idea who it was but silently moved a couple of steps to my left to escape this horrendous odour and at the same time so that others did not think that I was the perpetrator. Phil got it at about the same time as we had been standing next to each other, but he was not so silent about it. He also decided to escape its range and took a couple of steps in the other direction. The stream of expletives he was uttering, were interrupted abruptly by a short yell as he stepped into the void, followed by a very loud splash. The guide immediately turned the lights back on and we turned in time to see Phil surfacing for the third time. The water was quite deep but fortunately Phil could swim. He was unable to climb back up on his own due to the steep sides of the sand peninsular and so several of the group lent a hand and dragged him out of the icy water and across the wet sand. I would have given a hand myself of course but was on my knees by this stage, completely helpless with laughter.

Phil was absolutely furious, more so I think with me laughing than anything else, not helped when I suggested that perhaps next time he should enquire at the start of the tour if they had any lifejackets. Anyway, that put paid to Andy's afternoon rest as we had to go and disturb him so that Phil could borrow some of his clothes. We had a very enjoyable evening, or at least I did as I recounted the tale to the locals in the pub. Phil however was still not amused. It was a lovely pub but hard work with its bars, restaurants and B & B. Andy reckoned that taking the pub had proved to be the best contraceptive on the market. Six months later he was back on the ship as a Barman, as he had worked it out that he saw more of his wife during his one month leave following four months at sea than he did during five months running the business.

During this time, I heard nothing for several weeks, and then one Thursday evening, Mike phoned me to ask if I had heard anything, as he had to attend the Office on the Monday. I hadn't, but asked him to phone me Monday evening. Monday evening came and went and so did Tuesday evening. On Wednesday evening I phoned him and his news was not good. He had been fired on the spot. Over the next few weeks news reached me that Alan, the other Deputy had also been fired as well as the Storekeeper. Two other previous Deputy Pursers who had been there when I was SAP had been asked to resign. I had still heard nothing.

A couple of months later I received a letter ordering me to attend the Head Office a few days hence at 10.00am. I resigned from the factory as it had only been a temporary thing anyway and it looked now that I would be asked to resign or be fired and would have to rethink my future career, yet again. When I was ushered in to the Enquiry Room, there was a panel of three but Black Mac was not one of them. It was all very quick and I was not offered a chance to speak. I was told that the Purser had been fired along with several other senior Officers but that my services were being retained. As it had been my first trip as a Deputy Purser and that all my previous reports had been excellent I was being offered another chance. However, I would be demoted back to SAP and never considered for promotion again. Also any adverse comment on any future appraisal would warrant instant dismissal. I was then told to report to the Personnel Department where I would be appointed to a ship. I couldn't believe it. As I exited the room, another Deputy Purser, Richard, who had taken over from Alan a few weeks before I went on leave was just coming in. This was the same Richard who had been the Crew Purser on the Arcadia when we were trainee Cadets ashore in 1967. I had no idea he was also up for reprimand that day and I just managed to say to him out of the corner of my mouth to meet in the Hoop and Grapes over the road.

I went to Tommy, my Personnel Officer and was told I had to do a four day fire fighting course with the Royal Navy in Plymouth and then on the Monday following, I would report to the Oriana as SAP, do the five day wet dock and then sail for the series of Mediterranean cruises in and out of Southampton every 14 days. I have to say it didn't appeal at all but I was lucky to still have a job, even if it was back as SAP. I headed for the Hoop and Grapes and had a couple of gins while I waited for Richard to appear. I was just ordering a third when he appeared at my elbow. I merely said to him, "You still employed?" He nodded.   "You?" he asked. I nodded also and we both downed our gins and ordered more. We spent the entire day in the pub comparing notes. He also had to attend a fire fighting course up in Sunderland and was going to the Oronsay which by this time was based almost permanently in Sydney doing Australian cruising. He was joining as Deputy Purser Administration. He had not been demoted like me as he had been established for some time in the rank and I had only been in an acting capacity. I thought you lucky sod being out there whereas I would have the microscopic eye of the London and Southampton Management on my every move. Anyway, we wished each other the best of luck for future survival and looked forward to meeting again in the distant future, sometime, someplace, and staggered off to our respective railway stations, he to Lincoln and I to Brighton.

I drove down to Plymouth and reported to the accommodation which had been arranged. There were about 10 of us on the course but I was the only one from passenger ships and the only one who was not a Deck or Engine Officer. They were a fun bunch and we all got on well for the four days. It was a very thorough course, much more intense than the one day introduction to firefighting I had done at East Ham fire station as a cadet. The Fire Officers had a mock up of a ship in the yard which consisted of a Galley, Engine Room and Cargo Hold at ground level and two cabins above. On the final day we were formed into teams, and fires were set in the mock up. There were also 'bodies' made of fire hose soaked in water which had to be rescued. I was one of the fighters who had to go first, entering from above. I struggled down the iron ladder into the smoke filled Galley with my air bottle and hose. I opened the door to the cargo hold and seeing what I thought was flame gave it the full hose blast. I was in the middle of rescuing a fire hose body which was proving reluctant when my air whistle went, indicating my air was getting short. With a struggling body over my shoulder I tried to climb the ladder but by this time it was so hot I couldn't hold the ladder, and so had to cool it down with the hose before I could scamper up just as my air ran out. In the lecture room afterwards one of the Fire Officers ran through the salient points of each of our performances. When it came to my turn, he said that I had done quite well, except...that I should note that a torch light in smoke looked very much like flame because when the other Fire Officer had shone his torch at me, I had turned the hose full on him! That was why he wasn't there as he was getting changed. Also, he informed me that I had done quite well rescuing the 'bodies' but that I had tried to put him over my shoulder three times and he was beginning to quite enjoy it in the end.

CHAPTER 20

I caught the train to Southampton and joined the Oriana the day she arrived back from Australia and spent the next five days preparing for the first Mediterranean cruise of the season as we would be sailing on the Saturday at 6.00pm. During this few days I had to appear in Southampton Office in front of the Superintendent Purser who felt he had to add his bollocking to everyone else's and reiterate to me about being the model Purser's Officer and told me that any money I had made from the venture should be paid to a marine charity of my choice, a receipt obtained and sent to him. You'll be bloody lucky, I thought. No chance.

During this short break in Southampton, there was a Goan crew change. Fortunately all the hard work had been done by the ship's staff prior to arrival but the entire 280 of them had to appear before the UK Immigration on the ship the day before their flight. We had them all lined up in one of the rooms and eventually when all had been cleared for entry into, and exit from the UK, the clearance slip was filled with the name of the Supervisor and 279 others as per the attached list. This document was of paramount importance as without it, the Immigration at Heathrow would not allow their charter flight to depart. The document was given to John, one of the senior Supervisors who would be going with me to the airport with them. John apparently had done this on a number of occasions and the Management suggested I leave it all to him as he was well versed in the procedure at Heathrow. The next day, flight day, the Customs appeared to oversee the loading of a bonded air baggage van which was a facility afforded to the crew so that they could have any dutiable items such as liquor, cigarettes, electronic equipment, etc. transferred under bond to Heathrow and loaded on the plane. They would collect it in Bombay with their other air baggage. After lunch, I set off from Southampton with a convoy of seven buses of Indian crew and three baggage vans, including the bonded one, for our date with Air India at London Heathrow. The convoy had to make several toilet stops along the way as they were celebrating in high fashion having completed their 12 months on board and were at long last returning home to family. We pulled in at Heathrow Terminal 3 and disembarked the buses. I had them line up in ranks of three, military style while we did another head count just to ensure we had not left one behind at a toilet stop in a farmer's field. It was OK, they were all there.

The Air India ground staff was there to meet us and the first thing they requested was the Immigration document. I turned to John who reached in to his inside pocket. He tried both inside pockets, the side pockets, his trouser pockets and then seemed to turn the colour of a freshly laundered pillow case. He wasn't alone. "Oh my God", said he, "You know what?" "No", I said. "Do share". There was a sense of impending doom welling up inside me. "I remember changing my jacket just before we left and I must have left the document in the inside pocket of my other jacket, my uniform jacket". "Oh excellent", I said. "and just where is this elusive garment to be found?" He mumbled, "Hanging on the back of my cabin door back on the ship." The Air India staff made it quite clear that without the document there was nothing to be done and if the flight missed its slot for takeoff, as it was a charter flight, it could be days before they got another slot. The phone call I had to make to our office in Southampton was not one I was looking forward to. One of the Management had to drive to the ship, obtain a spare key to the crew cabin and retrieve the document which was indeed exactly where John had said it was. Then a motorcycle dispatch rider had to break the land speed record to deliver the document to me at Terminal 3. As we waited for him to arrive, all the crew were wandering all over the airport doing last minute shopping and I must have chain-smoked about 20 cigarettes. John had faded right into the background, as he had suddenly decided he was not that important after all and I was the one in charge. The rider duly arrived and clearance obtained in record time so the plane could be boarded and take off. Next, was the job of trying to round up 280 crew whose sense of urgency was practically non-existent. However, we got them away and collected the 280 incoming crew who were very docile after a long flight and already homesick with the prospect of a twelve month contract without a day off ahead of them before they would see home and family again.

I was just preparing to leave the Bureau around 7.00pm on the Friday evening, the night prior to sailing, when a familiar face appeared. Brian, who had been a Cadet in London with me entered and after exchanging pleasantries, I asked him what he was doing. He told me he was joining the ship as SAP and sailing instead of me. I was dumbfounded as to what was happening. I knew I had to keep my nose clean but they could have given me a bit more of a chance than just five days, even with a near disaster of a crew change, which had not been my fault. What was I supposed to do? I asked him. He told me he had a verbal message for me to go home and report to Fleet Personnel in London on Monday morning.

It was Friday night and there was nothing I could do until Monday. We spent a boozy evening together and I handed over to him Saturday morning and caught the train back to Brighton.

I was at the London Office in St Botolph Street, at 9.30am on the Monday morning, nervously awaiting my fate with Fleet Personnel. I was told to take a seat and wait as they were conducting interviews that morning. Frustratingly, I had to wait until 3.30pm that afternoon before Tommy, the Pursers' Personnel Officer decided he had time to see me. I am sure it was on purpose to make me sweat it out. I asked him why I had been taken off Oriana before it had even sailed. He explained that at the time he had not been able to get hold of Brian who was still abroad on holiday and had only returned two days before Oriana sailed. He explained that with all that had happened on the Spirit of London, he was worried that I would be targeted by what he called, 'the harassment department', meaning the Hotel Operations Department in Southampton Office. With sailing in and out of that port all the time, he would rather get me out over the other side of the world well away from Southampton. I couldn't have agreed more. He explained that what he really needed was an SAP for the Spirit of London but obviously could not put me back there so he would put another SAP there, John (who had been an Assistant Purser on Spirit the previous summer) who knew the ship and I would have to take over from John on the Oronsay in Sydney. I couldn't believe my luck. I was going back to Australia and Australian cruising. This was Monday afternoon and I had to fly to Sydney on Wednesday afternoon. I asked him if the ship was aware and he said not yet, but he would get a telex off to them straight away. He handed me a Qantas ticket and I asked him if I had any joining orders. He had not had time to have the secretary type them out but took an old lunch menu from one of the ships and wrote on the back of it my name, Oronsay, join as SAP in Sydney on whatever date, signed it and put his stamp on it. "There you are", he said, "There are your joining orders". I stared at them incredulously, folding it into my pocket, thanked him profusely and left the office. I was back. I was off to Australia again. Sod American cruising! It had only brought me bad luck and now I was going back to what I really enjoyed.

I had a good evening out in Brighton with some friends the night before I was leaving, stupidly of course, and only awoke at around Noon. It was a lovely summer's day and my flight from London was at 5.00pm. I leapt out of bed, dressed in jeans and T-shirt and threw my uniform into a suitcase. I left the bed unmade, my keys with a neighbour and dashed for the station to get the train. I made the flight with not much time to spare. If I thought the LA flight was long, this seemed interminable as although these days there is only one stop in the Far East, back then the flight took at least 24 hours stopping in Rome, Bahrain, Singapore and Perth. I was practically broke by this time and flew to Australia with only five pounds to my name. When we arrived, I recognised a fellow Officer, a Second Electrical Officer by the name of Jack whom I had known on the Oriana. He had just been promoted to First Electrical Officer and was also joining Oronsay. Arriving at our hotel, the first thing I did was to phone an old girlfriend, Diane, whom I had met on the Oriana from Southampton to Sydney in 1969 and was the girlfriend who used to come with me when we took a sailing break up the Hawkesbury River during my years on the Orcades. Fortunately she was free that evening and came for dinner. She had suggested a little bistro not too far away but not wishing to admit that I had only $10, I suggested that we ate at the hotel so that I could put it on the bill. We dined on lobster that night with all the alcoholic trimmings.

The next morning as we were about to settle our bills, Jack asked me if I had any cash. I had seen him entertaining three friends at dinner and had assumed he had cash. Not so. Neither of us had a bean so we signed for our rather extravagant bills and waited for the company to come after us later on for the excess. They never did. Now the Oronsay was the only ex Orient line ship that I had not set foot on, so on reaching the top of the gangway with my two cases in C Deck foyer, I was trying to get my bearings to find the Bureau. As luck would have it, John, the SAP Catering whom I was to relieve, came flying down the stairs and I called out to him. He stopped in his tracks and came up to me disbelievingly and enquired what I was doing there. Before I could answer, he said, "Are you living out here now?" Many in the Company had assumed that I had been fired along with the other unfortunate ones. "No", I stammered, rather taken aback by the question.   Before I could explain further, he said "You're coming on for a cruise?"   "No", I stammered again. By now it was obvious that the promised explanatory telex from Fleet Personnel had not arrived. John, by this time quite perplexed asked me why I was actually there. I informed him that I was joining the ship. "Fantastic" he said, and then after careful thought, said, "But hang on we don't have anyone leaving. Who are you taking over from?" "You", I said. He paled as I explained all to him, especially the fact that he had to fly to Los Angeles to join the Spirit of London. He obviously felt the same about Australian cruising versus American cruising as I did. The Purser had said nothing to John so we were correct that the magic telex was still in the pipeline somewhere. What John was most upset about, which he ex-

241

plained to me, was the fact that he had spent the past three weeks trying to get the Beauty Salon Manageress into bed and two nights previous, he had finally managed it. I told him not to worry, but to just include her on the handover, which didn't seem to appease his mood. We went up to the Catering Deputy's office and I waited outside while John went in to explain to him. He was also someone I had never met before and when he saw me, he looked at me as if I was something he had just scraped off his shoe and strutted off to speak to the Purser. I waited outside the Purser's Office while a conference was held before being told to enter. The Purser, Mike, I knew of, but had never met before. He greeted me with the words, "Who are you? Who are you? I've never heard of you, you're an impostor, get off my ship! "

And nice to meet you too, I thought. I explained my record of events and that Tommy had promised a telex on Monday afternoon which had obviously not materialized. "However", I said, "I have just flown all the way out here from London, but if you don't wish me to join, then you had better arrange an air ticket back to London and I'll go home". He sat there pondering this and then with a gleam in his eye, said, "Where are your joining orders?" I reached inside my jacket pocket and pulled out the rather creased lunch menu card and handed it to him. He looked at it with its signature and official stamp, stroking his beard with disbelief and muttering that it was 'incredible'. Whilst he was deliberating his next move, the other Deputy Purser, Richard, my partner in crime from the Spirit entered with something for the Purser to sign.   "Morning, Richard", I said   and   he   spun   round. "Good grief", he said, "What on earth are you doing here?" Before I could answer, the Purser sprung to life and said to Richard, "You know this   man?   You   know   this   man?". "Of course I know him", replied Richard, "we were both Deputy Pursers on the Spirit of London." After the Purser had consulted with the Captain, another delight by the name of Dennis with a double-barrelled name for effect, one I had not met before but heard all about, he decided that I should stay but that John was not leaving. Suited me, I thought, two people for one job should be quite cushy. He stated there was no spare cabin so I would have to sleep on John's couch in his cabin. We sailed from Sydney for Auckland on a sun and fun cruise and on the day after leaving Sydney, the magic telex eventually materialized and John left in Auckland to fly very reluctantly to Los Angeles to join the Spirit of London. I took the Beauty Manageress out for a drink that evening to console her.

We only had two Australian cruises to do before the ship would sail back to the UK, spend three weeks in Southampton, two in dry dock and one in wet dock before she sailed back out to Australia again. I was quite thankful that I was working for the Catering Deputy and not in charge of the Bureau as it was imperative that I did not get a bad appraisal or negative comments as the Head Office would be keeping check on me, certainly initially and keeping a low profile was the only way I felt I could manage this. My job mainly was keeping all the accounts of the food and beverage on board, checking stores on the dock when we loaded. I had done the job as an Assistant Purser on the Orcades so it wasn't anything new. Dickie, the Catering Deputy for whom I worked was not the easiest or the most popular and was nicknamed 'the corporal' due to the way he held his shoulders and my day to day function was to act as a buffer between he and the Chef, Chief Butcher and Storekeeper. Fortunately, I knew Arfon, the Storekeeper and Alan, the Chief Butcher from before, but this was the first time I had worked with Jack, this particular Chef. Alan, the Chief Butcher, as mentioned previously, was a practical joker and he seemed to spend most of his day planning the next wind up.

One day apparently on the Arcadia, Sean, the Irish Chef had decided to take a group of passengers round the Galley. Sean was a larger than life figure, with a good Irish singing voice. The problem was, it was difficult to keep him off stage. On several occasions when he should have been supervising the Second Sitting Dinner service in the Galley, he would be discovered up in one of the lounges in his tuxedo, singing all the good old Irish favourites. It was at the end of one of these evenings that he arranged with a group of First Class passengers whom he wished to impress, to have a tour of the Galley the next day and he would meet them outside the First Class Dining Room at 11.00am. Word of this reached Alan, the Chief Butcher. After breakfast service was finished, Alan got dressed up as a typical Australian passenger in shorts, a colourful shirt, long socks and sandals, a bush hat with corks dangling, sunglasses with camera and binoculars cross strapped and joined in on the end of Sean's tour of the Galley for VIPs. Sean had not noticed at first but when the 'Australian' asked if he could take various photos of the Chef 'peeling a potato' and 'icing a cake', Sean realised who it was. Naturally he was unable to say anything without alerting his VIPs whom he was trying to impress and so had to go along with these inane requests and smile for the camera. He was absolutely furious.

CHAPTER 21

During the final cruise we called at Nuku'alofa in Tonga. A few hours after sailing a stowaway was discovered who was trying to get to Australia. He had no papers on him and Australia would not accept him. Nor it would seem, would anyone else. He was placed in the brig on C Deck near the aft mooring station. It was basically a jail cell and it looked as if we would have to take him all the way back to UK and for the three weeks we would be in Dry Dock, he would be accommodated in Winchester Prison until the ship sailed again from Southampton. At this time he would be placed back on board in our brig and we would have to take him all the way back out to Australia and on our second cruise from Sydney we were scheduled to call again at Nuku'alofa where we would finally disembark him. To think people pay thousands of pounds to do a round the world voyage like that.

We stored heavily in Sydney prior to setting off and our next major storing would be Vancouver. I had kept a pretty low profile as had been my intention and was quite happy remaining out of sight and just getting on with my job. We were sailing from Vancouver at 4.00pm and with 30 minutes to go, I still had quite a few pallets left on the dock. I knew the Captain would not wait as we had a fast speed down to San Francisco. 15 minutes later my stores through the gunport were completed and the conveyor came out and the door secured. 10 minutes to go and I still had four pallets of potatoes to be craned into No.3 Hatch. We should just do it, I thought. Just then a car screeched to a halt, a guy jumped out and came up to me clutching a small package. He explained that it was a very expensive valve for the Radio Office and could I take delivery of it. I said I was sorry but he would have to go on board and take it to the Radio Office. Off he went and returned to the gangway, about five minutes later without the package. He thanked me and said he had put the package in the hands of the Chief Radio Officer but had forgotten his delivery note so would I mind just signing for it as there was not time to return on board. He was right, my last pallet was just disappearing down the hatch and we would be away in about three minutes once the gangway went. I thought there can't be a problem, I have seen him go on with the package, come off without the package and he even knew the name of the Chief Radio Officer. I signed. As soon as we sailed, I flew up to the Radio Office to check the package was received and the Chief Radio Officer, David thanked me. With relief I handed him the delivery note.

That evening, he must have been having a drink with the Purser and casually related the story to him. The next morning I was in front of Mike, the Purser having the arse ripped out of me for accepting the package. I was told radio spares were nothing to do with me and I shouldn't have signed for it. Each time I tried to explain that I wouldn't normally, but time constraints dictated otherwise and I was just trying to help another department. I was shot down in flames and told, "The moral of the story is never to sign for anything unless you sight it." Was the man demented? I had already explained that I had noted the guy go on with the package and come off without it, therefore it had to be on board, so I had sighted it. Not only that but I did not see what the problem was, the package had been received and all was well. I had to face the fact that he didn't like me and that was it. I had been in trouble with the Head Office and was obviously 'persona non grata' and the sooner he was rid of me the better. I got nowhere trying to explain to this martinet. No wonder inter-departmental co-operation was so bad back then. I left his office with no more to say but in a steaming temper at this small-mindedness, so I went and had a beer.

After leaving Vancouver the ship called at San Francisco, Los Angeles and Acapulco on the way down to the Panama Canal. However, in Los Angeles when all was quiet around lunchtime, the Hospital Steward took a tray of lunch along to the brig for the stowaway. Once inside, the Tongan knocked the steward over the head, locked him in the brig and disappeared down the gangway never to be seen again. The ship sailed at 5.00pm and about an hour after sailing the Doctor was alerted to loud shouts coming from the brig. Obviously the Hospital Steward had come round and was trying to attract attention. Apparently he had been trying to do this for some time but the medical staff just assumed it was the stowaway wanting to be released. Of course the keys were nowhere to be found, the Tongan had probably just dropped them over the side of the ship so the spare set had to be retrieved from the Captain's safe, for the Hospital Steward to be released. A report had to be sent back immediately to the Immigration Department. The next day was at sea and it was the Purser's birthday. He had invited all the Purser's Officers for a lunchtime drink at noon, using Dickie, the Catering Deputy's office and adjoining cabin to host this. I was doing an inspection of the Galley and so was about the last to arrive. When I did so, it was not so much a party, but more of a wake. There was just silence while the Purser related to everyone about the stowaway's disappearance and to make matters worse, he had signed the papers with the US Immigration Department to state that the Tongan was on board at the time of sailing. There was a $50,000 fine for an inaccurate statement and he was extremely worried that the company might make him pay for it personally as he was the one who had signed. There was silence while we all contemplated this. I know that I shouldn't have said anything, just kept quiet, but that's not me I am afraid and I just could not resist it. "You know Sir", I said, "There is a moral to that story".   "Oh really? What is that then?" he asked, taking the bait. I prepared.   "Never sign for anything unless you sight it", I said. There were gasps from the others and then silence. The Purser stood, slammed down his glass and stormed out. The two Deputy Pursers were horrified, most of the other staff faintly amused but not   really   knowing   why. Richard said to me, "What did you say? What have you done? You've really upset him". "I am sure he'll get over it", I said and thought perhaps I had better stay well out of sight for the foreseeable future. This worked well for the next few days until I decided to go out one evening for a drink or two. I was standing at the bar about to order a beer when I was suddenly conscious of someone else standing next to me. It was the Purser. We exchanged greetings and he asked if he could buy me a beer which I reluctantly accepted, as I knew I would now be trapped into conversation. Eventually he said to me, "You know, I have been furious with you for the past few days for the comment you made...but I have to say it was a good one, a real gotcha". From that time on we became the best of friends. He lived just down the road from me in Hove and we would often get together on leave for a beer or two.

Alan, the Chief Butcher had been quiet for a while, so it was no big surprise when he resurfaced. One of the Third Bakers had been to the Assistant Surgeon with a problem. He was a tall lad, pleasant enough but not too much of the grey matter between the ears and therefore just right for one of the Butcher's jokes. He had known that the Baker had been to the crew clinic and so at lunchtime when the Bakery and Pastry Shop were in full swing, the Butcher phoned to speak to the Chief Pastryman, nicknamed King Alfred as he was always burning his cakes, disguising his voice and pretending to be the Assistant Surgeon. He told the Chief Pastry that he was sending along a specimen jar for the Third Baker to perform a stool test, so could he give it to him, explain what he had to do and bring it along with him to the crew clinic at 7.30am the next morning? The Butcher had retrieved a large one gallon pickle jar, washed it out, shined up the top and stuck a label to the lid with the Third Baker's name, rank and article number on the top. The jar was duly received in the Bakery and given to the Third Baker. The next morning, the crew waiting room outside the Assistant Surgeon's office already had several waiting when the Third Baker walked in and sat down placing this large pickle jar on his lap which proudly displayed as fine a specimen of a stool that anyone could wish for. It curled round the jar unbroken several times and I am sure he must have been proud of it. Everybody else in the waiting room gave him a wide berth. After all, anyone who could produce something like that deserved respect. Eventually, it was his turn and so in he marched and placed the jar on the Assistant Surgeon's desk. The Doctor sat there for a while looking at it, before he asked, "What the hell is this?" The baker, somewhat offended said, "Surely you can see what it is." "Yes, Yes", replied the Doctor, "of course I can...but why have you brought it to me?" Once the baker had explained, the Doctor realising the lad had been the victim of a practical joke, said to him, "But did it not occur to you? Why on earth would I ask you to bring me this sample when what you have is an ingrown toenail?"

Shortly before arrival back in the UK, Richard, the Deputy Purser told me he wanted me to change jobs during the refit. He wanted me to switch back to the administration side and be the working boss of the Bureau and all the Assistants and Junior Assistants. I did not like the

idea at all as it would put me back in the lime-
light again and although I had one good appraisal
under my belt, I needed more to be safe with my
future. However, it was not an option and the
financial rewards were very tempting. For a start
I would be in charge of the slot machines. There
were many of these spread around the bars. Also
most of the ships possessed a couple of machines
which the company didn't know about, as they
were privately owned by the Senior Purser's
Officers and were not on any list. Richard and I
had to remain on the ship in Southampton for
the three weeks and sail again for Australia, although I would be disembarking in San Francisco and flying home for leave.

Several days after the ship sailed from Southampton and we were about half way across the
Atlantic heading for Bermuda, the Head Office in
London received a phone call from 'someone
with an Irish accent' saying that a bomb had
been placed on board during the refit and was
due to detonate that evening. The information
was relayed to the Captain. Announcements
were made and passengers were told to go back
to their cabins and make a thorough search and
if anything not belonging to them was found,
not to touch it but to report it to the Bureau.
Meanwhile the crew all had to do the same with
their cabins and then start searching public
areas, storerooms, machinery spaces, working
areas,   everywhere.

The ship having been in dry dock for a while and then the heavy storing of the last few days meant the storerooms were over-stowed and chaotic as it normally took the first week at sea to sort things into proper order, but this was normal. The Dockers would go slowly until the last day so that they could enforce overtime and then for the last day they would go all out. They would usually have everything on board by sailing time but there would be mixed stores all over the ship and on outside decks, total chaos until the crew got it safely stowed. Often storerooms would be over-stowed so that sorting within was impossible until stores depleted to a reasonable level. Management ashore was no help in this as very often they would have us take enough lamb on our last call in New Zealand to take the ship back to UK, operate the Mediterranean cruising season and back out to New Zealand. Of course, with the older ships, some of the large stores could be used as dry stores or cooled to chill (normal refrigerator) temperature or reduced right down to deep freeze. They were quite versatile. Anyway, trying to check some of these spaces for a hidden bomb was just about impossible. The search went on all morning and afternoon, with nothing suspicious being found. It was generally thought to be a hoax but this was not something we could take for granted. That evening's dinner was brought forward earlier as the ship's clocks had altered a couple of hours by then, and nobody knew whether the caller had taken this into consideration. Passengers and crew were all told that they would have to go to their Muster Stations after dinner as a precaution. This meant we, the crew would be standing out on deck in the cold for several hours, whether we had to take to lifeboats or not. I borrowed a freezer coat from the Butchers and had one of the Indian Stewards sew large pockets on the inside during the course of the afternoon. When the emergency alarm sounded, the Bureau closed and we all went to our crew alert stations. Some twenty minutes later the General Emergency Stations sounded, indicating that passengers should go to their Muster Stations, which were the main public lounges on the Veranda deck and the crew muster out on deck below their designated lifeboat.

On my way past the Bureau, I slipped in quietly and locked myself in. I went to my safe and opened up. I spent about five minutes stuffing the pockets that had been sewn in the freezer coat with all the large denomination notes. If the ship was going to be sent to the bottom of the Atlantic, I did not want it going down with all that cash. I quietly locked my safe back up and was about to exit the Bureau to go to my lifeboat station, looking very much like a Sumo wrestler, when I heard a sound from Richard, the Deputy Purser's office. I froze. Very quietly I tiptoed round so that I could see in the doorway to his office. There was Richard with his back to me, his safe door open and stuffing bundles of large denomination notes down his trousers. I silently entered his office and said, "Securing ship's papers are we?" He spun round, panicking at having been caught and said to me tersely, "Christ, what the hell are you doing here?" I opened my freezer coat like a flasher and said, "Exactly the same as you are". We went to our stations and remained at them until 1.00am when it was decided between the Captain and the Head Office that the call had been a hoax after all and everyone stood down and went to bed. However, it was with heavy heart that we both had to return all the money back to the safes.

I was in charge of the passenger berthing once the ship sailed and as always there were numerous passengers who didn't like their cabins. Some complaints are genuine; many cabins are very noisy, for one reason or another, mostly due to being directly above or next to a noisy piece of machinery or towards the stern where the props at certain revolutions can cause so much vibration that you can't hear yourself speak. There are also the 'try ons'. These are people who have booked a cabin on a share basis and don't want to share so they go out of their way to be incompatible with the strangers with whom they have been berthed and drive them to come and complain. Sometimes they will develop undesirable habits to hurry things along. However, on many occasions, it had all been a 'mistake on the part of the travel agent'. It was like dealing with children at a nursery school a lot of the time, and the recordings of Joyce Grenfell always came to mind. Even if I had empty cabins, I couldn't let them out as they were usually booked later on in the voyage and there was no guarantee the person would move out. For instance if a person booked from Southampton to Sydney wanted to move cabin, I couldn't just let them have an empty cabin that was booked from San Francisco to Sydney, in case they got comfortable and refused to move back. Knowing I was disembarking at San Francisco, I would try and give a bit of hope by telling them to check with me after departure from San Francisco in case there were any cancellations or no shows which did sometimes happen. John, the SAP whom I had replaced when I first joined the Oronsay was due to come out to relieve me while I had two months leave. San Francisco arrived and we would be overnight. John boarded and we agreed to hand the safe over the next morning as I had to balance. That night, after balancing, I was horrified to find I was exactly ten thousand pounds missing. I rebalanced and rebalanced until I was stir crazy. John had gone ashore with one of the Assistant Pursers to the Red Garter Club and I suddenly remembered I had sold him ten thousand pounds of Travellers Cheques the week before but never got the cash off him as he was busy. I waited for them to return and finally they did, helping each other up the gangway wearing the Red Garter boaters after what certainly seemed to be an enviable night out. The Cashier was in no fit state to balance his safe that night and was not too impressed when I told him he would have to do it at 7.00am. However, bleary eyed as he was, he did and found my ten thousand pounds. I started to hand the safe over to John who was not feeling at all well and had to keep leaving to go to the bathroom to throw up. The ship was sailing at 11.00am and we finally got the safe handed over at 10.30am. John went to see the Surgeon while I flew to my cabin and tore off my uniform and threw it in the case. 10 minutes before sailing, I had just stepped on to the gangway with my case when the Purser caught me by the arm. He told me John had just been admitted to the ship's Hospital and I would have to remain to Honolulu. I went back to my cabin, opened my case and put my uniform back on which was still warm from when I had taken it off.

On my way back up to the Bureau, I called in to the ship's Hospital to get the safe keys back. John was very apologetic, and what could I say? Shit happens. The worst part was as soon after we sailed, I had to face all those passengers whom I had told to come and see me after departure from San Francisco to see if there were any spare cabins. So, I really got my comeuppance. John was released from the ship's hospital but the night before Honolulu, he had a relapse and was readmitted for a couple of days. I was told I would have to stay until Sydney. After John was released a second time, we had quite a lot of fun as we had about ten days in which to do our handover. This came to a head when we were in Suva. We were both ashore at the beach and tossed up to see who should return early to oversee a mini-embarkation of passengers who were travelling to Sydney. John lost and returned to the ship. When I got back, I found out that instead of overseeing the embarkation, he had turned in for a nap and things had not gone smoothly. We were both in front of the Purser who wasted no words on us and told us we were on final warning until Sydney. I for one could still not afford to get a bad appraisal and had one coming up very shortly. I was being very careful and had wandered into the Night Club to have a drink around Midnight as I had been abstemious all evening. A group of friends were seated at a table in front of the bar and invited me to join them. Across the room was the Second Engineer, who went by the name of 'the Bopper'. He did not like me much for reasons I won't go into, but I was leaning back in my chair and just kept going. I caught my foot under the lip of the table to save myself but still kept going. The table went up in the air, all the glasses broke, the music stopped and the lights came up to reveal me struggling on the floor trying to crawl out from under the bar. Everyone naturally thought I was drunk but I had not had one drink during the course of the evening. I suddenly realised the Bopper had disappeared and I thought, the bastard, he's gone to get the Purser, I've really had it this time, so I left quickly and went to my cabin. The next morning I decided to come clean and get in first so I knocked on the Purser's door. He listened without interrupting me as I explained the whole unfortunate scene and that whatever the Bopper had said, he was totally mistaken. It appeared that the Bopper had merely gone to the bathroom and the Purser did not have a clue what I was talking about.

Some of the Stewards who had been around for a few years were real characters. One such Waiter, an Irishman by the name of Lou was wonderful with the old dears. Each waiter station in the dining rooms had a top for the waiters to place the tray when bringing food from the galley and which also served to collect dirty dishes, etc. before taking them back out. Lower down was a hot box where plated food brought from the galley could be temporarily placed to keep hot for a few minutes prior to being placed on the table. However, it was only for temporary storage as the food would carry on 'cooking' and would easily dry up. The Maitre

D' was always on the lookout for any Waiter who would 'cowboy' by bringing extra dishes in during first sitting for storing in the hot box to serve at second sitting or bringing them in during second sitting for his own consumption afterwards instead of subjecting himself to the crew fare in the mess room.

Lou had two lovely old ladies on second sitting who always ordered the same thing for breakfast every day for the six weeks out to Sydney. Lou would obtain their breakfasts during the first sitting and store them in his cabinet. Each day at the beginning of the second sitting, Lou would go through the routine of asking them what they would like and then open the door of the hot box and call their orders 'down to the galley', assuring his two charges that the Chef was taking care of their breakfast right away. Lou would chat to them, giving them plenty of blarney and then five minutes later, open the door of the hot box and declare that their breakfast had just arrived. With a flourish, and ensuring the Maitre D' was not in the immediate vicinity, he would place the plates in front of them and remove the chop covers. All went well for several weeks until one morning as the two ladies were leaving the dining room, the Maitre D' asked them if everything was to their satisfaction. If they had just replied that it was, things would have been fine, but one of them decided to comment on what a complicated system it must be down below in the galley with all the dozens of little lifts going down from each waiter station. Cottoning on, the Maitre D' agreed that it was, and immediately went off to look for Lou with a look that suggested that when he found him, he would be serving afternoon teas for the rest of the voyage, the ultimate punishment.

The Oronsay did not have launderettes for passenger use like the cruise ships of today. There was of course the main ship's laundry and passengers could make use of that for a charge. However, although, there were no launderettes as such, there were ironing/drying rooms. Should someone choose to wash items in their cabin, they could take them to this room where there were drying racks and ironing boards. I was busy working in my safe one day when one of the JAP's asked me to come to the desk to deal with a problem. At the desk were about ten middle-aged ladies all holding up their smalls for me to see. When I say smalls...there was nothing remotely small about them. An average hippo would have had trouble keeping them up but that was not the problem. All of them had the crotches cut out of them. The spokeswoman explained to me that they had all left their knickers to dry in the ironing room the previous day and today when they went to retrieve them they had discovered them in this crotchless state, and what was I going to do about it? I have to say

I was lost for words. The ladies were not going to go away until they received some reassurance that action would be taken and so I assured them that I would make enquiries as to try and track down the phantom knicker crotch remover. I was going to make light of it and say something to the effect that at least in these tropical temperatures, things would be cooler, but the ferocious snarls I was getting, suggested I should keep quiet and try and take it seriously. How do you even start to investigate? The ironing rooms were open all the time and it could have been anyone with a warped sense of humour among either passengers or crew to do such a thing. That narrowed it down to about 1,500. I never did find out who did it but Alan, the Chief Butcher was top of my list of suspects.

Sydney arrived and Richard (Deputy Purser) and I disembarked and flew back to London. We had a full day working on board and our flight was at 7.00pm that night after the ship had departed. We had technical problems with that particular flight and were delayed at each of the stops at Perth, Singapore, Bahrain and Rome before arriving at Heathrow after some 48 hours of travelling. I can never sleep on planes, certainly not in goat class anyway, so we were pretty knackered when we arrived. The other thing I had not thought about in my rush to leave back in the summer was that it was now winter (February) in the UK and there was snow all over. Had I thought about this, I might have taken clothing more appropriate, but here I was dressed in the same jeans and T-shirt I had flown out in. Naturally all the trains were delayed as there had been a couple of inches of snow and after several hundred years of the same thing happening every winter, 'British Rail was not prepared for it'. By the time I eventually got to Brighton at 6.00pm on the Saturday evening, I was knackered, frozen to the bone, thoroughly miserable and missing the Australian summer. I collected my apartment keys from my neighbour and entered. I flicked on the light and nothing happened. I had been late settling my electricity bill and had been cut off. The apartment was dark and like a refrigerator. The planned hot bath and hot meal was not going to happen as being Saturday night, I could not do anything until Monday morning. I found a torch and went in to the bedroom. There was the bed still unmade just as I had jumped out of it the previous summer. I just got under the covers and slept till the Monday.

We were both supposed to fly back to Sydney after seven weeks leave but I was two weeks delayed as I had set fire to my flat with a chip pan and burned my hand very badly. Not bad for someone who had attended a fire fighting course only a few months previously. Anyway, I did get back to Sydney and rejoined the Oronsay which was by now permanently cruising off the Australian coast. I was well settled in there but drinking far too much. As SAP, I hosted a table of passengers in the Dining Room. One couple on my table was an elderly English gentleman and his much younger Dutch wife who were going back to Tasmania where they had bought some land. I had pulled a muscle in my back and was in pain. The wife said she was a masseuse and would give me a massage. This seemed very agreeable but unfortunately the husband insisted on being present. Her massage was quite erotic and certainly helped, though I did feel a bit uneasy with the husband watching and wondered if it might be a set up. Fortunately it wasn't and she and I had some follow up treatments without the husband knowing.

The Himalaya had just gone for scrap in Taiwan, but not before offloading all her stores to us on the Oronsay. Our No.3 Hold was crammed full of boxes loaded by sling and crane and it all had to be sorted out. We had two Cadets with us this voyage, Simon and Sean and each sea day we went down the Hold via the vertical ladders to try and sort it all out. It had just been loaded haphazardly and pots and pans mixed with linen and stationery. It took us weeks to sort it all out but it saved us a lot of money in stores in the long run.

CHAPTER 22

I had a really nice cabin on the after end of D Deck. There was one alleyway in the passenger accommodation there and my cabin stretched the whole of one side of this alley with three cabins the other side, the outboard occupied by an Assistant Purser, the middle by two girls from the Beauty salon and the inboard was a passenger cabin. My cabin was the main venue for parties and so depending who was in the passenger cabin, they would either be invited (if young girls) or if not they would be given a better cabin to move to on the grounds that some maintenance needed to be done. My contract this time was nearly six months as we were doing some very long cruises out of Sydney. One particular cruise took us up to Japan, and across to Hong Kong and then up to Mombasa, Zanzibar, Madagascar, Seychelles, Mauritius, Durban and then back to Fremantle and round the south coast back to Sydney.

Although the new white shorts uniform had by this time been introduced to the rest of the fleet, there were still some places we visited where shorts were not acceptable for either religious or cultural reasons. Zanzibar was one such place. We had to beg, borrow or steal a pair of long white trousers for the day and there were some strange sights indeed. It was easy for many such as Engineers who just remained in their boiler suits for the entire day but for the Deck and Purser's Officers this was quite a challenge. It had been some time since I had been to Fremantle, but good old Tom the Customs Officer was still there. I was also able to catch up with a good friend who was the Manager of the Bank of New South Wales there. I had met Peter on the Oriana in 1969. He was a fun guy and very helpful when we needed some banking assistance for our personal finances for which the Oronsay was a generous contributor.

The new style of entertainment which was prevalent on the American coast had not stretched to Australia yet and we were still doing horse races and casino nights which was quite lucrative for the Pursers, especially for me as I used to run them. The Staff Captain on the ship however, was not keen on me, as he had been on the Spirit of London when the trouble had occurred, and went out of his way to try and trap me. One particular horse race, he was very much in attendance and I saw he was noting down figures. I played the next few races straight until he had disappeared and then hammered the last one when I thought it was safe. Just as we were about to take our leave at the end, he appeared from nowhere, took the clipboard out of my hand and noted the figures. I spent the next several hours in the office behind locked doors with all the ticket rolls and their serial numbers reworking the figures for the six races. Showing I had made a mistake on the fourth and fifth races and overpaid the winners, I clawed the money back on the last race. Everything balanced and I did a statement to that effect for the Purser as I was sure the Staff Captain would raise this at the Captain's meeting in the morning. I was right and he did. I was lucky in that this particular Purser, Big Jim, who had been the Purser on the Oracdes when I was a Cadet, did not like the Staff Captain due to his interference. The Purser sent for me on his return from the Captain's meeting and shut the door. He told me I had been right and the Staff Captain had accused me of embezzlement. He was completely deflated when the Purser produced my statement and all the reworked figures and said that he had already investigated it, it was a genuine case of inaccurate figure work on my part. He had given me a reprimand and told me to get my figures double checked next time. He also told the meeting that I had been astute enough to have clawed the overpayment on the previous two races back in time as there would otherwise have been a loss to the company. The Staff Captain was furious but we got away with it. My punishment was to give my share of the ill-gotten gains to the Purser.

I liked the Oronsay, it had a great crew, I was making money, the Australian girls were endless and we went to fantastic ports. Life could not be better. However, nothing lasts forever and with the Orcades, Iberia, Orsova, and then the Himalaya having gone to the scrapyard in Taiwan, it was another blow when it was announced that the Arcadia and Chusan would follow suit. The two small ships, Cathay and Chitral were also on borrowed time. The Cathay had already gone to a Chinese company and the Chitral after an unsuccessful attempt at Mediterranean cruising would follow suit. The fleet was shrinking at an alarming rate. Six mid-sized ships of approx 30,000 tons were gone and more were to follow as the days of the liner were numbered. We had built the Spirit of London and bought the Island Princess but they were small ships compared to those we sent to the scrapyard. Admittedly, as previously mentioned, we had bought British India Steam Navigation Company. However, the number of officers who came with them was quite unbelievable, especially in terms of Captains, and senior Officers in the Deck and Purser's Departments. How all these Officers ever managed to go to sea, I have no idea as they must have spent most of their time on leave waiting for a ship. Many however were getting near retirement and some dropped out before that, when they found out they would have to do a whole four months on a ship in one go. Still, it did not look good for promotion prospects and I was still intent on getting promoted back up to Deputy Purser in spite of what the Company had said. I was determined to keep my nose clean. I had a feeling that they thought that if they told me I would never be promoted again, I would be pissed off enough to resign. However, perhaps if I toed their line for a while, I would embarrass them enough to promote me again. I had to be a bit patient.

One of my duties on arrival in each port was to obtain clearance from the local authorities such as Customs and Immigration before passengers would be allowed off the ship. With being in and out of Sydney every couple of weeks, we made lasting friendships with Sydney Customs Officers and the Water Police who patrolled the harbour. One of the girls who worked in the Sydney Office was nicknamed Squizzie and she had many drinking friends among the Water Police. The Chief Boarding Officer for Sydney Harbour was Harry who had originally hailed from Lancashire but migrated to Australia as a youth. When we had completed all the formalities, Harry and his chums would often feel a thirst coming on and we would retire to one of the bars. However, the bars of course would be closed due to Customs regulations so Harry would give 'special permission' for one to be opened and we would go in behind closed doors. These sessions would go on often until late that night. Between the Police and the Customs, they were fairly boisterous and one night I spent the entire night handcuffed to a full beer barrel behind the bar. On another occasion I was handcuffed standing up with my hands over a water pipe that ran through the bar. Not an ideal way to spend the night, especially after consuming a good quantity of beer.

We had a lot of fun though and they reciprocated in kind. Whenever we arrived in Sydney, they would come to my office and ask if we had any troublesome passengers who had made themselves a nuisance during the voyage. There were always one or two who had been obnoxious to the crew, difficult in every possible way and stretched us to the limit. The details would be given to the Customs who would 'randomly' select them at disembarkation as they cleared customs. By the time their luggage had been searched, they would usually start giving the Customs some lip as well which then usually had to involve a strip and internal body search. Whether they ever suspected any collusion or not is unknown but we never had problems from the same people again.

Alan, the Chief Butcher was back on board again. There was a different Chef, Jimmy this time who was rather anti-gays. Alan, himself was not gay but liked to pretend he was. After a run in with the Chef over something, he went round collecting several of the gay pornographic magazines from some of the crew. They contained some very explicit photos and Alan went to the Chef's office whilst he wasn't there and stamped them all up with the Chef's office stamp. He then printed on the top of each magazine, 'When finished please return to Chef'. He then distributed these magazines under the cabin doors of all the old Stewardesses and Telephone Operators. A couple of nights later, when the Chef was in his office, he was absolutely fuming to have several of the female crew come into his office and discreetly drop a magazine on his desk in a plain envelope and thank him very much for the loan, with a nudge, nudge, wink, wink.

On our way back to Australia at the end of our long cruise, we picked up passengers in Durban who were returning to Sydney. We were pretty tight on accommodation and I had nothing spare. There was a very attractive Australian girl who approached me at the desk to ask if I had any other accommodation as she was sharing with an old lady who retired early in the evening. I was most apologetic and understanding but explained I did not have any spare cabins to place her on her own. That evening I invited her round for a drink and she still ended up sharing...but with me. We left Sydney, not for the ship's last time, but it was for me, and headed for the Far East. Richard and I would both be disembarking in Hong Kong along with the Captain. The company had not yet got round to flying the senior officers in business class so the three of us were together in goat class. We arrived in Heathrow and as the Captain was in the aisle seat he was the first one up and in opening the overhead locker, my jacket fell out. My passport was poking out of the inside pocket and he went to reach it to see the name. I immediately claimed the jacket before he did so, catching Richard's eyes nearly going through the top of his head. We said farewell in the terminal and Richard and I shared a taxi to our respective railway stations. Once inside the taxi we shared a hip flask in relief that the Captain had not gone right in to my pocket. We both were carrying cash we did not wish him to see. Still, I had five months paid leave due to me and I was looking forward to it.

CHAPTER 23

After three weeks I received a call from Tommy, the Personnel Officer asking me how I was enjoying my leave. This was not a good sign. Personnel Officers only get in contact when they want something. He urgently needed a Senior Assistant Purser for the ss Uganda, one of the educational cruising ships we had acquired from British India. When I moaned that I still had over four months leave due, he explained that it was only for three cruises (six weeks) and if I did him that favour he would see about getting me promoted back up to Deputy Purser. Eventually I did agree but only on condition that I could have my full leave once I returned again after the six weeks. Of course I could, no problem. I joined the Uganda in Southampton as she had just completed her season stationed in the Med and we sailed empty up to Leith in Scotland to begin our North Cape season. She had been built in 1952 some 23 years previously and had been an old design then. Once on board, I found that in addition to my normal SAP duties I also had the responsibilities of the Crew Purser but as most of the crew apart from the officers were Indian, this did not seem to be a problem, even though their system of paying Indian crew from Calcutta was a lot different to the way P & O paid the Goan, Indian and Pakistani crew.

What Steve, whom I relieved, had omitted to tell me was that on the day I would disembark six weeks hence in Dundee, there would be the annual Calcutta crew change and I would have to agree all the deductions and earnings for the entire Indian crew for the previous twelve months. This turned out to be a complete nightmare as their pay was not consolidated like in P & O but had all sorts of different bonuses of which I was totally unaware. There were storing bonuses, bunk making bonuses on turnround day, boiler cleaning bonuses, just about every damn thing they did carried a bonus, and I began to wonder if they were making some of them up. I was at a loss as to what duties their monthly wage actually included. To top all this off, the ss Nevasa, the other B.I. ship had gone to the scrapyard, but not before being destored in Malta when both ships were there a couple of months previously. Some of the crew from the Nevasa who were not time-expired had transferred to the Uganda at that time to replace some of the Uganda crew who were. The transfer of all the Nevasa stores naturally involved a storing bonus and a destoring bonus. Of course it did. Why not?

In the Hotel or Saloon Department as it was

called in B.I. the Butla was in charge whereas the Deck and Engine Departments both had a Serang. Trying to get an agreement between these three as to who should be paid the bonus was only one obstacle. One insisted the bonus should only be paid to the Uganda crew, another thought it should only be paid to the Nevasa crew and the other thought it should be paid to both. There was only a set amount of money and so the division made a difference. It took many days of discussions to get an agreement but we got there in the end.

On my second cruise, we were to visit Leningrad (now St Petersburg) and we had to get the entire passenger and crew lists visaed prior to arrival. This meant long hours for the two girls in the office after leaving Dundee and we had to have the lists back on board with visas by arrival Helsinki. I had visited Moscow and Leningrad 10 years previously on a school trip so was aware of the tight regulations and bureaucracy that prevailed. I also recalled that the things the citizens wanted most from any tourists were chewing gum, ball point pens and little clip on tin badges. Fortunately with 1,000 school children on board, they were reasonably easily regimented. I had heard that during the previous season, one of the Assistant Pursers had gone ashore on an occasion with a few pens sticking out of his top pocket and within minutes he had given them all away to people wanting to pay good money for them. On the next cruise, realising the cash potential, he had taken a large bundle of pens with him and sold them all during the afternoon. However, his actions must have been noted and on the third occasion he took with him a cardboard carton full of pens and was busy flogging them in the street. A car drew up and he was bundled inside, blindfolded and driven to a location approximately 10 minutes away from where he was picked up. He was taken out of the car, up some stairs and into a windowless room where the blindfold was removed from this terrified individual who by now must have been giving thought to the new colour of his white uniform trousers. He was told to watch a screen. He sat there watching a piece of cine film of his wife picking the milk up off the doorstep and his two children playing with a ball in his garden. He was told to go back to his ship and not to step ashore again. He was bundled back in the car and returned to where they had picked him up. He immediately returned to the ship and never set foot in the USSR again. It sounded like something from a spy novel, but when you think about it, easy enough to do. They had the name and address from the crew list and it was an easy thing to do to order the London Embassy to take a few minutes of footage so nothing very complicated. However, it was extremely effective.

On my third and final cruise we had a new Junior Assistant Purser by the name of Dean join the ship. Dean was older than most at 28 and was an Old Harrovian. He had the gift of the gab and had done a variety of jobs since leaving school. He never knew any of the answers to passenger enquiries but would engage them in such entertaining conversation, by the time they left the desk, they had forgotten what they had come to ask. Dean decided to invite David, the Assistant Purser and myself up to the Wardroom for a drink one evening. When we arrived, Dean was already there looking resplendent in blue mess kit. Blue mess kit was the uniform which had been discontinued in 1970 and we now only used the white. I asked him where he had obtained it and he told me he had bought it off someone prior to joining who had convinced him he needed it. I explained it all to him. He was not bothered though, as he said he would keep it for fancy dress.

During that last cruise, as I said earlier I had precious little time for anything else due to the preparations for the forthcoming annual Indian crew change. The entire Indian crew was flying back to Calcutta and the new crew would have arrived in Dundee the day before the ship docked. Bearing in mind I had only been on the ship for the last six weeks of their 52 on board, they took advantage of this and questioned every deduction and payment and I spent hours looking up records before obtaining a thumbprint as a signature. By the time we arrived in

Dundee, I had not slept for 72 hours and could not wait to disembark. The crew change went according to plan fortunately and I had to rush to get the train from Dundee. Dean was also disembarking after his familiarity cruise and as he lived in Hove and I lived in Brighton, we travelled together. We spent most of the train journey from Dundee to Edinburgh in the buffet car and once in Edinburgh airport after finding out our flight to Gatwick was delayed through fog, we decided to make for the bar which was closed. We were told the only way we could get a drink was in the Dining Room provided we had lunch. Why the hell not? I had hardly eaten for three days due to work and was starving. When the waiter came to take our lunch order, Dean ordered six gin and tonics while we read the menu, three each, he explained to the incredulous waiter. Once on the flight we had another good session and again in the buffet car on the train from Gatwick to Brighton. I said farewell to Dean, wishing him the best of luck wherever his next appointment might be and silently sympathising with the poor sod who would have him on his staff.

Anyway, at least I was now going to have my promised five months leave.   Two weeks later I received a call from Tommy wanting me to go out and join a ship called Pacific Princess as Senior Assistant Purser. Now, the American arm of P & O who had the Spirit of

London out in the USA plus the newly acquired Island Princess (originally called the Island Venture), knew that there had been a sister vessel to the Island Venture and eventually found the Sea Venture on the New York to Bermuda run. So P & O acquired this vessel also and renamed it the Pacific Princess. As Princess Cruises was better known in America than P & O, it was decided to market the American arm under the name of Princess Cruises although of course it was still part of P & O S N Co. Only one problem, the three ships marketed under Princess were the Pacific Princess, Island Princess and the Spirit of London and so the Spirit was renamed the Sun Princess.

I really did not wish to return as SAP as by agreeing to the six weeks on Uganda I had been promised that not only would I get my full leave but also that I would be promoted back up to Deputy Purser. I told Tommy this and he stalled and said that if a position came up for Deputy Purser during my time on there, he would trans-ship me. Like hell he would. Once I was there, I was there for the contract so I wasn't falling for that one. We agreed that I could have my leave and he would find someone else. I managed about three more weeks of my five months leave and he called again. This time it was for a Deputy Purser's position on the Oriana during Mediterranean cruising. I obviously wasn't going to get my leave and felt I was now out of bargaining chips and so I joined the Oriana. I reached South-ampton and when I walked in to the Bureau, I was greeted with a 'hello old boy'. It was Dean.

I was appointed as Deputy Purser Administration which meant that I was in charge of the on board accounting, all the complaints from passengers and everything controlled from the Purser's Bureau. Of course I had an SAP, my previous position but it appeared as I got promoted, so certain tasks were taken away from junior personnel and given to the next rank up so that tasks I had been glad to be rid of as I was promoted, I seemed to get back again as their importance was re-evaluated by Management. This was happening on the Food and Beverage side also.

It had now been announced that the Oronsay was also to head for the scrapyard in Taiwan. There were other changes afoot also. Suddenly there was an on board Accountant on the two large ships whose task was to audit just about everything. This was a most unwelcome addition as far as Purser's Officers were concerned. There was also a Slot Technician put on board supposedly to relieve us of the burden of emptying and repairing the slot machines. This was also not good news. The company knew only too well how much revenue was going astray with these machines and so their answer was to place a technician on board. Of course it did not solve anything as the technician was up to the same tricks as we all had been. The Accountant was a different matter though. We now had to be far more careful in everything we did and feign ignorance at times. Not so, one Entertainment Officer who was so disturbed to see the Accountant present at one of his bingo sessions counting heads and making notes, that at one of the Captain's meetings he threatened to throw the Accountant over the side of the ship.

The Oriana was the only ship in the fleet left now with British Deck and Engine ratings and the company was anxious to get rid of them too. However, allegedly there were various deals done with the National Union of Seamen and certain concessions had to be made. The Island and Pacific Princesses were manned with Italian Cooks and Waiters and Mexican utility positions. These crew members had to be officially members of the NUS and the company paid their union dues as well as agreeing to British Deck and Engine crew remaining on Oriana. For that simple reason, many tried to avoid being appointed to Oriana as they were such a source of trouble and expensive to employ for such little work output. There were other changes happening within the company regarding training also. It had been decided to do away with the Purser Cadet training scheme which to this day I believe was a huge mistake. The training scheme was excellent and stood P & O out from many other shipping companies but times were changing, no longer in the business of transportation as jet aeroplane travel was expanding fast and holiday or vacation cruising was the only ways ships would remain in a competitive business. Costs had to be reduced. It was decided that new Junior Assistant Pursers, instead of being employed as Cadets when 18 years of age, would be taken on directly as JAPs having gone to College or University and qualified in HND or HCIMA at 21. No longer was a career being offered, just a job to fill a place.

Existing personnel such as myself would be put through the three year course at company expense. First of all they tried to get us to do it in our spare time at sea by correspondence course. This was a complete failure naturally as the Management had not realised that when you are on the ship 24/7, you don't actually have any spare time and grabbing the occasional couple of hours sleep is a necessity. The Officers did not actually have a union as such but we were made to join the Merchant Navy and Airline Officers Association. They were a complete waste of time and were not at all interested in Purser's Officers, only Deck and Engine Officers, though they did welcome our enforced subscriptions.

After it was realised that not one of us had managed to submit one single module of the correspondence course, it was decided to take us ashore to attend college. Six Purser's Officers would be seconded ashore for six months to attend the last six months of the twelve month intermediate stage and a couple of years later we would be taken ashore again for another six months to attend college for the last six months of the twenty four months final stage of the HCIMA at Ealing Technical College. These six month sessions started in January each year and as I would be disembarking the Oriana in November, it would seem sensible to have my leave and start College in the January. I applied and was accepted.

I was quite friendly with the Ship's Surgeon, Tony and also one of the Guest Entertainers, Billy who was a rock and roll guitarist. Billy hailed from Redcar in the North of England, was very tall and had a habit of punching his fist through the deckhead of the Stern Gallery when he did his act. He was forever up in front of the Staff Captain and being made to pay for new deckhead panels.

These two were big mates and one day had been having a pretty good lunchtime session when they decided to call in my cabin for a drink. I had just had my siesta and had promised to see the Cashiers at 4.00pm to give them more currency as they had run out. These two arrived and both being very large would not allow me to leave my cabin. I explained what I had to do but they thought it was just an excuse not to entertain them. The Cashiers phoned me thinking I had overslept and I assured them I would be down in a couple of minutes. These two thought I was making it up. The cashiers' opening time came and went and then the Purser phoned me, shouting down the phone to get there immediately. Still, these clowns thought I was having them on and would not allow me to leave. When they eventually tired of their game I shot down to the office and fixed the two Cashiers up who had queues for foreign currency half way round the ship. The Purser gave me a right rollocking, assuming I had overslept and it took me some time before I was on speaking terms with Tony or Billy again. They were however apologetic when they eventually realised the impact their stunt had made but this was not going to help my appraisal from the Purser as I was still on probation.

Communications between shore and ship were still pretty basic thankfully. Telex had not arrived on the ships yet, they were still a land based operation and so whenever we reached port, our agent would arrive with a large fistful of telexes which had been sent mainly from the head office but some from other ports as well requesting our requirements well ahead of time and reaffirming the paperwork required for a speedy clearance on our forthcoming call. Only very urgent messages were sent by telegram via Portishead radio but this was expensive and usually confined to messages only of a very urgent or confidential nature. P & O had its own code for confidential messages and it was only the Purser's Officers who were trained in the coding and decoding practice with the use of the confidential code book. This book had to be kept in whichever Assistant Purser's safe who was on call at night. As well as one of the four male Assistant Pursers on call at night, there also had to be one of the three Deputy Pursers for dealing with any important issue the Assistant may not be able to handle. Both Duty Officers had to inform the telephone exchange of their whereabouts during the course of the evening and then when finally retiring for the night. It could never be assumed that you would be going to bed in your own cabin. There were no pagers in those days, and the number of telephones was limited.

The Captain on the Oriana at the time was a strange person, not particularly popular, with enormous bushy eyebrows which made him look unusually fierce. And so it was around 11.30pm one evening, I was sitting in the Monkey Bar with Cyril, the Accommodation Deputy having a drink when one of the Stewards approached me to say I was wanted on the phone in the bar. I went and took the phone and it was the First Officer on the Bridge to say that the Captain had received a coded telegram and wanted me on the Bridge to decode it. I shot down to the Bureau and summoned the Duty Assistant from his bed as I needed the code book. He didn't have it. He had forgotten to take it from the previous holder. We ended up summoning the entire staff from their beds in our quest to locate the code book. In the meantime the Telephone Operator kept frantically popping round to the Bureau to say the Captain was going apoplectic on the Bridge as he had been kept waiting. Eventually after twenty minutes, the code book was located and I hared off for the Bridge, not particularly keen on what I knew would be waiting for me.

As I entered the Chartroom on the Bridge, my feet did not touch the ground. "Where the hell have you been?" was the first greeting. Before I could utter one single word, "Don't argue" was the follow up. "I wasn't arguing", I managed to get out before I was remonstrated again with, "I said 'don't argue'. When you are on duty you let the telephone exchange know where you are". "I did", I said. "How dare you argue with me", he reiterated and then proceeded to lecture me further. I knew better than to try and explain, he wasn't having any of it and besides, I guess it was my Duty Assistant Purser who had failed to take possession of the book, so one way or another I was going to take the blame. We decoded the telegram. Unbelievably, one of our ship's Musicians had bounced a cheque for twenty pounds and the company wanted us to recover the money from him. We were both dumbfounded that some pen pusher in the Accounts Department. had gone to the trouble of coding a telegram for such a trivial matter. However, this Captain was also RNR, which usually meant frustrated Merchant Navy Captains who had been unsuccessful in joining the Royal Navy. This particular one, 'Whacker' as he was known, was totally obsessed by war. It is common knowledge that Captains of merchant ships have sealed orders from the Admiralty held in their safes which are to be opened in time of international conflict and only on instruction from the Admiralty. Whacker obviously felt the frustration of such a trivial communication and was disappointed, and so, "As it was ...it was unimportant", he yelled at me, "but suppose a war had been declared?" I am not sure what response he was expecting, if any at all. However, without giving it a great deal of thought, I merely said, "I am afraid we would have been 20 minutes late for it Sir". He stood there mesmerised for a few seconds, not sure if he had heard this flippant remark correctly, and then exploded, leaping so high in the air, he hit his head on the Chartroom deckhead jamming his cap down over his eyes. Presumably he was wearing his cap in case he had to go to war, had the need arisen. He stormed off the Bridge and left all the Bridge staff and myself standing there. To hell with him, I thought and went back to the Monkey Bar to finish my drink.

One of the Duty Assistant Purser's tasks as I have mentioned before was to meet the Pilot at the gunport door and escort him to the Bridge. I am not sure why it was our job to do it but in those days Deck Officers seemed to think themselves superior to all other beings, something which thankfully is no longer the case. It was one Southampton morning when I received a call at 6.00am from the Captain balling me out yet again regarding the Duty AP. My first thoughts were that the AP had overslept and not met the Pilot. However, this was not the case apparently. The Assistant Purser had met him and had given him a tour of the Galley before eventually one of the Cooks had shown him how to exit without going through the Dining Rooms which were locked. Once up on the Veranda Deck, he had given the Pilot a complete tour of all the public rooms and bars while the Captain and Bridge Officers waited for him to appear. Eventually the Pilot said to the AP that as he seemed lost, he, the Pilot would show he, the AP the way to the Bridge as he had seen the ship many times and really did not want a conducted tour. He proceeded to the Bridge with the AP in tow. I didn't need to guess who the AP was. It was Dean.

The last cruise completed, I had to stay for the dry dock and refit in Southampton, and then went on leave. This was going to be my first Christmas at home since going to sea. I had spent all seven of the previous Christmases on the high seas and being young and single, it was one of the best places to be. When married with children of course, it is a totally different story. Anyhow, it suddenly hit me that Christmas was going to be totally by myself in a cold miserable apartment in Brighton. Richard, my partner in crime from the Spirit and more lately Deputy Purser on the Canberra, was married with a three year old daughter, so I wondered if he might appreciate Christmas at home if I did the Canberra's Christmas cruise for him. I went down to see him and discussed it. He said he would be overjoyed to have the three week cruise off and be at home and would return at the end and do the World cruise, and I would go off to do my College course. I said I would contact personnel and let him know. On the Monday, I contacted them and suggested it. I might have well have asked them for the Moon! Quite impossible, they said. I did not understand why. I told them, that for one cruise over Christmas, he wanted to be at home as he had a small child, I wanted to be on a ship as I was going to be alone, we would swap over each time in Southampton so no flights or expense was involved and that I hoped that one day if I got married and had small children, someone might do the same for me, though I doubted it. However, they stuck fast without any proper explanation and Richard spent his Christmas away from his family and I spent a miserable Christmas by myself. Just bloody mindedness I suppose, as is their wont.

Whilst on leave I decided to take the train from Brighton to Bournemouth to see an old school friend, Tony, with whom I had been part of the tarmac team a few years previously. It was around 10.00pm when I changed trains in Southampton and decided to grab a beer in the buffet car. The buffet car had just closed and the attendant said he was sorry but he had to do his sales records before arrival in Bournemouth. There was something that seemed familiar about his tinted glasses but I couldn't put my finger on it. He was also looking at me and then said, "Didn't you used to work at sea? On the Orcades?" When I affirmed this, he said, "You were the guy that used to pay us our money", or not, as the case often was. I suddenly recognised him as one of the Waiters in the forward dining room and took a step back from the bar before acknowledging that he was correct; just in case a fist might have been coming my way. It didn't thankfully and once we had established each other's identity, he said, "Of course you can have a beer, sod the books, I'll have one with you". With that he grabbed four cold beers, wouldn't let me pay and came round to a table. We enjoyed the next half hour to Bournemouth reminiscing about the Orcades and he told me about all the fiddles there were with British Rail catering. At Bournemouth we said our fond farewells and it was the next day that I eventually remembered his name and that he was one of the main troublemakers amongst the Waiters.

CHAPTER 24

At the beginning of January 1976 I started at College in Ealing. It meant a train journey from Brighton to London at 6.00am followed by a long tube journey to South Ealing to arrive by 9.00am. However, fortunately the classes had been condensed into Mondays and Fridays only, so although I did not get home until around 11.00pm, it was only the two days a week, though they were very full days with classes from 9.00am until 8.00pm. At the end of January when my pay arrived, I was shocked to see they had dropped me back down to SAP wage. Obviously a mistake, I phoned up the office only to be told that it was correct as I had not actually been confirmed in the rank. There was no way I could exist ashore on that pay so I requested to go back to sea and was told 'no', as I had started the course. I had no choice but to take a part-time job. I became a bartender in a pub up in Rottingdean where they were building the new Brighton yacht marina. Being the nearest pub to the marina it was busy at night and at weekends with all the Irish labour living in digs locally and having nowhere else to go. I worked lunchtime and evening sessions at weekends as well as a couple of evening sessions during the week. The pay was lousy but the Irish were very generous and bought you a drink every time you served them so instead of having the drink I took the cash and basically managed to scrape through the course until its completion in June. The six of us had to catch up on the first six months that we missed but it was fairly straightforward as we had already been working in the industry for a few years, though the hardest thing I found was going back to a classroom after being away for so long and having to learn the theory of what you know doesn't always work in practice.

During this time, Robbo, my friend and fellow officer from London Cadet training and the Orcades was on leave and lived just up the road at Purley. Robbo had four younger brothers and it was a break for him to visit me in Brighton. I introduced him to a friend of mine, Maggie, one of the female Assistant Pursers with whom I had sailed on Spirit of London and Oronsay and who lived down the road in Worthing. They started going out together and eventually got married. However, we had all been invited to a party in London one Saturday night by a girl we knew who worked in our London office. Full of bonhomie and bullshit at the party Robbo invited me fishing on the Sunday with some friends and when we departed the party at around 5.00am, we agreed to meet at the pier in Newhaven at 9.00am. I got back to Brighton around 6.00am and went to bed for two hours. At 8.00am when I got up, I wished I had never agreed to go fishing but as we all know, these things seem a good idea at the time. I made salmon sandwiches for two and off I went. I could not find any trace of a fishing boat although I was there by 9.00am and when Robbo arrived a few minutes later we decided they must have left early. We drove back to my apartment and with the sandwiches I had made and Robbo's contribution of a case of beer enjoyed a relaxing day watching TV, nodding off and having our picnic on my lounge floor. Robbo stayed until 3.00pm on the Monday and then went home. By 5.00pm he was back, showered and changed and ready for a night out! I have very fond memories of that time as we were young and still unattached and made the best of that situation. We took the HCIMA intermediate exams in Food & Beverage, Accommodation, Bookkeeping, etc. and then waited for our next appointments.

I was appointed back to the Oriana again doing the Mediterranean season. I was Deputy Purser Administration again and I felt frustrated at not being given the Catering job as the extra money was considerable. A few days before I joined however, I received an agitated phone call from Stuart, the Purser's Officer from New Zealand who had relatives in Sussex with whom he had been staying. He asked could he come down and stay the night as he had to keep out of sight? It all seemed very strange but I would be glad to see him and met him at the station. He had just come on leave from the Island Princess, had spent a couple of days with cousins in Sussex and was flying to New Zealand the next day. It was fairly standard practice to generate some extra cash from the Captain's cocktail party on every ship by upping the consumption slightly. However, it seemed the Bar Manager on the Island Princess had become increasingly greedy and not liaised with his opposite number on the Pacific Princess because the consumption for the same number of passengers was vastly different. A team from Management in Southampton, spearheaded by Eric the Axe had flown out to the ship and boarded in Mexico unannounced and put locks on everything while they did an inventory and conducted interviews with various members of the bar staff. Naturally, cash finds it way upwards as well as down and the Purser was fired. This happened after Stuart left the ship but he had heard they were trying to get hold of him to ask him questions in the London Office. I knew how that felt. I told him he was being a bit dramatic when he said they might try and catch him at Heathrow when he boarded the flight. Anyway, off he went and I heard no more for several weeks and then I heard that he had left the company. I assumed it had not been his choice, but I was to find out more later.

The day I joined there was threatened union action from the National Union of seamen and we were told to report to our warehouse in Peel Street, Southampton, rather than go directly to the docks as usual. Once at Peel Street, we new joining crew were put into the back of an armoured security van and driven to the ship through the picket lines. When I went to sign on the Ship's Articles, I was told by the representative from the MNAOA that my subscriptions had lapsed and I would not be able to sign on until I brought them up to date. I was aware they had lapsed as the Officers' union was so damn useless as far as non technical officers were concerned. I went in search of the Shore Management to seek their advice. I was told that if I did not wish to bring my subs up to date, then I need not and the Management would give me full support. That seemed reasonable until I asked what the full support meant. They explained that although they would not be able to let me work on the ships, they could let me work in the office on a temporary basis and then... they would have to let me go. Full support that was! What a bunch of arseholes. I had no choice but to pay up reluctantly. I thought about cancelling the cheque but it would not have solved anything. The cruising season progressed slowly and for the first time I actually wished I had been in England for the summer as the 1976 summer was a scorcher. We were short of Junior Assistant Pursers and so in order to fill our complement, the company kept dragging Senior Assistant Pursers off leave for a couple of cruises so we had one of the most efficient teams with all these SAPs filling the slots normally taken by inexperienced JAPs. This meant that at 6.00pm when the Bureau closed, instead of having to work till about 8.00pm, we were all finished and there was a mass exodus as we all headed for the bar to do some serious damage to the entertaining account.

The threatened NUS action sorted out, the next hurdle was a dock strike in Southampton. This meant that we were unable to take on any stores so everything was put into containers and sent by truck to Copenhagen, our first port, where the sight of about 20 x 40-foot containers lined up made my counterpart, Nigel, pale. Of course 20 containers is not a lot these days as ships are designed with easy storing in mind and there are large areas where forklifts can drive around inside with storeroom entrances at deck level, but this was an old liner and the new design had yet to come. Our method was usually confined to pallets being craned down one of the hatches from where dock labour would move it to the storeroom entrance or up a conveyor to the gunport door from where ship's crew were allowed to handle them. On arrival in Copenhagen we decided that we could manage two conveyors through different gunports, a crane to lower pallets down No.3 Hatch and another crane to lower pallets on to the open deck. This would give us a fighting chance of getting everything on board in time but the problem was labour as we still had to give passengers a full service. The Pursers Officers had a party the previous night and were pretty hungover and looking forward to a few hours rest during time off during the day. I left the girls in charge of the Bureau and had all the male Officers change into boiler suits and we took care of the bar stores, chaining the cases from the container to the conveyor. Beer and soda came in cases of 24 cans and two cases at a time are quite heavy, particularly when not used to it and especially with a hangover. Among these Officers were two fairly new to the company, Paul and Grahame, both of whom would eventually end up in senior positions ashore in the Princess office in Los Angeles. We sweated and toiled that day until we had emptied and loaded 4 x 40-foot containers of bar stores as our contribution to the day. We dragged ourselves back on board, hangover sweated out and arms bruised, backs aching... but very thirsty. The crew did an incredible job that day and we had everything on board prior to sailing although we worked long into the night at sea still moving stores from the outside deck. Still, hopefully it sent a message to the Southampton dock labour, that they couldn't hold us to ransom.

Every ship has noisy cabins. The numbers and locations of these are known to all on board, the Purser's staff, Accommodation staff, Engineering staff, Management ashore, but none better than the Deputy Purser who would be on the receiving end of the complaints every cruise. The worst four cabins on the Oriana were the two aftermost cabins on both port and starboard sides of F Deck. There was a G Deck on the ship but due to the rounded stern they finished quite a bit forward of the propellers, the F Deck cabins continuing until they were right above. Not only did they have the props directly beneath them but also the Laundry directly above. The Laundry was an all day and all night operation and so if the propellers did not keep you awake, the constant trundling of laundry carts over a tiled deck between washers and driers certainly would. The worst night was always the first night out of Southampton when the ship would be going full speed to get to the Mediterranean and some civilised weather and at the same time the Laundry would be going full belt trying to catch up on the dirty linen generated from a full turn round and not being able to operate in port due to the fact that when people designed ships, they never considered what you were supposed to do with the dirty water. Just pump it over the side was the old idea before everyone became eco-conscious, after all it was not like having to refrain from using the loo while the train is standing in the station.

Anyway, never mind the romantic slosh of waves upon the side of the ship to lull you to sleep, when the ship was going full pelt trying to bust a boiler, you could not even hear yourself shout to one another, let alone stand still as the vibration would move you around the cabin at no extra charge. I always dreaded 8.00am that first morning at sea when the Bureau opened as the Receptionist would immediately be in my office saying there were four people from one of the cabins outside waiting to see me. The occupants of the other three cabins would materialise to join the queue to see me within the next 20 minutes. In spite of my hangover after the usual sailing night parties, I would smile and ask them what I could do for them trying to ignore their haggard looks derived from no sleep. I usually had to raise my voice as the night's experience had left them partially deaf as well as knackered. They would explain to me the terrible noise from both above and below and I would listen attentively feigning surprise that it had affected them so badly as 'this was the first time' any problem had been reported. I would go on to explain that there was always a certain degree of 'ship's noises' associated with a vessel at sea, but this was very tongue in cheek as I knew only too well the torture to which they had submitted themselves. Naturally, I had no spare cabins as the company would do the normal practice of filling ships whereby it is oversold by a certain percentage and then they hoped like hell that last minute cancellations would ensure 100% capacity. It used to infuriate me that they sold every cabin, that I had nothing to play with when perhaps there was a burst pipe or other disaster but in the Corporate Office they don't have sobbing little old ladies in front of them who have saved up for their cruise of a lifetime, merely robotic accountants. After explaining to them I had no spare cabins and of course nobody ever believes you, I would offer a glimmer of hope that maybe, just maybe, later in the day I might be able to offer them something. It would not be a whole lot quieter but it would be slightly better than what they had and I would contact them later on. Tears were dried, smiles reappeared and they would exit my office clutching at the straw I had waved at them. I would then go through exactly the same inter-view with the occupants of the other three cabins. After that I would find out from the Maitre d'Hotel what meal sittings they were on. Just before lunch I would contact them all in turn to say I had another cabin, not quite as bad as the one they were in and to save them missing lunch, if they put their things together in the cabin, we would handle the swap for them and deliver their new keys to their table in the Din-ing Room once complete. This was so that the different cabin occupants would not meet and get into conversation. The Supervisors and Stewards were all primed and ready once the lunch bell went, as after all we used to do this every cruise, and within ten minutes we had done diagonal swaps with all four cabins. By lunchtime on that first day, the speed would have slowed and the vibration and noise abated very slightly but at least noticeable, convincing them that although still noisy, I had done my very best against all odds to move them to somewhere slightly quieter. In spite of trying to avoid bumping in to them during the next thirteen days, it would sometime happen and in trying to ignore the pale and wan looks of the tortured, I would enquire as to how things were. Inevitably they would admit that it was still noisy but so much better than the original. I would smile and say how glad I was to be able to help. Of course from the company's angle, they would sell the cabin at full fare and if they received a letter of complaint post cruise and they had to offer a 20% discount on the next year's cruise, so be it. They were probably going to get that discount from the travel agent anyway.

During this season, we had a visit from the notorious Jimmy Saville. As well as hosting the programme, 'Jim'll Fix it' on TV, he used to also present a radio programme called, 'Saville's Travels' on BBC Radio on Sunday afternoons. On this particular Sunday when the ship was in

Southampton, Saville would present the programme live from the Monkey Bar on the Oriana.
The Captain and some senior officers hosted him
at lunch and afterwards he toured the ship, ending up in the bar from where he would do his live
broadcast. As the party walked down one of the
alleyways, a deckhead was down and one of the
Radio Officers was up on a pair of steps with his
head and arms up amongst the pipes and cables,
struggling to make a repair to a cable. As the
party passed, the Officer leaned down and trying
to be funny called out "Hey Jim, can you fix this
for me?"   Jimmy
stopped and looked up and said, "Hello son,
what's   your   name   then?"
"Gavin",   replied   the   Officer.
"Well, fuck off Gavin", replied Jimmy.

Whacker, the Captain from the previous year
was still on board and clearly not having forgotten our 'war' discussion from the previous year,
he chose to completely ignore me which suited
me fine. At the end of August he went on leave
which also suited me fine and he was replaced
by Peter, previously the Staff Captain when I
had been a JAP in 1969 and had by now been
promoted to Captain. As I said before he was a
delightful man and loved by everybody, passengers and crew alike. The day he joined in Southampton, I had to go up to his office to get some
papers signed. I had been holding on to them so
that I did not have to get Whacker to sign them.

I asked him if he had enjoyed a good leave and he told me had taken his family on a narrowboat on one of the English canals and they had thoroughly enjoyed it. The only thing, he told me, was that on the Saturday afternoon they had run aground on the mud and had been unable to get off and so had to phone the boatyard owner. He did come out but not in the best of moods as he had intended to watch the soccer on TV. He apparently had towed them off so they could continue on their way but Peter said his parting shot to him was, "You weekend sailors ought to learn how to drive boats before you take them out!" The Captain said to me, "You know, I just kept quiet; I didn't dare say a word".

During this season in the Mediterranean, we called at Alicante which was not too far from Javea where the Des, the ex Barman from the Orcades had set up his bar, when he left the sea and I had visited him in 1972. I rented a car and drove up to see him only to find out that he had sold the bar and met a girl from Rhodesia (as it was then) and had gone out to Salisbury to be with her, especially as her father was allegedly quite wealthy. No other details to be had, it looked as if we had lost touch.

Sue, the SAP, was a great character, larger than life, was a natural when it came to organising people and had a great sense of humour. We got on well and this was the start of a great friendship which still exists to this day. We would sail together, and take over from each other many times during the ensuing years. One sailing night from Southampton, we had been having a rather raucous party in Sue's cabin which was just forward of the passenger cabins on A Deck. Grahame, the Duty Assistant Purser had been called out by a couple of cabins about the noise and when he returned, he had told us we had to keep it down. The next morning, at 8.15am these passengers were waiting to see me to complain. Whilst I sympathetically listened to their complaint about the noise, I looked on a deck plan to see what machinery was in their location to cause disturbance. However, they were most emphatic that it was not machinery noise, but party noise, and one particular female laugh that they would recognise anywhere. I promised to have the Night Stewards keep an eye on the area over the next few nights as I prayed that Sue would not suddenly laugh whilst they were in my office. For the rest of that cruise we had to hold our parties elsewhere. I checked with the complaining passengers a few times afterwards, telling them that I had received no reports from the Night Stewards. They assured me everything had been fine since, it had obviously been a one off and they had not heard this raucous laugh since. I assured them that I would continue to monitor for the rest of the cruise to ensure their continued comfort and they thought I was wonderful. I did, however have to ban Sue from laughing until after disembarkation in South-ampton.

Nigel, the Catering Deputy Purser and I were both leaving the ship after the dry dock prior to the ship going out to Australia. A new Beauty Salon Manageress, Sian had joined the ship and in some ways I was sorry to be leaving as I was very attracted to her. Still, leave beckoned. Nigel had hurt his head one day during the storing operation by ducking under a conveyor and coming up too soon. He had to have some stitches in the back of his head and his blues jacket collar was covered in blood. At 6.00pm the night the ship sailed we disembarked, it was cold and pouring with rain. I only had to drive to Brighton but Nigel lived in Inverness so I suggested he followed me back to Brighton and stayed the night and continued his journey the next day. We got back to my apartment and went out for a meal and quite a few drinks. He ended up staying the weekend and left on the Monday morning. About five days later I received a call from Tommy in Fleet Personnel to say that I would be getting a call from the police in Inverness to verify a story of Nigel's.

It appeared that there had been a murder in Inverness around that time but before Nigel had arrived home. On his second day at home he had taken his uniform jacket in to the dry cleaners to have the blood stain removed from the collar. A zealous dry cleaner had reported this to the police and Nigel was duly 'assisting the police with their enquiries'. Naturally he had been working on the ship when the murder had occurred, and then stayed with me at the weekend and the police wanted to verify with me, the time scale and also the accident on board when he cut his head. The Inverness police phoned about an hour later and after verifying my identity asked me if I knew Nigel. I was very tempted to say I had never heard of him, but decided to come clean, as I had a feeling Nigel might not have appreciated the joke, let alone the Inverness police.

CHAPTER 25

Another lonely Christmas ashore and at the end of January, I received instructions to rejoin the Oriana in Sydney, for Australian cruising and the line voyage home to Southampton. There was to be a large crew change in Sydney and the company had chartered a plane. Fortunately there were too many for the charter and 18 had to go by Qantas. I was relieved to receive a phone call to say I was going on the scheduled flight but not so relieved to find that the other 17 were Deck and Engine ratings and I was to shepherd them and be responsible for their behaviour. Great! However, they were very well behaved, no problem at all, so when the customs and immigration forms came round, I thought I would try and help, so I asked the steward to announce over the public address that if any of the other seafarers wanted assistance with their form filling, they could find me in seat number whatever it was. There was soon a line stretching down the plane and after about two hours, I realised I had done about 50, not just my 17 charges and there was still a line down the aisle. I asked one of them if he was joining the Oriana and he said No. It appeared there were seafarers on the flight from Shell, Esso, BP, OCL and a dozen other different companies. Still, it was one way of killing a few of the 24 hours in the air.

This time I found that I had to share my office with the onboard Accountant, which made any dubious transactions even more difficult. Fortunately, John was one of the best and did not take things too seriously. He was engaged to one of the female Assistant Pursers and so that helped. He also had a good sense of humour which is unusual for an accountant. There was a strict ruling about promissory notes. These were never to be accepted under any circumstances. Officers on the payroll and not paid on board like the rest of the crew could cash a cheque if they required cash. However, John the Accountant never had his cheque book with him and whenever he wished to go ashore, he would just sign a promissory note, and I would give him the cash, and he would promise to settle before I did my safe balance. A safe balance for me would take around six hours as being the main safe holder, all floats on board to Bars, Shops, Salons, Cashiers, Photographers, Radio Office, Slot Machines all came from my safe and so with different currencies, credit cards and travellers' cheques, I was balancing on well over a million pounds. Once complete, John, the accountant would have to check my balance and physical cash. He had just completed it one time when he queried the fact that he had not settled his debts with me. "What promissory notes?" I asked him. He started to explain and then realised that I had him right where I wanted, and realised his mistake. However, things were much easier from then on.

Before we arrived in Auckland, I made contact with Stuart, who had stayed with me in Brighton, one night before flying back to NZ and had said he was in trouble with company. Stuart was working as Front of House Manager at one of the more upmarket hotels in Auckland. He invited us over for lunch and we were able to catch up. It seemed that he did board the plane at Heathrow that day, without incident but in Los Angeles, they had to change planes and wait in the Transit Lounge. Whilst there, the Hotel Operations Manager from Princess had entered the lounge and found Stuart, handing him a ticket back to London and telling him to get back there as he was wanted for questioning by the company. Stuart knew he would be fired at the end of it and so just thought what the hell and continued on his journey to New Zealand. There was never any contact between he and the company again. However, he and the Purser from the Island Princess who had also been fired went on to work for a large consortium in the Middle East which accommodated and fed about 10,000 multi-national oil workers. They earned a packet and never looked back.

On the way back to the UK, I had to start tidying up the cash operations on board as we would be audited on arrival in Southampton and so John, the Ship's Accountant and I decided to have a dummy run and complete stock take and balancing act after leaving Panama so that any nasty surprises would hopefully reveal themselves then rather than on arrival and we would have time to deal with them. There was in fact one which was the Shop which balanced up considerably. The Accountant, Shop Manager and I sat in my office until 3.00am trying to locate where this excess had come from. It was a well known fact that Shop Managers bought in all sorts of goods during voyages with private funds and the sales of these kept separate for private gain and although he maintained that he had accounted for all that side of the business, he must have underestimated his own expertise. I kept the cash separate and by Southampton, everything still balanced and a nice little windfall was had by all.

By now, I was going out with the Beauty Salon Manager, Sian which made life much more pleasant, and I looked forward to returning to the ship after my leave for the Mediterranean cruising season again. However, the company had other ideas. I had been confirmed as Deputy Purser the year before after the successful HCIMA intermediate exam results and now they decided I should go back to the West Coast of America to one of the Princess ships. I was appointed to the Island Princess in Alaska and Sian was appointed to the last voyage of the S.A.Vaal, the last of the Union Castle ships out to South Africa and back. When I flew to Vancouver, I found myself sitting next to Joy, the newly appointed Social Hostess, and who had been the Beauty Salon Manageress on the Oriana the year before. I joined the Island Princess for the whole Alaskan season which nearly drove me out of my mind. All the time, I bore in mind what had happened to Stuart and Mike, the Purser when they had been on the Island Princess. The scenery in Alaska is absolutely stunning as I mentioned before, and the quaint little towns, at least they were quaint before the cruise ships ruined them. These days they are full of lewd jewellery shops and other rubbish, shopping malls have sprung up, roads have become highways and they have lost all the charm and character that they had in the seventies. The last time I stepped ashore in Ketchikan, I took 10 minutes to decide how spoiled it had become, went back on board and never stepped ashore in Alaska again, I was so disgusted to see what the greed of the bureaucrats and cruise ships had done. However, back then, an Alaskan cruise was very scenic and enjoyed by the 'almost dead...but not quite brigade'. One Purser described his ship as a 'Palace of Senility'. And that just about summed it up. I always reckoned that we would empty the nursing homes of the western seaboard each week to take them for one final outing before the inevitable. I have nothing against this so long as people bring the appropriate assistance with them to look after their requirements but so often the poor Cabin Steward is expected to help them on and off the toilet or in the shower. The Waiter is expected to cut up their food for them at the table and practically feed them, that is for those that don't need the food to be blended so that they can suck it up through a straw. And all the time, Stewards are having to push them in wheelchairs from cabin to lounge, lounge to dining room, dining room to lounge, lounge to cabin. We always felt this was over and above the job description and customer care. This was taking the piss, but the Company didn't care; it was a fare, it was an occupied berth and so money in the bank.

The Purser on the ship was Alan (Simbo as he was known). Again he was someone I knew of but had not met until then. He could be charming one minute but scathing the next without warning. He was very much a loner, strange in some ways and had a reputation of being rather anti-Semitic. The Maitre D'Hotel was under strict instructions not to put Jewish passengers on his table in the Dining Room. One day the message had not been passed across to the relief MDH and he went to his table the first night, had a bowl of soup and left, and did not go down again until the following cruise. He would have a party in his cabin for passengers one night during the cruise. This was not out of choice; all the senior officers had to do this. It was eventually discontinued as it was an imposition on one's privacy. However, Simbo had to go along with it so on one of his party evenings I was surprised to find him at the bar about 10 minutes after the start of his party. When I queried it, he just said that he had met everyone at the door and got them all talking amongst themselves, so he slipped away to the bar for a quiet one.

As the Night Cleaners who cleaned all the bars and lounges during the night came under me, he would walk through them all with me at 7.00am each morning. We used to serve two sorts of bar snacks at the time, dry roasted peanuts and little cheese goldfish crackers. One morning we were walking through the Carib Lounge when he pointed out a couple of these under chairs which had obviously been missed when vacuuming. I apologized and reprimanded the Night Cleaners telling them to be more vigilant in future. However, about three days later it happened again in the Carousel Lounge. This time he was not so pleasant and told me in no uncertain terms to get on top of it. I couldn't understand it, especially when I tackled the Night Cleaners again who swore they had double checked prior to finishing their shift at 6.30am. I told them that for the next few days I would go round with them at 6.30am prior to my going round with the Purser at 7.00am. So for the next couple of days I did exactly that. However, on the second day, I had just finished around 6.45am when I noticed the Purser setting off for a walk through the lounges. I was surprised as he was early and did not wait for me to appear. I followed him at a discreet distance and watched him take a couple of goldfish crackers and place them under a couple of the chairs in the Carib Lounge. I followed him around, totally unseen and back to his office. At 7.00am, he collected me from my office and off we went on our inspection. Everything was fine until we reached the Carib Lounge whereupon he went ballistic with me, yelling at me that this was the third time. I stood there calmly until he was finished and enquired as to what the problem was. He pointed to a couple of chairs over the other side of the lounge and shouted to me, "There are two goldfish crackers under those chairs".   "No there aren't", I said, "they are peanuts". He splurted out, "No, they are not, they are goldfish crackers". To which I replied, "I saw you put them there...so I switched them over for peanuts". He glared at me and stormed off. The inspection was over but we did not have problems again.

Simbo lived in Germany as his wife was German. One of my predecessors, Mike had also upset him one day when Simbo was proudly showing him the plans of his lovely old house and his ideas for refurbishment. Mike calmly mentioned that as it was rather large, he couldn't understand how the RAF had missed it during the war. Simbo, without another word, rolled up the plans and stormed out.

The Island Princess was totally different to everything I had been used to and I was not sure that I liked it. For a start the food, but not the beverage was contracted out to an Italian company, rather than be in house which was what I was used to. The catering company supplied an Italian Chief Steward and Assistant, which on the P & O ships had been the Catering Deputy Purser and AP/SAP. They also had under their charge all the Italian Waiters and Cooks, Butchers and Storekeepers. It was a strange set up which was never really made clear to us where responsibility lay. Naturally the Chief Steward reported to the Purser the same as everyone else but when it came to standards, it was all very vague. It seemed that as a Purser you had the responsibility of the catering operation but without the control. We were never privy to any of the accounting on the catering side so we as a company could have and probably were being ripped off like crazy but without any access or control, how could we know? However, that didn't matter...we were responsible anyway, but it didn't make for easy sleeping at night. It did not help that some of the Princess Management were Italian and connected so we as P & O people were very much the outsiders. The Southampton Management were trying to control things from there but fighting a losing battle as Princess gradually distanced themselves and kept them informed only of what they wanted them to know. I felt we were just puppets for the Southampton Office and this was my first taste of the politics to come.

After we completed the entire Alaskan season and I felt ready for the funny farm, we set off in search of the sun again and I did three trans-canal cruises between Los Angeles, through the Panama Canal to San Juan in the Caribbean. One cruise, the Italian gentleman who owned the catering company travelled with us from Los Angeles to Acapulco with his Consiglieri. They were delightful people to us but commanded nothing but respect and fear among the Italians. They went ashore for lunch in Puerto Vallarta in Mexico and in 1977 it was still a tender port, a small fishing village and not the enormous port it is today. They settled on a local restaurant and ordered a steak. The steak was of very good quality and after settling the bill, the caterer enquired of the owner as to his supply. He was already thinking that if he could make a decent deal with this meat supplier in Mexico to supply the ships, it would be much more profitable than the current supplier in Kansas. The Mexican restaurant owner was happy they had enjoyed their meal and was only too happy to share with them the details of his supplier. "You very lucky today", he said to them. "Today big white ship come in to port and I buy from the Provision Master on board". This was neither the answer he expected nor did he want. Especially as it meant that he had paid for his lunch twice! By the time the ship sailed from Puerto Vallarta, the Provision Master was already at the airport with his bags to fly home and seek other employment.

I arrived home and was summoned to the office in Southampton to furnish a report. I had to be interviewed by the Deputy Hotel Services Manager, namely Eric the Axe whom I had not seen since the Spirit aftermath. I was quite honest with him and explained that I did not really enjoy the Princess operation as there were too many vague and political issues which made working difficult. He was reasonable on this occasion and decided to give me more Food and Beverage experience and appointed me to the Uganda. This would not have been my first choice of ship, but beggars can't be choosers. Although I had done six weeks on there as SAP in 1975, the idea of a full contract with 1,000 school kids was not one that appealed. However, my views on this would change later.

I had to join the ship in Ceuta which meant a seat on one of the kids' charter flights from Gatwick to Tangier and then a bus from Tangier airport to Ceuta. My cabin was right by the Bureau and my 'office' next to it. The 'office' was basically a broom cupboard with a shelf built into it just wide enough to accommodate the Kalamazoo board which was the food and beverage accounting system used on the ships, at that time. I had been used to operating this system when I was Assistant Purser Catering and then Senior Assistant Catering to the Deputy Purser Catering on the Orcades and Oronsay respectively but now here I was on the Uganda with no assistant so I had to do it all myself.

Now, I had mentioned earlier that the Uganda had originally been a two class liner with B.I.S.N. Co prior to being purchased by P & O and who had already converted the ship to educational cruising for students. The first class had been left more or less as it was and the 150 cabins used to accommodate the school teachers. The tourist end had been converted to dormitories and classrooms for 1,000 students. Girls' dormitories were on one side of the ship and the boys on the other, and a nightly patrol of four Masters at Arms ensured that it was kept that way. There was a ship's Headmaster and Deputy Head who organized the 'school timetable' and a host of matrons who looked after everything else including homesickness. The old tourist class Bureau had become the School Office and was manned by two Purser's Officers and four school office assistants who were mature students and worked for a few cruises at a time usually on break from university. The timetable included classroom lectures regarding the history of the forthcoming ports, people and countries we would be visiting, mingled with deck hockey or other sport. Meals were taken in the Canteen (a served buffet) and in the evening there was a disco and bar/shop dispensing soft drinks, snacks and other necessities. I soon learned what a slick operation it was and I had a huge respect for it.

All their tours were included in the price of the cruise which was paid in the main by parents, though subsidized by the local education authorities. Packed lunches would be provided by the ship and the day before a port a factory conveyor belt operation would be held in which 1,200 packed lunches would be made up. We had to provide them for bus drivers and guides and had to ensure we did not include something like a pork pie during a call in Haifa. The full day tour in Alexandria would consist of a trip to the Cairo museum to see the Tuten Khamun relics, the Sphinx and of course the Pyramids in Giza, a ride on a camel optional. The full day in Haifa would see them in Jerusalem and Bethlehem, with sufficient time to buy their 'genuine' splinters of wooden cross from the nearby Jesus Christ Superstore.

CHAPTER 26

The school operation was organized in liaison with the various education authorities in the UK, so that each cruise there were schools from a certain area which might be the West Country one cruise, the next Scotland, the next the Midlands, the next Wales, etc. etc. The whole ship was run on a shoestring in order to keep costs down and thereby the fares for which parents had to find the money. However these cruises for youngsters were excellent value not just for their educational content but for the life experience. Many of these kids had never spent a night away from home before, which is ridiculous I know, but it happens. I probably have a bit of a biased view on this as I went to boarding school from eight to 18 but it is important to condition children at an early age by lengthening the apron strings. It helps them stand on their own two feet and the wrench later on goes easier. And so, it used to amuse me to see some of these kids in tears the first night, absolutely distraught and then 14 nights later they would be in tears again because they did not want to leave their friends and go home. I met many Assistant Pursers both male and female over the years who had cruised on Nevasa or Uganda as students which was what had induced them to work at sea.

Whilst in the Mediterranean, we received all our meat, fish and most of the dry stores by container from the UK but all the fresh produce had to be picked up locally. I would have to get all the price lists from the various providores and convert their pesetas, francs, lire, escudos, shekels, drachma, etc. to sterling as this was pre-euro and work out where we would take on what. Storeroom capacity, price, and quality would have to be taken in to consideration as although the price of potatoes, say would be better in A, the quality might not be as good as at B, but you still had to reach B without running out. Then there was always the added risk of inclement weather preventing you entering a certain port where you were going to store, causing a real nightmare. The more you could stay within budget the more remunerative it was for us; I need not say more. The least wastage, a good Chef, Butcher and Storekeeper was essential for this operation.

The Purser was Jeremy, a delightful character whom I had first come across as SAP on the Cathay in Rotterdam when I was a Cadet. Our paths had not crossed for 10 years during which time we had both been promoted and now both serving on the 'punishment ship'. Jeremy was a real character who would sip brandy and dry all day until 6.00pm when he would switch to scotch for the rest of the evening. One day I was on the dock in Piraeus counting my stores to ensure I hadn't been short supplied when he beckoned to me from a porthole in the Galley. I was half way through counting cartons containing 360 eggs each and seeing whether they came to the 54,000 I had ordered. He was quite insistent and I had to leave off and go and see what he wanted. He was cooking himself a late breakfast in the Galley as the Chef had gone off duty. Jeremy wanted two fresh eggs from the new supply. I wasn't best pleased as I went and broke open one of the cartons, took two eggs and walked back, handing them to him through the porthole. I went back and had started recounting when he beckoned me again. Once more, I had to leave off my count and go and see what he wanted. This time he wanted two fresh tomatoes from the new supply. I could have throttled him.

Alexandria was not a favourite port of mine as I found the Egyptian officials very demanding without reciprocation. Everything was want, want, want, with nothing in return. One evening as we departed Alexandria the wind suddenly came up and the swell increased. The Purser received a call from the Bridge to ask if we had any spare cabins as the Pilot was reluctant to disembark in such a swell and was considering travelling with us to the next port and flying back. The only spare cabin was a deluxe cabin on the Promenade Deck which I was reluctant to use for the Egyptian Pilot but it was all we had. I took the key up to the Bridge and collected the Pilot and showed him to the cabin. Immediately he started issuing instructions to me to get him some bar supplies and a large platter of smoked salmon sandwiches. These I duly organized for him and as I went to leave I asked him for his passport. He handed it to me and I explained that I needed it to put his information on the passenger list and he would get his passport back when he attended Immigration on arrival. He asked when the next port was and I told him it was two days time and he would have tomorrow at sea to relax. As he stretched out, he casually asked where the next port was and I told him it was Haifa in Israel. He turned the colour of milk and leapt to his feet almost knocking me over as he raced to the Bridge. I followed him up and he screamed at the Officer of the Watch to raise the Pilot station immediately and have the pilot boat come out and pick him up. The pilot boat arrived after about 20 minutes and it certainly looked very precarious as the little vessel was tossed all over the place as it tried to get as near as possible to the rope ladder dangling from the gunport door. The Pilot was hanging on to the rope ladder for his life and finally he jumped as we watched to see what would happen. Fortunately he had timed it well and landed in a heap on its small deck. We were relieved he had made it without accident and waved him a fond farewell. The Captain was at a loss as to why he had suddenly changed his mind and I shrugged as he had not made any comment to me. However, I must have got it wrong as the next port was Athens.

One evening there was a good film on TV and the Purser asked Derek, the Accommodation Officer and I if we wanted to join him for a couple of drinks and watch the movie. It seemed a good idea but Jeremy was due at his table in the Dining Room. It was agreed that we would give him about 15 minutes until the end of the soup course and Derek would go to the Dining room and request his presence to say there was a phone call for him in the Radio Office. At the appointed time, Derek entered the Dining Room and approached Jeremy's table, and stood quietly to the side as Jeremy was holding court. When he had finished, Derek politely apologised to the table and then said to Jeremy, "I am sorry to bother you, Sir, but there is an incoming call for you in the Radio Office". "What? Now?" expostulated Jeremy, taking Derek aback. "I am afraid so", said Derek. "I am really very sorry to have to disturb you". "Well, can't Peter take it?" Jeremy asked. "They did say they wanted only to speak to you

Sir", Derek replied, fumbling for words at this deviation from the agreed script. By this time the others at the table were looking daggers at Derek, who in their eyes was totally incompetent and was responsible for interrupting their jovial repast. "Oh well, I suppose I have to do everything myself", exclaimed Jeremy getting up from the table and explaining that he would try and return if he possibly could. He left the Dining Room with Derek in tow and once out of sight and earshot, said to Derek, "Did that sound convincing? The look on your face suggested it did." To which Derek replied, "You bastard, don't ever do that to me again".

Those of us who had been on the Princess ships were used to Port Health Inspections by the CDC in USA and now the British Port Health was raising their profile. The USPH Service, part of the CDC, only inspects ships in American ports and only those of foreign flag. Well, there are only foreign flag vessels cruising out of America as the USA does not have any American flag vessels left. For a vessel to fly the American flag it has to not only be built in an American shipyard but be manned by all American seaman's union members. Nobody could afford to have a ship built in America and certainly not have it manned by union members, which is why the British, Italians, Dutch and others cruise their ships out of USA without American competition. Don't misunderstand me, the USPH keep the cleanliness and food handling practices very high which is a good thing of course but it's a pity they don't apply the same high standard to their own catering establishments on land. The British Port Health operates in a similar way.

Now the Uganda by this time was already 26 years old and was not the sort of vessel one could proudly present to an inspecting authority with any degree of pride or confidence. The main galley itself where passenger food was prepared was actually in good shape for its age but on the after end of A Deck, there were two Asian galleys for the crew, one on the portside for the Saloon (Hotel) crew and one on the starboard side for the Deck and Engine crew. Both had their own Bhandary (cook) but the facilities were very basic and antiquated beyond belief. During our stay in Southampton, two officials from the British Port Health arrived to have a look at the ship and its facilities. I showed them the main galley and they actually said that considering the age of the ship, they were quite impressed. I was about to show them back to my office when one of them asked where the crew food was prepared and could they see the area. This was an unwelcome surprise as they had only ever seen the main galley before and had assumed everything came from there but we suspected someone must have tipped them off.

Reluctantly I led them up to the after end of A Deck. To reach the entrance of the Saloon crew galley we had to climb over the after mooring ropes and a mountain of garbage which all had to be stacked there while we were in port. I began to feel a sense of foreboding as amongst the garbage the Assistant Bhandary was squatted on the deck chopping raw onions for the curry. Mouths fell open at this spectacle but more was to come. There was an ancient butcher's block outside the door of the galley and a live chicken was sitting atop, also waiting to join the onions in the pot. After a few minutes, one of the officials found his voice and asked me how the dishwashing was done. Now, each Indian crew member on joining was issued with a tin plate and mug. Outside the galley on the open deck was what at one time had probably been a stainless steel sink with a cold tap. Before I could answer, one of the Indian crew emerged from the mess room and with a big toothy grin, rinsed his tin plate under the cold tap and dried it on his lunghi which he wore round his waist. We all stood there agape for a few minutes and then I said, "would anyone like a cold beer?" There really did not seem to be anything else to say.

I was leaving the ship in Athens and catching the charter flight back to Gatwick. This was very convenient for Brighton as it was but a short direct ride on the train and also as it was a charter flight for the passengers there were very flexible baggage restrictions. In my position I was always being given gifts from suppliers and I ended up with eight pieces of luggage in one form or another but some of which would require deep freezing once I reached Brighton. Having reached the platform at Gatwick, I was at what would be the rear of the train when it arrived from London and so I decided to move all my luggage to the end of the platform by the front end to make it easier at Brighton. At some stage I would have to walk the length of the train with all this lot and so decided to use the time at Gatwick by carrying two pieces about 50 yards and then going back for another two until I had it all at the front end. When the train arrived I loaded it all in the front carriage and sat back for the 30 minute journey. Unfortunately there had been a landslide somewhere between Gatwick and Brighton which meant a slight detour. Not too far, but the train would have to swing left around to Lewes and then reverse back into the station at Brighton. That meant I was in the last carriage and not the front one and had to manhandle all this luggage the entire length of the 12 carriage train for the second time in an hour.

I had sold my flat in Brighton and was living in the spare bedroom of a colleague of mine, Malcolm who was the senior Chef de Cuisine in P & O. Sian, my girlfriend had left the ships by now and was working in Leeds. She had a flat in Harrogate in Yorkshire and I split my leave between

Yorkshire and Brighton. When Malcolm was at sea, I had his maisonette all to myself and she used to travel all the way down to Brighton from Leeds just for the weekend. Other times, I would drive up to Yorkshire but she was working during the week and I did not know anyone else up North. However, as our relationship developed, I moved to Yorkshire and moved in with her in Harrogate. I had heard that the company was shortly going to cease sending Pursers Officers on the HCIMA course and I was anxious to do the finals and not be left only with intermediate qualifications so I applied to do it the next year. The company accepted this and programmed me to be on study leave for the first six months of 1979. As it turned out, that would be the last year the company did it. In the meantime I was appointed to the Sun Princess for the remainder of the year. This would be the first time I had seen the Sun Princess since she was the Spirit of London, she hadn't changed that much. Except that, now a Princess ship, the catering was contracted out as were the Island and the Pacific so there was an Italian Chief Steward and Chef but instead of the Italian Waiters and Cooks, the British were in the Galley and the Goans still in the Dining Room and Accommodation. However, there were six Italian Head Waiters to enhance the service.

The Purser was my friend Dick, who had been the SAP on the Orcades when I was an AP, and it was good to see him again. As Deputy Purser I was in charge of Bars and Accommodation and had to share an office with the Accommodation Manager. This office was no larger than a cupboard with two desks in it. It was a mess most of the time as it was where the Cabin Stewards came to sign on duty and report any defects, etc. The Utility Cleaners were constantly in and out and there were always vacuum cleaners waiting for repair and piles of upholstery for dry cleaning. Amongst all this I had to do all my work for the Bars and interview passengers who wanted to arrange cocktail parties. Hardly an ideal arrangement and to cap it all the Accommodation Manager was Rod, better known as 'Big Mary'.He was the one whom the Waiter had hit over the head with a pile of plates a few years before. He was a great chap but his only fault was that he suffered with an unusual degree of flatulence. That meant that we all had to suffer it too. One day, the Front Desk (this was the new name for the Bureau) phoned to say they had a little old lady who wanted to arrange a cocktail party and when could I see her? I told them I could see her now and to show her in. Whenever I had a passenger to see, Rod would have to leave the office so that the passenger could sit down, and on this occasion Rod stood to exit the office. Just as he did he let fly the most horrendous fart and quickly stepped from the office. I immediately got up to head off the passenger and use the Purser's office but she was quick and was through the doorway before I could gather my papers. She was a lovely little old dear of about 80 and wanted to arrange a cocktail party for her birthday. We both sat there breathing in Rod's anal emittance and pretending not to notice. She had to think it was me of course and I felt so embarrassed, not made any better by the sight of Rod standing outside the office absolutely convulsed in laughter at my, and her, discomfort. I could have killed the bugger.

The Captain on the ship was Sammy who was disliked by just about everyone. On the other hand his wife, Pat was delightful and we always enjoyed it when she travelled as she would keep him under control and out of our hair. Most of the Officers were berthed on two of the top decks at the forward end and the Captain's cabin was on the starboard forward corner. The Ship's Surgeon was a chap named John who hailed from Bristol. He had been one of the UK's top kidney transplant surgeons and had been reaching burnout, always being on call for when a kidney became available. He decided to take a break and take six months off to work at sea. The hospital in Bristol where he transplanted was supportive when he told them and said to take as long as he wanted, his job would still be there when he returned. John spent six months as an Assistant Surgeon dealing with the crew and then was promoted to Surgeon. He stayed at sea until he retired and never returned to transplanting kidneys. One night on the ship, we had all had quite a bit to drink and John went off back to his cabin. He entered the cabin and being a bit worse for wear, couldn't find the light switch. He undressed in the dark and climbed into bed, suddenly being aware that there was someone else in his bed. He was starting to remonstrate about this intrusion when the bunk light switched on. John had got the right cabin but the wrong deck and was now sitting up in bed next to the other two occupants of the bed who happened to be the Captain and the Captain's wife in the middle.

One day just before the end of the cruise in San Juan, the usual notification of the crew change came through from London. I noted that there was a Bar Steward joining with the same initial and surname as Des, the ex Bartender who had gone to Rhodesia. It had to be a coincidence, as Des had been a Senior Bartender and anyway was now living the life of luxury in Africa. Surely not. But it was him. The ship had several of us from the Orcades on board including several Bartenders, Phil, now the Bar Manager, Andy, and Kevin (Whispering Jack). Des was very pleased to see some familiar faces and a few days later we were able to catch up and fill in the missing six years. Yes, he had gone out to Rhodesia, though it had now become Zimbabwe and his girlfriend's father had fixed him up with a job as Manager of the Salisbury Club. However, he needed to get a work permit and to do this he had to obtain a Rhodesian passport which meant handing in his British one. That was all very well until the war started between Zimbabwe (ex Rhodesia) and Zambia. Des was now a Zimbabwe National with a Zimbabwe passport and eligible for enlistment. He was called up and was in charge of a nine man patrol of a stretch of the border between the two countries. Many were killed, but Des survived his first six month patrol. After a couple of weeks leave he returned for a second one and managed to survive that but not before having all his teeth knocked out with a rifle butt and seeing most of his men killed. He was due to return for a third stretch. Nobody had survived three stints. On his two weeks leave, Des went on a visit to Capetown on a three day pass (with 12 suitcases) and never returned. He boarded a ship to Southampton and hitchhiked back to Javea in Spain where he still owned a house, bought with the proceeds from the Bar, but now let out.

He had no money and no job. He managed to get another British passport and tried his hand at delivering yachts in the Mediterranean. A pleasant enough existence but very little money and so in desperation had contacted P & O in London and cap in hand asked them for a job. He knew the Personnel Manager, Derek, quite well as he had been a Purser's Officer on the Oriana back in the mid-sixties when Des was a Bartender. After a six year absence, he could not return straight back as a Bartender but was offered a Bar Steward's job. He took it and it was pure coincidence that he should have been sent to the Sun Princess. Just prior to my going on leave, one of the Bartenders had to go home on medical grounds and I deliberately left it too late to inform the Personnel Department for them to find a replacement. They suggested I promote someone already on board. I promoted Des.

CHAPTER 27

Dick, the Purser from the Sun Princess was also on the HCIMA finals course and also lived in North Yorkshire so we had both hoped that we would be able to attend the course locally, as others had done the previous year. However, the syllabus had changed slightly and as we had done the intermediate under the old syllabus we would have to attend Ealing College in London again. To add insult to injury we had lectures start at 9.00am Monday and would take up all Monday and Tuesday. That was fine, but then all of Wednesday and Thursday morning were free but we had lectures again on Thursday afternoon and Friday morning. That meant we had to travel to London on Sunday evening and back home again on Friday afternoon. You could not have a more inconvenient timetable if you tried. We managed to find a small guest house run by an Indian gentleman and four of us shared two rooms. I shared with Grahame whom I had sailed with on the Oriana. We also joined the Student's Union in order to qualify for a student's rail card. Even so, there were no course expenses apart from one return train fare per month, nothing for living expenses. Tommy, our personnel officer had retired by this time and we had a gentleman called Dusty who had been a Deputy Purser at sea some time in the past. We had a meeting with Dusty at college one Wednesday. Unfortunately Wednesday was the only day he could see us and so not wishing to share the knowledge that Wednesday was a day off for us, the six of us had to front up and pretend we had a free period. It was pointed out to us that Deck and Engine Officers did not get living expenses when they were on study leave and we, in turn, pointed out that not only was it made clear at the beginning of their employment that at certain times they would have to take study leave for their next ticket but also they had a choice of colleges around the UK from which to choose. However, it was eventually decided we would receive expenses for two return train fares a month which with our student rail cards meant at least we covered the weekly return journeys.

As we were joining the course when it was 75% through, we spent the first month copying notes every evening that the regular students had taken during the first 18 months that we had missed. Again there was Preparation and Service of Food and Beverage, Preparation and Service of Accommodation, Accounts, Management, Hotel Law, and Economics. Again it was difficult to sit in the classroom learning the theory of what you know does not always work in practice. Grahame and I hated the housekeeping lectures and would often go to the cinema instead after a boozy lunch. Still, we got there in the end, and at least it helped towards promotion in the future. We became Members of the HCIMA.

It was July 1979, the course completed and time to go back to sea. Sian and I were in the middle of buying a house at the time, in a village near Harrogate and so it was convenient when I received an appointment to join Uganda just for six weeks. However, as often happens, once there I then received a telex to say that I had been extended for an extra four months so I ended up doing nearly six months taking me to December. I had to join the ship in Dundee as we were accommodating many of the schools from Scotland at the time. We would turn around usually in Tail of the Bank, an anchorage off Greenock, about a half hour train ride from Glasgow. We would be at anchor for the turnround which meant baggage, stores and people had to travel back and forth by tender. A shore tender was used and this service would stop around 11.00pm as the pubs closed. The first time, as I had not been to Glasgow before, I took the train from Greenock to Glasgow for the evening. I was surprised to see so many broken windows in the train and wondered why. About half way through the journey we found out as the train passed through a rundown council estate and it provided entertainment for the local kids to throw stones at the train windows. We had to spend about 10 minutes of the journey on the carriage floor amongst the broken glass. I did not stop long and caught the train back deciding to sample the local Greenock pubs instead with the rest of the crew who were ashore for the evening. When the pubs shut at 11.00pm, we would stop at the fish and chip shop on our way back to the pier for the last tender. Naturally this last tender was always crowded to the point where we hanging on the outside as it groaned its way back towards the Uganda anchorage and many a newspaper containing fish and chips was lost over the side. We would get back on board and settle down in the Crew Bar to watch the midnight movie on BBC2 with our supper and of course more beer.

The Captain on the Uganda was a tyrant by reputation. He was ex Orient Line and was known as Jumping Jack (without the Flash). He was less than five feet tall, hated the Pursers and made life as difficult as possible. Allan, the Accommodation Officer, whom I had known for a number of years on the Spirit of London and the Oronsay was also ex Orient Line and would tell me stories of back in the fifties when Jack was a Chief Officer on ships such as the Otranto and Orion. Apparently, Jack had a bathtub, as opposed to a shower, in his cabin which was salt water. The only hot, fresh water supply was in the Galley and so to have a fresh water bath his poor Steward had to go down about six decks using steep companionways as there were no lifts and fill two buckets of hot, fresh water, climb the stairs and gradually fill the bath. He would have to do this about five times to get sufficient water in the bath. Jack would step in to the bathroom with a thermometer and if it did not reach his required temperature, he would pull the plug and the poor steward would have to start all over again. There were many stories Allan told me about him of a similar ilk. Allan had known him since he first came to sea back in the fifties. Although Allan now lived in Newcastle, he hailed from the Shetland Isles and between line voyages as I mentioned at the beginning, most of the crew would get 10 days leave between four/five month trips. He would have to catch the train from Tilbury Riverside to Fenchurch Street and then the overnight steam train from Kings Cross to Aberdeen which took 13 hours. In Aberdeen he would have to catch the ferry to Lerwick and then another small ferry to Bressay, one of the other islands. It would take him two days to get home and two days to get back again so he only actually had six days at home. Life was pretty tough then.

Captain Jack would invariably go to his table in the Dining Room for breakfast. This was usually unheard of. Eating at a table of passengers was usually only done for dinner in the evening but Jack was different. He had the same thing every morning, a boiled egg and two slices of toast and it had to be perfect. As I was the Catering Deputy Purser, it was my responsibility of course to make sure the egg was four minutes and I had it drummed into me just how brown the toast should be. If the toast was too brown or not brown enough, the egg too soft or too hard, it was sent back and I would be sent for to his cabin and a stern bollocking delivered. Eventually we had it down to a fine art whereby, the Captain's Steward would phone the Maitre D' as soon as he left the cabin and the egg was started, as well as the toast. As Jack walked through the door of the Dining Room and headed towards his table at the far end, one Steward would set off with the egg from the portside galley door and another with the toast from the starboard side, all three arriving at the table simultaneously. What a bloody performance but it was the only way to a quiet life.

Once a cruise he would go to lunch with the students in the canteen and I could always expect a phone call afterwards with his report. One day he called and told me that his custard had been cold and was it supposed to be cold? I knew this was a trick question and so rather than fall for it and say 'no', it should have been hot, I merely told him that if the custard had been cold then it was supposed to be cold, if it was supposed to be hot, then it would have been hot. This flummoxed him a bit and he let it go at that.

Each cruise he would have a cabin party before dinner for passengers on the open deck adjoining his cabin. The nibbles always had to be the same, small cubes of cheddar cheese on cocktail sticks. It had to be cheddar cheese, no other would do. Whenever we reached anywhere humid, the inadequate ice making machines would cease to function and we would have to resort to freezing butcher's trays of water in the freezers and then chopping them up. One day, the Chef had an Indian Pantry Boy who was not well and the Surgeon, Frank had put him off duty. We were around the Canary Islands at the time and were short of ice. It was the night of Jack's party and I wanted to get up there to check all was ready before the start. I was just changing into evening dress when my phone rang and it was the Nursing Sister to say that the Pantry Boy could go back to work but not to handle food for the time being. I was in the middle of thanking her for letting me know and reassuring her that I would make that clear to the Chef when a little voice kept interrupting on the phone. It kept going, 'Hello! Hello!' and I thought it was Frank the Surgeon on the extension fooling around as he often did. I told Frank to 'f' off and hang up. However the voice continued, 'Is that the Catering Deputy?' With horror, I realised it was Jumping Jack, the Captain and he had an over-rider on his phone where he could dial any number and if the line was busy he could just listen in to the conversation. I did recall the Chief Engineer telling me about this one time when he had been on the phone to the Chief Officer and had referred to Jack as a poisoned dwarf, and that's when he had discovered it. However, I had forgotten but now Jack was demanding I attend his cabin straight away. What the hell had gone wrong now? I finished dressing and dashed up to his cabin where I hoped everything was in readiness for his party.

I say in readiness but I use the term rather loosely. He screamed at me to take a look at the cheese cubes. I looked. 'They're mouldy', he yelled. As I found out later, the Indian Cook who had prepared them at lunchtime had placed them in a locker rather than the fridge because he was afraid someone would steal them! They were indeed mouldy with green spots all over them. I tried to tell Jack that it was Sage Derby, however he merely reiterated that he did not care what it was, the cheese must be cheddar. I whipped them all away to avoid any closer inspection on his part and reassured him I would have them replaced immediately with cheddar this time. Before I could leave however, he told me to look at the ice. Again I looked. Whoever had chopped up the ice we had made in the butcher's trays had not spent enough time on it. The chunks of ice were almost large enough to recreate the Titanic disaster and there was no way they would even fit in to the goblets laid out for the party. I assured him that they had been left that size on purpose due to the humidity and demonstrated balancing a chunk on top of a goblet and then once the drink was about to be served, the chunk would have melted sufficiently to slide in to the glass. I explained that as he had his party on the open deck in such humidity, normal ice would not last five minutes and we would be left with a bowl of water. This seemed to satisfy him as he muttered something that obviously I knew what I was doing, and I took my leave to go and investigate these traumas, surprised even myself at the bullshit I had managed.

Allan, the Accommodation Officer was going on leave for six weeks and was being replaced by Harry, the Officer from the Spirit who had helped me so much when I was first promoted in 1973. Harry, as I said before was always immaculate and had been on the Spirit and more latterly the Pacific Princess for the past seven years since he left the Canberra. By now he was well brainwashed into the American ships' way of doing things and he was not too impressed to be relieving on the Uganda as he felt it was beneath his dignity. He was always complaining about how backward the ship was in its methods and its standards, there was nothing right and he couldn't wait to disembark, he hated it. One night, he and I went up to the bar for a drink. Harry could not resist criticising my uniform. He asked me where I had purchased my black evening trousers and I told him I had bought them at BHS for six quid and he proudly told me he had his tailor made and although they had been twenty pounds the difference was worth it. Next he started on my shoes. I informed him I had bought them at Supershoe for five quid, they were plastic covered and not patent leather like his which had cost him around 30 pounds. Later in the evening Harry went to the bathroom and after about 15 minutes when he did not return, I went to look for him, as knowing Harry of old, he had a habit of falling asleep on the loo when he had a few drinks. I found Harry standing in front of one of the urinals cursing like crazy and struggling with his zip which had broken. We found some safety pins to keep things together for the rest of the evening and I told him he should consider buying trousers from BHS as I never had any zip problems. Harry was not amused. Around midnight, we decided to retire for the night and half way down the stairs, Harry decided to perform a somersault down the remaining stairs, landing on his back in the foyer. I thought this was strange for Harry, even after a few drinks, especially as having gained his feet he was turning in circles and looking for something. I picked up a shoe heel from the stair from which he had departed to perform his somersault and asked him if that was what he was searching for. I gave it to him, suggesting the carpenter might be able to glue it back on for him, but in the meantime suggested he consider buying shoes from Supershoe as I had not had any such mishaps. Harry had not had a good evening and put it all down to the fact that he was sailing on the Uganda.

We were doing a couple of cruises up to Scandinavia and the North Cape. Although I do love the Scandinavian countries, especially the Norwegian fjords, I have never really liked cold weather. We were overnight in North Cape and Chris, the Staff Captain had gone ashore on arrival at 10.00pm to set up the Shore Party as we would be using the ship's tenders. He filled his hip flask with something to keep the cold out prior to going. Around midnight when he was about to return, one of the Customs Officers must have seen him taking a nip and arrested him for bringing liquor ashore without duty being paid. The message reached me around midnight that he wanted me to go ashore with some money for the fine and bail him out. I did of course, but not till 8.00am the next morning which didn't please him.

CHAPTER 28

Now, although the Uganda was essentially a ship for students, she undertook two cruises per year for adults only. One of these was primarily for ornithologists and the ship was chartered by the Scottish National Trust. The cruise would take in many of the Scottish Islands, the bird watchers would all sleep in the children's dormitories, and would be up early at sparrow-fart, out on deck with their binoculars, retire early and generally be well behaved. The other adult cruise in August could not have been more different. The ship was chartered by the Augustinian Monks from Dublin.

The ship disembarked its last students in Southampton and we sailed empty over to Dublin to start the Irish cruise which would take us to the Canary Islands, Casablanca and back to Dublin. Allan the Accommodation Officer rejoined in Southampton but as Harry lived in Dublin, it seemed sensible to remain on for two days, help prepare the ship for the Irish adult cruise and save the company an air flight. Of course, these two had not seen each other since the Spirit of London in 1973 and had quite a bit of catching up to do. When the ship arrived in Dublin, Harry's wife and two daughters came down to the ship to collect him. By this time, and without any passengers on board we had all had quite a lot to drink. Allan and I stood on the outside deck and waved farewell to Harry and his family as they crossed the car park. We could not hear anything due to general dock noise but it was like watching an old silent slapstick comedy. The two girls got in the back of the car whilst Harry and his wife, judging by the gesticulating, were having an argument as to who was going to drive. Harry's wife eventually gave in and got into the passenger seat and Harry into the driver's. The car started and we could only assume that Harry's wife must have left the car in reverse when she parked. The car shot backwards, ramming into the front of the parked car immediately behind. Both front doors opened and Harry and his wife climbed out and crossed over round the front of the car, Harry's wife getting into the driver's seat and Harry into the passenger side. The car drove off and I should imagine there was total silence all the way home.

Embarkation started in total chaos. There weren't the restrictions on visitors that there is nowadays and practically the whole city of Dublin had come down to see someone off, it didn't matter who. I also think the charterers had not been completely forthcoming with their passengers about their accommodation and many were expecting a nice outside passenger suite without realising they would be sleeping in children's bunks in a dormitory with 29+ others. The alleyways were packed like the London tube in rush hour, trying to get from one place to another was impossible, and wearing a uniform was the worst thing. I look back now and try to imagine what it would have been like if there had been a fire; an absolute disaster. The restrictions on visitors which were to come in, albeit for a different reason are a benefit in disguise from a safety aspect.

I would suddenly be accosted by someone asking me, "Have you seen my wife anywhere ?" The first couple of times, I would naively ask what she was wearing which of course the husband couldn't remember, but after the first couple of times, I would just say, " Yes, I have, she just went down there", and point the other way. Off he would scurry in pursuit of her. It was much easier. How we ever got all the visitors off the ship prior to sailing from Dublin, I shall never know. I think one of the charterers must have announced over the PA system that the pubs were open.

The priests were in charge as they had chartered the vessel for two weeks. Constantly the public address system was being used as they advertised various charity raising events for a new church roof or the Bishop's Mission in Nigeria.

One of these was that each passenger should purchase 'a little bottle' to donate to the Fathers. This referred to the ready availability in the Canary Islands of purchasing miniature bottles of spirits, and it was advised that one of these per person should be purchased in one of the ports and donated. Presumably these would be sold at some future Church event to raise money. In order to keep a tight check on this, one of the Fathers would sit outside the Dining Room each evening at dinner to collect these as passengers entered. So that nobody should be missed, he sat there with a passenger list and crossed off the names of those contributors. After departure from the Canaries, anyone who had not contributed 'a little bottle' had to fork out five pounds in lieu.

The first morning at sea, I took a walk around the ship. As I passed the dormitories at around 9.00am. I was amazed to see a few of the middle aged women sitting on the edge of their bunks wearing baby doll nighties which barely covered their modesty, with a glass of scotch in one hand and a fag on the go in the other. A glass beside the bunk with her teeth in was not unusual either.

Apart from the dormitories, the Uganda also had classrooms, just like a school and each classroom was named after some historical figure like Samuel Pepys, Francis Drake or Walter Raleigh. These classrooms were obviously not used during this adult cruise and had been locked up. It was with some surprise that I noticed a long queue forming outside one of them and enquired what they were lining up for. I was told they were all waiting to see the Doctor. This particular classroom was labelled Doctor Johnson.

When I passed by the Purser's Office, one of the Fathers was in the middle of purchasing a couple of tour tickets for Tenerife. He told the young lad on the desk that he wanted one for himself and one for Bishop (some almost unpronounceable Irish name). The lad asked him to spell it and so the Father replied 'B-I-S-H-O-P'.

One evening, Allan and I went up to the bar for a drink while the Fathers were running their Wheel of Fortune. We watched for a couple of spins and it looked to stop on 'Green 37'. Over the microphone, came 'and the number is Red 76'. How the hell did that work? We counted the heads in the room, some couple of hundred, all who must have spent about five pounds each on tickets which was a reasonable pot. The first prize was a bottle of crew whisky which cost around two pounds and the second prize was a toy sailor doll from the shop priced around 50p. Still it was all in the name of charity and the winners seemed happy enough. Not half as happy as the Fathers were, I'll wager.

We were just about to depart from Casablanca and I was at the top of the gangway. The crane had the gangway on hook and was just about to land it when I saw two ladies on the dock casually leaning against the rail of the terminal with cameras up to their faces taking photos. I felt sure I recognised one of them as a passenger and signalled the crane driver to wait a moment. I shot down the gangway and asked the ladies if they were passengers on the ship. When they confirmed that they were, I told them they needed to board immediately as the gangway was just being landed and the ship would sail. They looked at me and said that it was quite all right as they had asked one of the ship's officers if it they could take a photo of the ship sailing and he had said it was OK. Quite unbelievable.

Arrival back in Dublin was around 2.00pm and after clearance by the local authorities, we started disembarkation. Needless to say the Fathers were the first to disembark having gathered all their goods and chattels at the top of the gangway. Amongst all this were several tea chests, all marked 'SACRAMENTS' in bold letters. These of course were the 'little bottles' so generously donated by the passengers for charitable religious causes, and each one was carefully manhandled by two of the Fathers down the steep gangway. Once at the bottom, two Irish Customs Officers wagged their fingers at the Fathers and told them there was no way they were coming ashore with that lot! Not to be outdone they struggled back up to the top of the gangway with their 'sacraments'. They opened the lids and disembarkation started properly. Every passenger was given two little bottles to take down the gangway and through Customs. On the other side of the Customs Hall were two more Fathers collecting them back off them.

Disembarkation complete, we still had a couple of hours before sailing and so the Agent took Jeremy, the Purser, Allan and I out to a local pub for a few pints of Guinness. Normally I am not a Guinness drinker but the draught Guinness in its native Ireland is like nowhere else, creamy, smooth and you have to order the next pint whilst drinking the first as it takes so long to pour. In small talk with our agent, he told us that Sunday was his day for relaxation. He would go to the pub at lunchtime and sink about 14 pints. We stared at him agape…14 pints! After that, he informed us, he would have his lunch and a bit of snooze before returning in the evening for a further 16 pints. I don't know about a bit of a snooze, but I probably would not have been able to get into work until Wednesday.

We were sailing empty once more back to Southampton from where we would pick up students again to resume our role of educational cruising in the Mediterranean where we would be based for about the next eight months. We had a hell of a party during the two nights and one sea day back with a sumptuous T-bone steak dinner the night before Southampton. As there was no passenger disembarkation, none of us raced to get up for arrival thinking we could have a bit of a lie-in. Management however had other ideas and were down on arrival. Realising what had probably gone on the previous night, they searched and found the T-bones from the steaks amongst the garbage and were not best pleased with any of us.

The Mediterranean season progressed. The Indian crew had a Hindu feast coming up which meant they would have a celebration after their fasting. This meant I had to purchase 72 live chickens in Piraeus. That wasn't the problem though, the problem was where to keep them for two days until the day of the feast which was a day at sea. I had to get the supplier to deliver these hens when the kids were all out on tour so they would not be upset at seeing live chickens taken on board and guessing their fate. We loaded them discreetly through the bunkering gunport and kept them in a large crew toilet on the after end, until they were required for the pot.

As I mentioned before it was important for budget control to take advantage of prices for various food items in certain ports and Israel was excellent value for citrus fruit. I consulted with Mick, the Chief Butcher as to how many oranges and grapefruit we could take. On Haifa day, the cartons just kept coming until every chill room was block stowed and there were still more. In the end I had to get every Purser's Officer to take so many cases of fruit in their cabins leaving them a small tunnel through which to crawl from the door to their bunk. They weren't best pleased of course but a sweetener took care of that and they were the first ones to be used.

I would have happily returned to the Uganda, it was a ship on which you could keep a low profile and not be permanently under the spotlight. However, it was looking as if they had other candidates for the 'punishment ship' and after Christmas, I was going to be heading back to Princess.

It was not that I had anything specific against the Princess ships apart from the fact that it was boring in that you just went round in circles the whole time doing seven day cruises with the same itinerary and it may as well have been a cross channel ferry...except it was in the sunshine. Well, for the majority of the year anyway. Unfortunately there was always the Alaskan season to get through but with carefully timed leave, this could be reduced to the minimum.

It did mean giving up my beloved Australian cruising but there we are, nothing lasts forever and the American market, although not so much fun was where the money was, at least as far as the company was concerned.

CHAPTER 29

The Sun Princess in January was based in San Juan in Puerto Rico. Flights to join the ship meant either via New York or Miami. I was relieving Dick, my old friend from Yorkshire as Deputy as he in turn stepped up to Purser to relieve him. Once again I found myself working in the broom cupboard sharing it with the Accommodation Manager, about 30 cabin stewards and Uncle Tom Cobbly and all. You had to be careful using that expression in America as it was not one with which they were familiar, and I once found after casually mentioning it to someone in our office in Los Angles that a memo arrived and on the bottom of the distribution was Uncle Tom Cobbly. Not quite sure where Tom's copy ended up.

As soon as I walked on board the Sun Princess, a surprise awaited me. "Hello old boy" was a familiar greeting and I turned round to confirm the inevitable. It was Dean. How had Dean managed to get on Princess? The American passengers loved him of course, the Harrovian accent and manners went down a treat on the Front

Desk as they struggled to understand him. He was actually a delightful chap as long as he was kept on a short leash, which of course was not easy.

Around this time, the latest cruising fashion was to find your own island in the Caribbean and have a beach day, no shops, no traffic, just a day swimming and sunbathing with a simple bar and barbeque. NCL had started this when they bought the ss France from French Line and re-named her the Norway. She sailed out of Miami on a seven day cruise and apart from St Thomas was too large to call anywhere else and so they purchased their own island. Naturally everyone else in the cruising industry had to follow suit. We did not buy ours at first, we had a contract to call at Palm Island, owned by John, a retired American. He was quite eccentric but a really nice and energetic guy. We called there every Wednesday. He would have his local lads put out our umbrellas and beach mats prior to our arrival as we kept them there for the season. He also started the barbeque for us with charcoal we had left the previous week. Alan, the Accommodation Manager, Gerry, the Assistant Chief Steward, Pat the Bar Manager and I would be in charge of the operation and we would have to go ashore first with all the food and punch prior to the passengers disembarking. Once into the weekly routine, it all ran like clockwork and essentially it was as good as a day off for me. I spent the day on the beach, my skin becoming darker as the season wore on.

One week, Steve, the Marine Ops Manager from Los Angeles asked a few of us if we would like to visit Mustique. Seven of us flew over there from St Vincent, a neighbouring island, and we toured the island in the back of a Land Rover, careful not to disturb anyone's privacy. We had pointed out to us Princess Margaret's villa, Mick Jagger's, Rachael Welch's and several more belonging to the rich and famous before having a drink at Basil's Bar. Princess Margaret was there holding court to a private lunch party. We had to sit well away from this party with her two bodyguards sitting between her party and ours, their shoulder holsters bulging conspicuously under their T-shirts.

The Caribbean cruising routine, although boring doing the same itinerary week in and week out did actually make for quite a pleasant lifestyle. Saturday turnround in San Juan started off fairly busily but after 10.00am when the ship was empty, things quietened down. Often, I would go ashore for lunch with some of the senior Bartenders. Embarkation of new passengers did not start until 4.00pm and so we always had about six hours free. I have to admit I did feel a bit guilty as some of them who had arrived early in San Juan depending on flight and had come down to the ship expecting to board at 11.00am, had to wait until 4.00pm. They may not have liked it but they knew the time of boarding, if they had only read it of course. Many seemed to think it was like a bus where you just hopped on and off at will, and had to find out the hard way. Sunday, the only day at sea was usually busy, basically getting most of the week's work out of the way. Monday was Barbados and most of the day spent at the beach. Tuesday was La Guaira in Venezuela and apart from the odd walk ashore, I stayed on board knowing the next day I would be ashore in Palm Island for the entire day. Thursday was Martinique and again I stayed on board as it was expensive ashore. Friday was St Thomas, and after loading the week's bar stores, we would go off to Magens Bay for the afternoon. I soon discovered that the large pink hotel near where we docked had a new General Manager, Rob who had been one of my Assistant Pursers on the Oronsay back in 1975. He had done well for himself and occasionally would invite a couple of us over for dinner with he and his wife. Well, that took care of the seven day cruise in the Caribbean and then the next day being San Juan, the routine was repeated. Things could have been worse of course, I could have been working in the cold and wet of the English winter and commuting by train every day. That thought was always in my head and was never going to be an option.

When the ship had ceased to be the Spirit of London and become Sun Princess, the administration for Princess came out of Los Angeles which included all the stores. As the catering for Princess at the time was contracted out, the bar supply no longer came by container from the UK as with all the other P & O liners, but came from a local supplier. The crew beer on all P & O ships was Allsopps, known as the yellow peril due to its yellow can. Supplies were gradually depleted until the very last can on board stood on display behind the crew bar and was not for sale. After about six months when everyone had depleted their cabin supplies, it was decided to raise money for the Crew Club by holding an auction in the crew bar for the very last can of Allsopps. The auction took place at midnight one evening when everyone had finished work. The can had been chilled to the correct temperature and the auction began. Phil, the Bar Manager eventually won the auction paying no less than $78 for this one last can of Allsopps. He sat at a table in the Crew Bar wearing his white tuxedo and the Allsopps was presented to him in a silver ice bucket, the top of the can pulled and the contents poured into a frosted glass. Phil stood up, held the glass high, and to everyone's envy proceeded to drink and savour the amber nectar.

At this point, one of the Goan Night Cleaners ambled through the bar on the way to his cabin, completely unaware of the momentous occasion which was taking place. It could have been staged, though it wasn't, but it drew gasps from the crowd assembled as they realised what he had on his shoulder. An unopened case of 24 cans of Allsopps lager that he must have had stashed away in his cleaning locker and was taking it to his cabin. Phil almost threw up his Allsopps after paying $78.

The Caribbean season was coming to a close and we were going to be headed through Panama, up the West Coast to Vancouver to start the Alaskan season.

Again our Alaskan Cruising was a repetitive seven day cruise. Vancouver turnround day was Saturday, Sunday at sea travelling the Inside Passage, Monday was Ketchikan, Tuesday was Juneau, Wednesday cruising round Glacier Bay, Thursday was Skagway, Friday, the Inside Passage again and back to Vancouver. American cruising always reminded me of that movie years ago, 'If it's Tuesday it must be Belgium', where a group of American tourists travel by coach 'doing Europe', one day one country.

The bars in the various ports always sported at least one pool table and it must have been the most popular of the limited activities available. The local rednecks were all expert pool players and it was easy to be taken in by their friendly approach to an innocent game. They would allow you to win a couple of times, holding back their potential until they had upped the stakes. Dean was just their cup of tea. He had gone ashore in Skagway to the Igloo Bar (later to catch fire and burn down, though nothing to do with Dean, I am happy to say) and as he consumed more beer was playing for larger stakes. Eventually he ran out of cash and convinced he could still beat these local guys, literally started playing for the 'shirt off his back'. The ship was sailing at 7.00pm and I was concerned that Dean had still not returned. At 6.40pm however, a local pick up stopped at the end of the gangway and deposited Dean dressed only in a shabby old raincoat. He still had his undershorts but no shoes or socks, he had lost the lot by playing pool with locals and it was only through the generosity of the Bartender in the Igloo that he had he lent Dean an old raincoat.

I had carefully engineered my leave programme so that of the four months in Alaska, I would only do the first month, have leave for the middle two and return for the final month. That meant not only did I have the UK summer at home but my next contract would take me to the middle of December which meant I would be home for Christmas and New Year. I managed to maintain that pattern for the next four years.

CHAPTER 30

Times had indeed changed over the previous 13 years. There were now only two ships left of the 1967 P & O fleet when I had joined, the Oriana and Canberra. The Oriana was about to be based permanently in Australia, which left only the Canberra and the Uganda, though the company had by now acquired the Kungsholm which they renamed the Sea Princess. She had been very luxurious in her day, built in UK, and had been designed for round the world cruising. She was still in good shape superficially but technically she was a mess and became a bottomless pit in which money was constantly poured. The idea at the time was that she would take over from the Canberra for the annual round the world cruise as the Kungsholm had been built as one class and was more suitable. The Canberra was becoming increasingly outdated, expensive to run, and there had been a number of times when the company had seriously thought about scrapping her. Each time, however, she was reprieved as she had a tremendous following, apart from the fact that it would have left P

& O with only Sea Princess and the Uganda, plus the three small ships of the Princess fleet. The Uganda was already on borrowed time and besides which had her educational role.

The Canberra in fact was to be given several more years of service after Brian, previously the head of the Insurance & Claims Department, persuaded the company to give him a certain amount of money and time to turn the Canberra around into a money making concern. He was given two years and a fairly generous budget. Brian had a totally different approach to the previous Management by actually talking and consulting with the people who did the work. For instance, he would talk directly with the Chief Pastry Chef as to what he needed to enhance the dessert trollies. Often this would involve a small outlay, easily provided within days, whereas all previous requests through the normal bureaucratic system had been refused without thought or enquiry. Brian spoke to everyone in all areas of the ship and it inevitably paid off.

There had been an old isolation hospital on board, necessary in the days of mainline voyaging but now no longer needed for her cruising role so this was a wasted space. Brian had it converted to a night nursery fitted out with children's bunks. Parents could take their children (up to the age of seven) and put them to bed there and enjoy the evening on board without having to constantly worry if their child was wandering the alleyways looking for them, or finding their way down to the Engine Room to play with the propellers. They just had to pick up their sleeping child by 2.00am from the Nursery where there was a Stewardess in charge. As I said, these changes he made cost very little but made a huge difference to the cruise experience and Canberra's popularity increased almost to cult status. Brian also had the support and backing from all her crew as at last they felt they had a voice and someone who would listen to their suggestions.

The conditions for us had changed somewhat for the better also. No longer would we only get 10 days leave after an eight month voyage, with the remainder being accrued until after a few years, taking a long leave of a few months. Now, with flying backwards and forwards to join and leave ships, it meant that we now went to sea for four months at a time with two months leave in between which meant a much more bearable existence, especially for those with families. Mind you, the four months away was often around 18/19 weeks, and the two months leave, around seven weeks. The arithmetic sometimes left a lot to be desired, but then leave still accrued but it did present the Personnel Department with a greater logistical challenge.

Captains had for the previous year been allowed to have their wives on board for part of their contract and this was now being extended down to other senior officers, the stipulation being that it had to be the same wife and not a different one each voyage! In 1980, Sian and I decided to get married. Dick, my friend from North Yorkshire and his Australian wife, Anne-Marie were our witnesses at the Registry Office.

When I went back to the Sun Princess after leave, I was able to have my wife out for the first time which certainly made the difference to the time away. However, to start with it was not a popular introduction with everyone. One evening, having a drink with the Purser prior to dinner, my wife asked him if his wife had ever been on board. He admitted that she hadn't, as he had not yet got around to telling her she was allowed to.

On one particular occasion when I was flying home from San Juan, the Second Engineer, John was already waiting in the taxi with his suitcase in the boot (trunk) when the Assistant Electrician, Bar Steward and I arrived who were also going home. I had a particularly large suitcase and could not fit it in the boot with John's case so I took his out and placed it on the pavement to get mine in first. The Electrician and Steward only had hand luggage and leapt in the back of the cab. Suddenly seeing his suitcase on the pavement, John got out of the front seat and went to deal with it. I assumed he would take care of it and so leapt into the front seat. The cab driver seeing we were all there took off to the airport with the three of us and left a bewildered Second Engineer standing on the pavement with suitcase in his wake. It could not have happened more smoothly if it had been stage-managed for a comedy clip. Needless, to say, he was not in best of moods when he arrived at the airport some 30 minutes later, puffing and panting.

Sammy was still the Captain on the ship but would be off fairly soon to join another vessel. He used to cause a lot of controversy on board with his master key which gave him access to anywhere on the ship. As Master, of course, he could go anywhere he wanted, as it was his ship and he was responsible for it, but it was the way he used this authority which got up everyone's nose. He would just use his key to enter cabins whenever he wanted, not bothering to knock. There were more and more females among the crew these days, and his brash disregard for privacy caused much bad feeling.

One turn round day in San Juan, the ship's Doctor had a visitor on board and was energetically entertaining her in his cabin when he heard a jangle of keys. Leaping off the young lady, he threw a cover over her. He knew who it had to be, but there was no time, and the key was already in the lock. The Doctor desperately looked round for something to wear, but he only had time to pick up his officer's cap. As Sammy opened the door and entered the cabin, he was treated to the sight of the ship's Doctor standing in the middle of the cabin, stark naked, wearing only his cap on his head. He was saluting with his left hand and holding a very presentable erection in his right. Sammy stood there, gobsmacked and spluttering expletives, turned on his heel, and exited the cabin, locking it again on his way out.

Inevitably about ten minutes later, the Doctor's phone rang and of course it was Sammy, summoning the Doctor to the Captain's office straight away. The Doctor dressed in his full uniform and went to see the Captain. Sammy gave him a huge bollocking, not mentioning anything about the lady in the cabin, but reprimanding him for saluting with the wrong hand.

28353303R00220

Printed in Great Britai
by Amazon